Five of the Many

Five of the Many

Survivors of the Bomber Command Offensive
from the Battle of Britain to Victory
Tell Their Story

Steve Darlow

GRUB STREET · LONDON

Published by
Grub Street
4 Rainham Close
London
SW11 6SS

Reprinted 2009, 2011

British Library Cataloguing in Publication Data
Darlow, Stephen
  Five of the many: survivors of the Bomber Command
  offensive from the Battle of Britain to victory tell their story
  1. Great Britain. Royal Air Force – Airmen – Biography
  2. Great Britain. Royal Air Force. Bomber Command – History
  – World War, 1939-1945 3. World War, 1939-1945 – Aerial
  operations, British 4. World War, 1939-1945 – Personal
  narratives, British
  I. Title
  940.5′44941′0922

ISBN-13: 9781904943983

Line drawings by Pete West

Typeset by Pearl Graphics, Hemel Hempstead
Printed and bound by MPG Ltd, Bodmin, Cornwall

Grub Street only uses
FSC (Forest Stewardship Council) paper for its books.

Contents

Acknowledgements

I am indebted of course to the Five; Joe Petrie-Andrews, Benny Goodman, Harry Hughes, Tony Iveson and Tiny Cooling, who gave up their time freely and were so supportive of the project. Thanks also to Joe Petrie-Andrews's navigator John Backhouse, who helped fill in some of the gaps. John Davies and the Grub Street team have, as usual, supported my endeavours.

The BBC have been kind enough to allow me the use of extracts from their WW2 People's War website – an online archive of wartime memories contributed by members of the public and gathered by the BBC. The archive can be found at bbc.co.uk/ww2peopleswar.

My appreciation also extends to Pete West, Maisie Goodman, Doug Radcliffe, John Stopford-Pickering at the IWM sound archive, Jonathan Falconer, Lee & Sue Chambers, Chris Webb, Patrick Bishop, Steve Fraser, Jim Sheffield, Rob Thornley and Mark Postlethwaite. A special mention also to Andy Baxter, whose previous research into Joe Petrie-Andrews's wartime days was of great value.

NB: All the aircraft illustrated in the book are in the markings as actually flown by the pilots themselves.

Introduction

Airmen of RAF Bomber Command were immediately into action against the enemy when World War Two began in September 1939. They would fight the air battle over western Europe continuously through to the end of the war in May 1945. It was an air campaign like no other before or since. A relentless and necessary assault upon the very fabric of the enemy. Bomber Command's contribution to the defeat of the Axis powers was immense but the relative cost in men and material was high. Herein lies the term used in the title of this book – the 'Many' – in contrast to Fighter Command's 'Few' who kept the Luftwaffe at bay in 1940. Bomber Command lost a staggering 55,500 men killed from the 125,000 men serving in both the aerial front line and the training units. In Sir Arthur Harris's 'Special Order of the Day' written a few days after VE day he commented, 'your chance of survival through one spell of operational duty was negligible; through two periods mathematically nil... In the whole history of our National Forces, never have so small a band of men been called upon to support so long such odds. You indeed bore the brunt.'

This band of men played their part in thwarting German invasion plans in 1940. They countered the U-boats on the seas and in the factories. They hindered German military industrial production, and disrupted German V-weapon plans. They cleared the way for the D-Day landings and seriously, crucially, disrupted German reinforcement on the Normandy battle area. They supported the land advances to Germany and the crossing of the Rhine. Amidst this were special operations such as the Dams raids, confounding German radar on D-Day, supplying the Resistance, minelaying, and seeking to destroy the *Tirpitz*.

Throughout, the controversial attack on the German nation escalated. It was not all success, serious and costly mistakes were made and hard lessons had to be learned. But what comes through is the unquestionable bravery and commitment of Bomber Command's young men, who had to carry out the truly devastating offensive to defeat the unquestionable evil of Nazism.

Five of the Many tells the story of a few distinguished Bomber Command airmen who 'bore the brunt'; their motivations, their aspirations, the perils of training, the forming and bonding of the crew, the mental and physical challenge of operations, the long cold night flights over hostile territory, corkscrewing amidst the glare of enemy searchlights, being buffeted by flak, combating enemy nightfighters, fighting to control lame aircraft, baling out, sustaining injury, and witnessing the violent deaths of fellow aircrew. This book puts the reader in the pilot's seat of a Mosquito over Berlin, in a Halifax over the flak-infested Ruhr, in the cockpit of a Lancaster as the pilot focuses to keep his aircraft steady on a bomb run, next to a navigator as he guides his crew around flak to a blacked-out target, and in a Wellington bomber watching Dunkirk burning.

Rupert 'Tiny' Cooling opens the book, providing a graphic account of Bomber Command operations and service life in the early stages of the war; then going on to serve in North Africa. Jack 'Benny' Goodman's story follows, the account of his extra-ordinary career taking the reader from the early days of inexperience both at command and personal level to the days of precision bombing in 1944. Joe Petrie-Andrews tells of the aircrew experience during the escalation of the bomber offensive in 1943, going on to record his accounts of operations flying as a pathfinder. Navigator Harry Hughes's operational flying during the Battle of the Ruhr in 1943 then provides an insight into the intense air battle over Germany. Harry goes on to fly a second tour on Mosquitoes as part of the Light Night Striking Force, a stark contrast to Tiny Cooling and Benny Goodman's night flights over Germany in previous years. Finally Tony Iveson, who went from a fighter pilot in the Battle of Britain, to a bomber pilot with 617 Squadron in the last year of the war, tells of his time flying Lancasters on precision raids on specific targets. Collectively these men flew one short of three hundred operational sorties!

I would like the reader to note that the telling of Harry Hughes's experiences with 102 Squadron contains continual reference to the death of airmen. I make no apologies for this repetition, as it brings the point home. At the time the men on the squadron had to deal with such repetition of loss.

The language that is used in books about the RAF during World War Two has been a concern of mine in that it does open itself up for misunderstanding. So here I would like to qualify the use of one particular term when employed in this book. When one talks of 'success', or words to that effect, in terms of a bomber raid that has caused considerable destruction and death, it is used with respect to the achievement of the objective, as set out for the operation. My books are absolutely not intended as celebrations of war; they are accounts of war activities, and how people are affected by them, and how they respond – notably of course focusing on Allied airmen. The vast majority of material I have used has been from primary sources and my objective is to put in the public domain the experiences of the respective airmen. I have never come across any veteran who has revelled in, or celebrated, war. But they do reflect upon the journey they went through and how it changed them. They will celebrate lifetime friendship, and acts of great skill and invention. They will remember the loss of good friends. They do not, and I do not, celebrate the evil that is war, although no one can disagree with the fact that to leave Germany unopposed would have resulted in a far greater evil overcoming humanity. The war to defeat Germany has full justification. And in that context, and without the advantage of a precision bombing capability, the use of the blunt instrument that was Bomber Command came from necessity.

Bomber Command's motto states, 'Strike Hard, Strike Sure'. The five men featured in this book certainly fought hard and flew sure, along the flightpath to victory in Europe.

Air Chief Marshal Sir Arthur T Harris KCB, OBE, AFC – Special Order of the Day – 12 May 1945

Each crew, each one in each crew, fought alone through black nights rent only, mile after continuing mile, by the fiercest barrages ever raised and the instant sally of searchlights. In each dark minute of those long miles lurked menace. Fog, ice, snow and tempest found you undeterred. In that loneliness in action lay the final test, the ultimate stretch of human staunchness and determination.

Chapter 1

Early Nights

Dorothy Stapleton (née Geater) served with the RAF during the war as an MT driver, working on a bomber base.

My duties were driving crews to their aircraft and driving the ambulance when needed. I used to sit at the end of the runway with the senior medical officer waiting for the aircraft to return. We got to know our crews really well and I used to really enjoy our evenings in the NAAFI with them. But it was very distressing when I had to collect some of them in the ambulance after they had been shot up on raids.

There were Australians, New Zealanders, Canadians as well as the British boys and it was heartbreaking that many of them did not return or returned badly mutilated or dead. I suppose thinking back on it now one had to become quite hardened to this constant loss but it saddens me even now to think of those boys who were so young, happy and frightened.

Sometimes I even had to drive the bomb tender with coffins on the back for burial at the colonial cemetery in Haverhill. Very sad. We each had a flight to look after and you watched for the numbers as they landed to see if any were missing. Sometimes aircraft would return badly shot up and if they were the rest of the crews were very upset as they were all great friends. Some of the boys returned with their nerves shot to pieces and I expect for many the rest of their lives were affected.

I don't regret leaving my sleepy village for the war effort. I am old now but I remember it all as if it were yesterday. Despite the horrors we witnessed the whole event was, in a way, life enhancing.

'A beautiful sunny day', is how Rupert 'Tiny' Cooling recalled the conditions on one flight early in his flying career, 'and I was diving down into these cumulus valleys, shrieking with delight.'

When John Gillespie Magee later penned his famous poem, 'Oh! I have slipped the surly bonds of earth, and danced the skies on laughter-silvered wings...' I knew exactly what he meant. When I came back from this flight I landed and was asked if it was alright. My response, 'It was bloody marvellous.'

Tiny had been given the opportunity to take to the air by the Royal Air Force Volunteer Reserve, the 'Citizen Air Force', established and expanded in the years leading up to the Second World War to bolster the RAF Regular force when hostilities broke out. The RAFVR had sought out men just like Tiny, 'Your country has a job for you – a job that calls for fitness, dash, initiative, intelligence, responsibility. A young man's job – a war winning job. We're getting the planes – we must get the men.'

Tiny was one of many that succumbed to the promises of the RAFVR recruitment and he thrilled at the opportunity to fly. He definitely had the ability and not long after he had completed his 'bloody marvellous' flight he was to receive the coveted 'wings' recognising him as a qualified pilot in the Royal Air Force Volunteer Reserve. Tiny was proud of his new status, so much so that he couldn't wait to receive the insignia to stitch on to his uniform, 'So I went to a shop in Hull and bought my first set of wings for half a crown.' Tiny, having a nickname that belied his true stature, then had to wait for a uniform. 'There was a delay getting my uniform because it had to be made to measure. I couldn't be served from stock and I didn't get my uniform until about a month before war broke out.'

Flying, however, was not Tiny's chosen profession at this time. He was merely flying part time with the Volunteer Reserve. But that was to change towards the end of August 1939.

> My indentures as a pharmacist ended on 28 August. I had a motorcycle and I went down to a friend in Bournemouth. It took me a couple of days as I stopped with an aunt in Birmingham and then went on the following day. The balloon went up the day after that. We went to the cinema in the evening and I remember feeling grotesquely important telling the cashier which row I would be in and that I might get a telephone call. As we were coming out at the end of the performance, a commissionaire came up to me and said, 'By the way. We've just had a call from where you are staying. They have had a telegram saying that you are to return to your unit immediately.' So big stuff this. I left my motorcycle behind, went to Bournemouth station and then to Waterloo. The train took forever. We got to Waterloo at first light and there were big newspaper placards on the book stall GERMANY INVADES POLAND.

Rupert 'Tiny' Cooling was born on 10 March 1920, in Northumberland Avenue, London, an only child. His father had numerous jobs as an under buyer but as Tiny recalls, 'he always seemed to pick a loser', financial problems becoming more acute during the great Wall Street crash, 'and by god did it crash' and the economic slumps of the 1930s.

I can well imagine that my parents had a pretty rough time, although I never went without. The only thing that I yearned for was a bicycle and a cricket bat. Eventually I got the bat, which was a throw out from the company's sports club. I remember one Christmas getting nothing more than a very large tin of toffees. That told me something.

Early in the 1930s Tiny moved with his parents to Leeds, and then his father's work took them to Hull in 1934, following which he opened up his own shop, a ladies outfitters – from reels of silk to hosiery to summer dresses. 'Nice little shop on the north-western edge of Hull.' Tiny, at this stage, 1936, was at college.

I was mad keen on chemistry and when I left school in July of that year, I became an apprentice at a pharmacist. I thought that would get me through to where I wanted to be, a research chemist. Then one day in 1938 I joined the RAF because the chain came off my bicycle. My father had been in the Honourable Artillery Company and was called up at the beginning of the First World War. I decided that I was going to join the territorials. It was really the gung-ho attitude of every lad in his early teens, talking about joining some military formation. One February evening I was coming back from work on my bicycle, which I hadn't looked after very well, and there was a howling easterly wind with heavy showers. Suddenly the chain came off. As I put it back on again down came a ghastly shower, really vicious. I looked up and just above my head was a board that said 'Number 8 Reserve Centre Royal Air Force Volunteer Reserve'. I darted up the path, opened the front door and a chap whom later I knew as Corporal Lamb welcomed me with open arms, 'Ah just the sort of young man we are looking for'. So I asked him to tell me more. Now at that time, as an apprentice pharmacist, I was getting between ten shillings a week and twelve and six a week. Corporal Lamb said, 'Right. What you do is sign here. We teach you to fly. For one day only you will be an Aircraftman Second Class; the next day you will be a sergeant pilot under training at ten and six a day. And when you have got your wings it goes up to twelve and six a day. And you come here three nights a week and we will pay you two shillings an hour plus travelling expenses. And all you have to do is fifteen days training and if you have a word with your boss he might give you the extra time off'. Not that I was particularly bothered about that. 'And on top of that you get a bounty'; if I recall about twenty-five pounds. I thought this was riches beyond dreams. I took the papers home and went through them with father and mother who were sort of in agreement; although my mother was really not very enthusiastic about the idea of her sole fledgling suddenly flinging himself into the air. This is the time when newspapers made great play of aircraft plunging out of the sky and bursting into flames and aviation didn't have a good name in 1939. Nonetheless I pressed on.

Tiny was clearly keen at the prospect of flying with the RAFVR, although he had to wait until he came of age.

I had the forms filled in but was not allowed to apply until my eighteenth birthday. I went in and I pushed the forms through the letterbox on the night of 9 March 1938 so that they would be opened the following morning, my birthday. I was called down for a medical, which was carried out by our family doctor. I remember that one of the things they asked you to do, which I was aware of before I went, was hold your breath for as long as possible. I realised I could improve this with practice, so I practiced and practiced and practiced. At the medical I remember he asked me to hold my breath. When I got over the two minutes he said, 'You don't have to hold it forever.'

A further requirement was that minimum leg length had to be 30 inches. Tiny had passed that requirement many years before, his leg length now at 37^1/$_2$ inches, so he was certainly not diminutive in stature – hence of course his nickname. He passed and became one of the many thousands of young men that the RAF would try to mould from a novice into a wartime fighting pilot.

Tiny took his first flight 'air experience', in a Blackburn B2 biplane, with a Flying Officer Morris at the controls, on 22 March 1938, flying from Brough.

We did a circuit, and all it really involved was that 'Chuff Chuff' Morris took off, climbed up to 1,000ft and said, 'Now there's the horizon. See the position of the nose. If we pull back the stick it goes up and if we push it forward it goes down.' And he showed me left and right. Then he said, 'Now hold the nose on the horizon.' And so it went on and on. I had done about five or six hours on the B2 when we were issued with a Miles Magister, the 'Maggie' [a two-seater monoplane basic trainer], which was just coming into service. A couple of the instructors looked me up and down and one said, 'I think you might be better off in the Maggie, it's got more room.' So I made the switch. The B2 cruised at about 70 knots and the Maggie cruised at about 90 odd. It seemed an incredibly fast ship, and I didn't settle down, eventually going solo after about 13 hours. Then I was on 15 days training but I'd lost the touch and I either came in too high or too low. I could handle the aircraft alright but didn't seem to be able to land it. Eventually I was put up for a test by a fellow called Flight Lieutenant Hastings, from the central flying school. I was told I would be flying with him, to be assessed, which I felt very unhappy about.

Miles Magister

I remember leaning against the wall outside the flight hut, watching another Maggie take off. It went partially round the circuit and then disappeared behind the hangars, which were on the riverbank. This was quite usual, you would lose sight of it and eventually it would come in and land. On this occasion it never came in. All of a sudden there was a god almighty clatter and hooters and people running all over the place. The pilot had stalled off a gliding turn and dived into the Humber. When they got him out he was dead, knocked out by the impact and drowned. I then had to go up with Flight Lieutenant Hastings about three-quarters of an hour later. I consider it a very very cruel thing to do, because he took it up to 3,000 feet and spent the first part of the test trying to find out what had happened to the other Maggie. He would be flying along, cut the engine and keep the nose up. I knew bloody well that we were going into a spin and he would do it one way, then the other, then this way, then the other. He spent 15 minutes playing with this thing then said, 'Alright over to you now. Let's carry on with the test.' By that time I was so thoroughly discombobulated that I made a complete pig's ear of the whole thing. We landed and he said, 'unless you make significant progress for the next two or three days I am going to recommend that you cease further training.' The next morning I found that all the Maggies had been grounded following the accident.

It was decided to put Tiny back on to B2s, 'and they modified the rudder by pushing it out to give me the maximum leg length'.

I never looked back and I went on and on through the B2s and onto flying the Hawker Hind and Hawker Audax. I did my height test in July 1938 when I was on my 15 days, in an Audax and learned something which I was to discover later was anoxia [an inadequate supply of oxygen]. The briefing was go up to 15,000 feet, stay there for ten minutes then come down. Well what the hell do you do at 15,000 feet for ten minutes. I just carried on climbing up and up and up and of course I ran into an anoxia. All I remember was that I got up to 15,000 feet still climbing and the next thing I remember I was at about 14,500 feet and it was 20 minutes later. I'd passed out and the aircraft had just sort of waffled down until there was sufficient oxygen in the air to bring me round again. It was a disconcerting experience.

Through the remainder of 1938 and the first half of 1939 Tiny accumulated flying hours and experience, receiving his wings. But of course this experience was gained in a peacetime environment. The challenges of wartime flying were now fast approaching. The German invasion of Poland on 1 September 1939, whilst Tiny Cooling was in London, could only mean that a declaration of war was imminent. Hence the call for Tiny to return to his unit, taking the train from London to Hull, 'which again took forever'.

> I signed in and they told me to come back at 11 o'clock the next morning. We listened to Chamberlain's speech very quietly. He finished and somebody said, bravado, embarrassment, uncertainty whatever, 'Never mind let's all meet up again here when it's over.' People replied, 'Oh yes. Of course.' Then about 15 minutes later the air raid siren went and people didn't take a great deal of notice of it. 'Oh what's that funny noise? It's the air raid siren. Oh let's go out and see if we can see anything.' Then the all clear sounded and we went home. We came back again the next day at 11 o'clock, nothing happened and we repeated that for about a week.
>
> Then out of the blue, three of us, 'Clark, Cooke and Cooling' were told to go on a flying instructors course. Obviously somebody just stuck a finger over an alphabetical list. I had just turned 19. So I went and flew around in a B2. Flight Lieutenant Alison was my instructor, hell of a nice chap, and we just got some more hours in. It was of no consequence and we finished the course on 30 September.

When war broke out Tiny had approximately 120 flying hours to his name. Following the instructor course he was then posted to Number 1 Initial Training Wing, Selwyn College, Cambridge, 10 October 1939, 'and I was there for a couple of weeks whilst they inoculated us, vaccinated us, issued us with kit and then said, "well you've got your wings you had better go home on indefinite leave."' Tiny duly did so and spent the next few months eagerly awaiting his opportunity. Frustration set in as the 'Phoney War' ran its course.

> The wait went on and on and on. I was just hanging around the house with nothing to do. I didn't have to report to anybody or do anything; I think my mother was beginning to feel that if this was war it was fine! Then just before Christmas I had a posting notice saying go to 15 Service Flying Training School, RAF Lossiemouth, Scotland, on or about 21 December. This really put the cat amongst the pigeons because my poor mum had decided I was going to be home for Christmas and she was really going to try and

push the boat out. Next door to us was the butcher's shop and she had been to see him and got this, that and the other, but now I had received a posting. Then another telegram arrived saying my move was postponed until after Christmas so there was relief all round. Well to some extent. My mother was now very perturbed because I was going to Scotland and would be there for Hogmanay. I was 19, and she knew the Scots were prolific drinkers. Her brothers unfortunately were also very much inclined to knock off a bottle or two and she had visions of her little chick going up there and being thoroughly debased and degraded on the fire water of Scotland. Of course it was nothing like that at all. I got up to Lossiemouth after an arduous journey, an interminable journey. I left home about ten at night and got to Lossiemouth at about seven in the evening the following day, settling into these wooden huts. Hogmanay fell on a Sunday and it was decided that we would go and see these 'riotous Scotsmen'. We walked to Lossiemouth and the place was as dead as a doornail. There wasn't a light showing, there wasn't a pub open, there wasn't the sound of music, there was nothing. I had overlooked the fact that in this Calvinistic country, the Sabbath was holier than Hogmanay.

Tiny spent his time at Lossiemouth learning the controls of a twin-engine Airspeed Oxford. A mere 19 year-old, Tiny was mixing with service men almost double his age.

I was just an ordinary plain sergeant pilot under training. I was a bit horrified in a sense because I was one of about eight injected into a mess where sergeants had sweated for 15, 16, 17 years. They had worked their way up to become sergeants and here were these kids wet behind the ears walking in bright and shiny. We were ignored generally apart from one chap who was coming to the end of his time, if it hadn't been for the war he would have been retired at the end of the previous year. He became quite a father figure to us, with many words of encouragement and advice.

Initially I carried out a circuit with an instructor, who showed me the way around. Then following another couple of circuits, we landed, taxied in, and he said, 'Right off you

go.' 'What by myself?' 'Yes.' I said, 'But this is the first time
I've flown an Oxford.' His response was that I had my
wings so 'go and fly it'. I thought that was a bit harsh.
Anyway I did and I got it down in one piece again. But I
never did master the Oxford. It was excellent for training
but a cow of an aeroplane. They expected you to three
point them, and the Oxford didn't like three pointing. The
only time I ever greased an Oxford onto the ground was my
first night solo. I was frightened of that, everybody was.
Only birds and fools fly and birds don't fly at night. On the
night I took off, it felt magical. I headed north and there
was the Moray Firth in very thin moonlight. I could see the
flare path behind me, it was a crystal clear night, and I just
seemed to be hanging there looking at the light sliding by.
Then I came to land, lined up, got the green and thought
well this is it. Feeling for the ground, all of a sudden I felt
this rumbling and was down. It did everything for me. No
problem.

Tiny's logbook continued to fill with all-important flying hours.
He spent Easter 1940 at home and then received news of a
posting to Harwell, to an operational training unit. At the OTUs
individual airmen, trained up in the various trades required to
operate a bomber, gained experience on operational aircraft
types. Tiny Cooling however had 'no idea' what he could expect.

I was just posted 'to number 15OTU'. I thought what the
hell was an OTU? I had no idea what it was and what was
going to happen. On arrival I went into the mess then
walked up to the hangars to see what sort of aeroplanes
they had. I was faced with a twin-engine Vickers-
Armstrong Wellington, an enormous thing, it seemed to go
on forever. There was a wooden ladder sticking up under
the nose and an airman came clattering down. I asked if I
could go inside, was given the OK, so I climbed up. There
was this sort of magnificent green leather throne and I
touched some of the knobs, dials and levers that were all
over the place. I sat in the seat, put my head out of the
window, my feet on the rudder bar, and way back in the
distance I could see the rudder. I thought, 'God how am I
supposed to fly this?'

The Wellington, or the 'Wimpy', has been described as 'one of the outstanding bomber aircraft of the Second World War'. Its geodetic construction meant that it could absorb battle damage; which was understandably much appreciated by aircrews. Tiny Cooling was one of many who developed some affection for the aircraft he would go to war in.

The Wellington was a perfect partner. If you treated her with the respect of a very gracious willing lady, she would do whatever you wanted. I wouldn't care to take liberties with her but providing you realised that there were certain things that you shouldn't do, you were alright.

She wasn't easy to fly on one engine, so you didn't try that too much. When you were airborne you would look out at the engine nacelles and the wingtip, and as you flew along you'd see this seagull attitude. The wings were flapping. I remember commenting on it to one of the chiefs one time, saying, 'it's a bit disconcerting seeing the wings flap.' He said. 'Mate, time to be disconcerted is when they don't flap.' But it was a good, thoroughly good, aeroplane. Relatively easy to fly although it was heavy and it was slow in response. You would put the aileron on and have to wait two or three seconds before there was any noticeable change in attitude. You wouldn't classify her as nimble, but she was a stately, very robust steed and once you got confidence in her, and that was easily obtained, she'd no vices at all. If she was forgiving I don't know. I never had an occasion to demand her forgiveness. I know I did some mad things in it which when I think about it later makes my blood run cold and wonder how the hell it was I managed to get away with it.

Tiny would fly Wellingtons of various marks throughout his operational flying career, leading to further praise for his steeds.

I flew the Mark I, IA, IC, III and the Mark X, and each was better than its predecessor. The latter was a joy to fly, with the Hercules engines, which I flew in North Africa where the climatic conditions were a bit more arduous. Because of the heat you had to watch things like cylinder head temperatures. I remember once taking 6,500lbs in one load on an outside air temperature which probably at take-off time was about 28 degrees. By the time I got up to about 1,000ft, the collector rings on the front of the engines were growing a bright pink cherry red. It really was a bit off-putting. When we went out over the coast and tried to get altitude, it was a bit difficult so I shed one of the 500lbs. But apart from that the Hercules engine was a delight. Coming back half empty and bombs gone, we used to bring the rpm down to just over 1,600. You had to keep it over 1,500 to keep the generator turning sufficiently to give you electrical power. She just sighed through the air, it was lovely. Back in to the circuit and you got lined up, got your pitch levers up and flaps down and set her at about 95 on the approach. You put her into the landing attitude and just lowered her with the throttle. You got a winner every time. There were no runways in North Africa, it was just baked earth. The ground was a bit rough, but she just used to settle like a bird on a nest. She was a forgiving aeroplane and you had total confidence in the aircraft, utter and complete confidence.

You knew that as long as she had got that geodetic construction she'd get you home. I did see one flying once at a gunnery school where the stitching had come lose from the fabric after the trailing edge. The rear gunner was sitting there looking down a tube of fabric. Rather like somebody pulling a sock off. It had split either side of the fin and it was flapping. I thought, 'God that's half as long again, it shouldn't be. Where's the bit in the middle?' The rear gunner was rather disconcerted when he landed, thankful to be on the ground.

Like any aeroplane, you didn't want to be foolish with it, get cocky with it, I have heard people say, 'Oh yes you can barrel roll a Wellington without any trouble at all', and people did. These people had the skills, but if you were bloody fool enough to try it when you only had about a couple of hundred hours you were asking for trouble. She wouldn't forgive that. But if you treated the aeroplane with respect, recognising that there where limits, limits that were published, which you could reach and perhaps go over slightly, you were alright. But if you tried to do anything damn silly believe you me like any aeroplane she would bite and probably bite hard.

In North Africa, when we moved base, we transported the entire unit in the aircraft themselves, which meant we were loading tents and ammunition boxes. I don't think we carried bombs, but I know I took my groundcrew and our own tent and everybody else's tent. People were just stuffing it in.

At the end of OTU Tiny had accumulated about 270 hours of flying, 'most of it was daylight, although there had been some at night. They were beginning to realise that the heavies would need to operate in the dark so in the latter stages the weighting was toward night flying.' On 7 May 1940 Tiny was posted to 3 Group's 9 Squadron at RAF Honington, about to join the air battle as part of the RAF's Bomber Command. Later on in the war 'tours' would be introduced, limiting the number of operations aircrew could expect. There was no such arrangement when Tiny began his operational flying, not that he felt in a position to question what the RAF required of him, 'This was an awesome major organisation. Wing commanders were gods and you had to move up to heaven before you got to air vice-marshals.' Bomber Command's activities during the early months of the war were noted for the largely ineffectual leaflet raids and some costly daylight operations on German shipping. An international consensus on avoiding civilian casualties had limited its operational scope. An idealistic stance that would steadily erode amongst all the warring nations as the war progressed and the limitations of air war technology became apparent.

Importantly two significant operations occurred on 14 and 18 December 1939, when 17 Wellingtons in total were shot from the sky whilst searching for German shipping, seriously putting into doubt the belief in well armed bombers defending themselves against enemy fighters in daylight. When Norway and Denmark became the focus for German aggression, further evidence of the risks of daylight operations were provided, notably on 12 April 1940 when six Handley Page Hampdens and three Wellingtons were lost on a shipping attack at Stavanger. Bomber Command policy unsurprisingly adjusted. Bomber crews, with the odd exception, would henceforward operate under the shroud of night. Following the opening of the German invasion of the Low Countries and the Blitzkrieg through France, further evidence of the dangers of daylight operations was provided by the crippling attrition rates suffered by the Bristol Blenheim and Fairey Battle squadrons operating in support of the hard pressed Allied armies.

Notably, though, the losses amongst the Wellingtons, Hampdens and Armstrong Whitworth Whitley's operating at night, were small.

When Tiny arrived at 9 Squadron he was crewed up with Sergeant 'Dougie' Douglas, who had been a second pilot and had flown on the fateful 18 December 1939 raid.

> Dougie was a pre-war direct entry sergeant pilot. When I crewed up with him he was about 24, a lot older than I was and a sort of elder brother figure. I don't remember socialising with him, he had his own circle of friends having been with the squadron since the outbreak of war and I was very much a new boy and wet behind the ears. He and his mates would be at the bar chattering away, and I had my contemporaries who had also come in at that time and we formed our own little group.

Following a few days of circuits and landings and cross countries, so that Douglas could check out his new second pilot, Tiny prepared for his first operation, which took place on 10 May 1940 when, 'the balloon went up in Holland'; the Germans opening up their Blitzkrieg on the Low Countries. Tiny recalls the day.

> The harsh voice of the Tannoy woke everyone up. 'All aircrew to briefing rooms.' It was scarcely 8 o'clock and, somewhat unkempt, all the crews gathered. Wing Commander Andrew 'Square' McKee, CO of 9 Squadron strode in followed by his flight commanders. Rumours were confirmed; the 'Phoney War' was over with a vengeance.
>
> Aircraft were tested, guns were cleaned, bombs were fused and ammunition belts made up. Meanwhile we could return to breakfast, wash, shave and then back to briefing at 1100 hours. The spectre of 18 December hovered over the airfield. For us new boys it was bewildering, ominous. The appetite failed, a ball of warm damp dough seemed to be located in my stomach and there was a greasy feeling in my gut. At 1100 hours there was little new; report back at 1600 hours and no one was to leave the aerodrome. A silent group gathered about the mess radiogram to listen to the news. The BEF was moving forward, the Belgians were withdrawing and in Holland there was fierce fighting with

the Luftwaffe everywhere. One thing was clear – this was the big one and we would all be in it. Dougie Douglas, calm and authoritative and our navigator Jock Gilmour, with his soft Scots brogue and cheerful mien gathered me in as we walked up to Flights to discover what lay in store.

The wing commander entered with his retinue of specialists, met, intelligence, navigation and signals officers. There was silence. 'The target is Waalhaven, the aerodrome at Rotterdam. German forces have seized it and are bringing in troops by air. The Dutch are to launch a counter-attack just before last light. The squadron will seek to crater the airfield and to soften up the Nazi defences.'

Take-off times were allocated. The met officer promised that the weather would be fine and cloudless. Intelligence surmised that there would be 'plenty of light flak, inaccurate over 5,000 feet. Heavy stuff unlikely, the enemy having no time to deploy it. And as for fighters, a few Me109s were reported, it was a bit far from their German bases, but Me110s were possible'. The crews departed, the observers and wireless operators going to their own specialist briefing.

In total Bomber Command sent 36 Wellingtons to Waalhaven airfield that night, to follow up on an attack that had been carried out by Blenheims earlier in the day. 9 Squadron would be contributing six aircraft to the attack.

It was two and a half hours to take-off and almost two hours before climbing into flying kit and going out to the aircraft. A long two hours with little to do but wonder and wait and wonder some more. The aircrew meal momentarily raised images of the condemned's cell. It was straight from the table to the crew room. Putting on the Mae West and parachute harness seemed to improve morale and climbing into the familiar environment of our aircraft L7777 was solidly reassuring. Dougie settled into his seat, checked his controls and secured his harness. The observer appeared in the hatch, straightening his back as he ducked out of the bomb bay where sand-coloured ovoids clung like insect eggs to the black beams. The port engine wheezed as the starter motor jerked the propeller into motion; the engine fired, free wheeled, fired again and steadied into a smooth rumble. The starboard engine expelled a cloud of blue-grey smoke to be dissolved in the slipstream before it too settled to a regular rhythm. I stooped to receive the wooden ladder, the face of an airman being briefly framed in the open hatch. A thumbs up, then with a thud the door shut. The grass of Honington, the ground of England, six feet away as isolated as another continent. With a lurch and a subdued squeal of brakes, the Wellington rolled forward. My journey into the unknown had begun.

The first three 9 Squadron Wellingtons took off at 1950 hours and began flying to the target in formation. The next three took off at 2000 hours, 2010 hours (in which Tiny Cooling was second pilot), and 2020 hours. Course was set and the English coast was crossed: 'As it disappeared so did my feeling of apprehension; an infusion of excitement took its place.' The enemy coast was reached and the first three 9 Squadron Wellingtons flew on to the target and in a shallow dive attacked separately. The next three Wellingtons followed up.

Ahead lights were rising rapidly in a curtain with a hem of billowing black. I remember Dougie saying to me, 'Right you go back, stand in the astrodome, and keep a look out for fighters, anything, and I'll do the flying.' I went back to the astrodome and looked around. My heart stopped when I saw another aircraft, then I recognised it was another Wellington. Straight ahead of us was a screen like those coloured bead curtains one sees in front of beach huts and doorways in the summer; coloured lights that twinkle as the wind catches them. And here was one of these hanging right across the sky straight ahead of us. It was flak and we were heading straight for it. I remember sitting there like a petrified rabbit watching these colourful lights going left and right. But as we got to them they appeared to separate.

Tiny listened in as his pilot and observer went through the bombing procedure, 'Bomb doors open. Right. Right. Steady. Left. Steady. Left. Steady. Hold it. Steady.'

Next came the 'bombs gone' and our Wellington bucked as nigh on two tons of steel-cased high explosive plunged from the gaping belly. Then there was a thwack and a piece of fabric danced up on the starboard wing. I called to

Dougie, 'We've been hit.' He replied, 'Where?' I said, 'Starboard wing.' 'Anything?' 'No it's just torn fabric.'

We pushed on through, across the coast, and came out over the North Sea again. Dougie said, 'Right you fly it and I'll go back and have a look.' I took over, flew our bomber back to England and as we saw the airfield beacon Dougie took over. We came in, landed and became very unpopular. We were the first or second to land. The light flak had punctured the starboard tyre, and as we touched down Dougie tried to hold it but couldn't. We came to a stop 90 degrees across the flare path, which meant that nobody else could land until either we had been moved or they moved the flare path.

They got us out and I remember climbing down and noticing the sweet smell of petrol. There was this sort of pustule carbuncle on the side of the wing where the self sealing had been pushed through, and petrol was dripping. You could hear the engines ticking and once you moved away you could smell the burnt exhaust. God the grass felt lovely under my feet! Wonderful! They bumped us into a wagon, drove us back and we had debriefing. Dougie looked at his watch, 'That's lucky. The bar will still be open in the mess. Tiny I'll treat you to a beer to mark a successful first operational trip.' It was nice to be back, to feel truly one of the team. We were probably half way through our first beer before the next man landed.

The 9 Squadron diary recorded that two Wellingtons came back from the raid with considerable damage and two with slight damage and one gunner suffered a slight shrapnel wound to the leg.

Over the next few days Bomber Command tried its best to disrupt the German advances. But there was little significant that could be done, and yet the cost was still high, notably the Command lost 11 from 42 Blenheims on 12 May whilst attacking bridges. German road and rail communications had been on target lists in the first days of the German offensive, but policy limited these to those west of the Rhine. The German bombing of Rotterdam in the middle of May was highly significant in initiating a change in policy. The RAF bombers were now allowed to venture further into the Nazi homeland. The night of 15/16 May 1940 holds a significant place in the history of Bomber Command as the occasion of the first strategic bombing attacks on German industry. The Ruhr was visited by 99 aircraft spread across 16 targets. This night was also the first time Tiny Cooling would fly over Germany, attacking Bottrop. The operational report in the 9 Squadron diary that night is worth recording, and can be contrasted with the operational reports related further into this book.

> In accordance with HQ No. 3 Group instructions... dated 15 May 1940, six aircraft of No. 9 Squadron carried out a raid against target A69. Aircraft proceeded singly, taking off at irregular intervals between 2050 and 2235 hours.
>
> On the route out between the English and Dutch coast weather was hazy up to 5,000 feet. Above that it was fairly clear. Between the Dutch coast and target, clouds gradually formed varying between 2/10ths and 8/10ths, between 5,000 and 11,000 feet. Over the target area, the first four aircraft found a cloudless sky, but very hazy. The last two aircraft, arriving at approximately 0045 to 0115 hours encountered 8/10ths cloud at 10,000 feet. Due to thick haze and clouds the target was very difficult to locate.
>
> Four aircraft encountered a violent thunderstorm between the Dutch and English coasts en-route home. One aircraft was badly struck three times by lightning, causing a valve to fuse in the wireless set, also terrific sparks shot off from the leading edge of the main planes, airscrews and front turret of the aircraft. The other three aircraft complained of receiving brush discharge of a less violent nature. The wireless sets [in three aircraft] were put out of action by the electrical storm. Due to this two aircraft were unable to definitely locate themselves [and made force landings on other airfields]... Two captains considered that they had bombed the correct target. The other four captains were unable to locate the primary target, and therefore carried out attacks on what they considered was the secondary target. Intense searchlight activity was encountered, but AA fire, which was fairly plentiful, was inaccurate. There was no opposition from enemy fighters.

This report provides an excellent snapshot of the operational difficulties Bomber Command crews had to face at this early stage of the bombing campaign. Throughout the war the weather conditions and target location and navigation tested the skills of the aircrews. And as we shall see, the use of bombers operating singly over Germany was a tactic that would not last.

Tiny and his crew returned unscathed from this particular operation, although they did encounter the severe electrical storm on their return. Indeed all but one aircraft came back from Bomber Command operations that night, the only loss being that of a 115 Squadron Wellington, owing to the adverse weather, crashing in France. A significant night undoubtedly, at little cost to Bomber Command, but with little damage to the targets. A report from Münster, where six bombs fell, which was in fact not on the target list that night, included, 'This bombing created a sensation and for days on end thousands of inquisitive people were attracted to the scene.'[1] Bombing at this stage of the war was clearly a novelty for the German people. Such scenes would in the years to come be all too familiar.

Tiny was next operational on 18/19 May attacking marshalling yards in Cologne. Sixty aircraft were sent out that night, only one was lost. The night before no aircraft had been lost from 130 dispatched. Compare that with 11 out of 12 Blenheims lost on a day attack on 17 May (the twelfth aircraft damaged and crash landing) and three out of 13 Blenheims lost on 18 May. Further evidence that for a bomber crew safety, at this stage of the war, lay amidst the shroud of night.

With three operations now inscribed in his logbook, Tiny had gained essential operational experience, but he was under no illusion about the seriousness and risks of the air battle he was involved in. He was beginning to learn about and understand the vital importance of crew unity that could certainly improve a crew's odds of survival. As Tiny recalled, 'We were a bunch of six youngsters, all really at the same level of experience and we had to rely on each other. We had total bonding and trust. The fact that you had no option may have been relevant, but the point was that you did. You had to have total trust, and it existed.' Each airman in a crew had his job to do, and he was an integral part of the fighting unit. The crew would have a shared experience of the war, which would forge a bond that would often last for years to come, into retirement and old age. But each airman would also have his own unique recollection of the war.

I would say that each individual in the crew experienced his own particular war. The rear gunner was 70 feet away down the back end in his tiny little cubicle. He was a disembodied voice over the intercom. The wireless operator had his headphones on and a mass of dials and couldn't see a damn thing. The navigator was in his cubicle. When you came up to a target the bomb aimer was looking straight down into it watching everything come up. Basically the others couldn't see anything, except the rear gunner and he saw it when we were on our way out.

I don't think I was ever scared, once I was in the thick of it. But the time that was least attractive was when you felt you had that ball of wet warm dough in your guts; between the time that your name went on the board and the time you took off. Once airborne and on your way, you were enjoying flying.

Tiny's next two operations took place on the nights of 20/21[2] and 24/25 May; as part of Bomber Command's attempts to delay the German advances. On the latter raid 12 aircraft were sent by 9 Squadron, the diary recording the task of the airmen, 'to interfere with the enemy movements and to prevent both rest and activity of troops in and about the target area throughout the hours of darkness'. Over the course of just over four hours that night, the 9 Squadron Wellingtons attacked what they could find, 'each aircraft made two to four runs, dropping the bombs in sticks. Aircraft carrying out low level or shallow dive attacks also attacked with the front and rear guns. Altogether 7,400 rounds were expended. There was considerable searchlight and AA activity, which was accurate and four aircraft were damaged'.

We felt we might do something. Towns and villages were out; farms and settlements of any kind were not to be attacked unless elements of German forces could be identified, such as tanks, lorries, guns. In the bright moonlight, from 1,500 feet, the landscape had the look of a photographic negative; shades of grey scattered with irregular threads and patches of moon-silver from reflecting streams, dykes and little lakes. Somewhere below lay the enemy but they gave no sign. Not a shot was fired at the Wellingtons sweeping their allotted areas. Bivouacked in towns, villages and farms, concealed in woods or moon shadow with camouflage nets and branches, there was no need for the advancing Wehrmacht to betray its presence. What was one Wellington when the whole British Expeditionary Force might be destroyed? We bombed deserted railway lines and road junctions, copses and woodland strips, and then, frustrated, flew home. Happily, our routes lay over enemy occupied territory; the air above our own forces was doubly dangerous offering but false security. Soldiers, British and French alike, fired at anything that flew.

It was a week before Tiny's next flight, 'over the top'. As a result of the German thrust to the Channel coast the British Expeditionary Force now had its back to the sea at Dunkirk and one of the most momentous events in the history of the European war was about to unfold. At the end of May and the beginning of June an all-out effort was made to extricate as many Allied troops from the beaches around Dunkirk as possible, using all kinds of sea-faring craft. Bomber Command airmen tried their best to protect the perimeter around Dunkirk, the Blenheims attacking German positions by day, the Wellingtons and Whitleys kept up the effort at night. 9 Squadron played its part and on the night of 31 May Tiny Cooling flew to Soex, a few miles inland from Dunkirk. Again the 9 Squadron diary provides a summary of the nature of the flying that night.

> 12 aircraft of this squadron carried out raids against the road junctions at Soex. Nine aircraft found and bombed the correct target, two aircraft bombed the roadway in the village of Warmhoudt, which was 5 miles away from the target. One aircraft was unable to locate the primary target and therefore bombed the secondary target which was Nieuport... High level and medium level attacks were carried out by most aircraft, varying in heights between 2,000 and 7,000 feet. Two aircraft carried out shallow dive attacks down to approximately 1,000 feet. The night was very dark and all aircraft had to use parachute flares to locate their objectives.

Three nights later Tiny would fly to the same target area. Earlier that day 3 Group had sent through orders to 9 Squadron tasking the aircrews to 'interfere with enemy movement and action by sustained attack'. The operational order went on to list the targets.

1) Berques – twelve sorties except one bomb from each sortie.

2) [Gun] Batteries situated along the coast from Point de Gravelines to two miles west of this point. Each sortie to drop one bomb on this position, some to drop on way out and some on way home. These batteries are interfering with the embarkation of our troops. No repeat no other alternative target is to be attacked except in the event of a sortie being unable to identify the target allotted to it and finding one of the other targets, the aircraft may attack that target... Owing to the close proximity of our own troops NO bombs are to be dropped except on the actual target which has been definitely identified.

As it was the 'miracle of deliverance', as described by Winston Churchill, had all but ended that day, 338,000 men eventually reaching safe shores. This was to be Bomber Command's last night of attacks on the German positions around Dunkirk. Tiny's recollection of the preparation for this raid and that night's events remain firmly lodged in his memory.

We all assembled in the briefing room in early evening sunlight. Take-off would be 2000 hours, the target Berques, German positions south of Dunkirk.

'For God's sake', said Wing Commander McKee, with uncharacteristic emotion, 'Make sure you drop your bombs over enemy-occupied territory. Our troops have enough to cope with without the added burden of someone's misdirected aim. And keep well away from the Channel. The Navy will fire at anything overhead. In present circumstances, who can blame them?'

Routine took over as the crews gathered their equipment, were taken to their aircraft, carried out pre-flight checks, started the engines and took their place on the runway. Tiny Cooling was to take on new responsibilities this night. 'It was the first time that I really carried out an operation with Dougie acting as second pilot.'

Prior to take-off Dougie said, 'Right you are going to do the take-off tonight and fly up to the target. I'll take over as we come up to the target and then you can fly it back again and land it.' As we approached the coast at

Orfordness there were two other Wimpys ahead of us, in several individual air currents. It was the time that the film Henry V was on, and I thought, 'We few, we happy few, we band of brothers.' It was great; you really felt that you were doing something. We got to the coast and turned right losing sight of the other aircraft. There appeared to be another sunrise; it was Dunkirk burning 90 miles away.

There was no real need for navigation. As darkness fell, the golden glow increased. We came into the north east of Dunkirk. We didn't want to go anywhere near the Navy or anywhere near the beaches. They didn't ask which side you were on. Dougie took over, it was my job to drop the bombs, whilst our navigator Jock Gilmour kept track of our wanderings as we sought out targets of opportunity. The target was Berques but really it was a gesture because there was nothing we could do; there was no target. Dougie said he wanted us to drop the bombs.

From the bomb-aimer's position the sight was awesome. Six thousand feet below, Dunkirk was a sea of flame glinting like a brightly spotlit plaque of beaten copper. In black intaglio, the gutted streets patterned its surface; large buildings were gaily decked with bunting but the bunting was pennants of flame. The sea beyond reflected golden light, itself like beaten copper but less bright. Somewhere, within that mass of fluid amber, the British Army was struggling to extricate itself. We turned and flew south, avoiding the coast, skirting the column of smoke thrust like a stake into the heart of the town. A flare ignited and drifted above a pale grey sea of smoke. We might have been flying over a lake of milky water. From its depth, bright flashes winked, small fires glowed: guns firing, transport burning.

Targets of opportunity! We were trying to pick something. We wanted to make sure that we didn't drop them within the perimeter. So it was anything that we could find on the other side, but there was nothing to see. I suppose the only thing we could hope for was that perhaps we had made some axis military unit duck and pause for a few seconds so that another boat got away. But really we had no idea what was going on down there. All we were doing was stirring the pot, but it was an incredible sight.

We left the burning beacon and headed home.

There was quiet in the mess when we returned, a very sober attitude. The post-operational release of tension somehow did not take place.

On 7 June Archibald Sinclair, the Secretary of State for Air sent a message to the RAF personnel, undoubtedly to try and boost morale:

> The War Cabinet have expressed their high appreciation of the fine work of the Royal Air Force in covering the evacuation of the British and French forces from Dunkirk. All ranks have done magnificently in this trial of strength with the enemy. The pilots and crews of our aircraft have gained an ascendancy over the German Air Force.
>
> They have inflicted on the enemy losses far greater than our own, and they have played an indispensable part in preventing the destruction of the British and French armies in Flanders. Throughout the battle our aircraft have operated with unparalleled intensity, sustained by the sure skill and unwearying work of the ground personnel. All ranks have worthily upheld the traditions of the Royal Air Force and have earned the country's gratitude.

The remnants of the BEF were now back on friendly soil but the battle for France continued, as did Bomber Command's commitment to doing all it could to aid an ally close to defeat. The Blenheim crews kept up their attacks on German troops and communications by day and continued to suffer. The Hampden, Wellington and Whitley crews continued to ply their destructive trade in the dark, and over Germany. On 5 June Tiny Cooling flew again to Germany – Duisburg, the squadron diary noting the experiences of the 9 Squadron crews and providing an example of the difficulties faced by bomber crews in addition to weather and navigation, the defences en-route and at the target. At this stage of the war the main threat at night came from the ground.

> Weather conditions over the whole route were good throughout the period of operations. The night was very dark, with a light haze up to 5,000 feet. Navigation was carried out by DR [dead reckoning] assisted by DF [direction finding]. All aircraft experienced very little difficulty in getting to the area of the target, but due to

darkness found difficulty in locating the actual target.

The night was very dark and parachute flares were used by all aircraft for locating and attacking the target. Four aircraft failed to find the primary target and bombed the secondary ones... All aircraft encountered intense light and heavy flak fire over both the targets attacked. One enemy aircraft was seen, but no attack was made. All captains complained that they were prevented from doing accurate bombing by the intensity of the searchlight activities. These were very accurate and although avoiding action was taken, captains found it impossible to get out of them. On previous nights it was found that by dropping a parachute flare the searchlights would concentrate on it, but on this occasion it did not happen. The aircraft were held all the time. Squadron Leader Peacock and crew who were carrying out a raid in the Ruhr area failed to return.

Squadron Leader Peacock's Wellington had fallen to flak shortly after crossing the Dutch coast. He lost his life along with his observer. The other four members of the crew were captured.

Tiny now had eight nights away from operations. The next time he took part in the air battle would be in an attempt to support the land campaign, one of 163 crews attacking communication targets in France, Belgium and Holland on the night of 13/14 June. One Wellington crew was lost that night, from 9 Squadron and Tiny, as we shall soon discover, would experience at first hand some of the human emotions surrounding such a loss. Tiny flew again a few nights later, on 18/19 June visiting Germany once more. This night has become fixed in his memory and many years later he recorded on paper the events that would unfold the next day.

Unusually it was an overcast morning. A thin damp mist from the summer anti-cyclone restricted visibility, a cloud layer began to creep in as we crossed the Suffolk coast homeward bound from a sortie to Germany. The night had been dark, the gibbous moon briefly mirrored the ghostly reflective Rhine in a landscape of deep shadow.

We got back at about three and were in bed an hour later. Sleep sodden, it was a major effort to claw back to consciousness as the wireless operator tugged at the blankets then took down the blackout screen.

'Wha'ssa matter? Why the panic?'

'We're on a search. Butler's missing in P – Peter. Looks as if they've ditched. We're off at 0930. The Wingco's out now. Took off at 0530 with the stand-by crew.'

It took a moment or two to sink in. A Wellington down in the drink; six men bobbing about in a little yellow dinghy – perhaps. But which six? Mentally the mind ticked off the names and images of close comrades.

Butler's navigator had the room directly opposite me in the mess, a fellow called Charles Naylor. Very nice chap, very quiet, desperately quiet, never drank, never smoked, never swore.

One morning about a week before, he had tapped on my door as I dressed. As he came in, anguish and disbelief were reflected in his face. I said 'Hello, What's up?' He looked at me, and said, 'Bob Hewitt's missing. His wife's expecting a baby.' [The night of 13/14 June 1940, his crew of six losing their lives]. He stood stock still a moment then, almost slowly, he collapsed to his knees to bury his face in the coarse blanket of the bed, sobbing like a child. What the hell do you do? I was just turned 20, he was about the same age. It was total embarrassment in a sense, a chap my own age blubbing his heart out with his head buried in my blanket. Totally nonplussed I waited for the flood of sorrow to subside. He part rose, sat on the bed and looked at me with a wan smile, 'Thank you very much,' he said, 'I had to talk to somebody.' I made a few platitudinous remarks. As he got up, I put my arms across his shoulder. He smiled gratefully. 'Thanks,' he said 'I'm sorry I knocked you up.' Then he went out across the corridor to his own room.

But now it was Charles Naylor who was missing and Tiny and his crew had been tasked with the job of searching for their squadron colleagues. They made their way to their Wellington, which had been refuelled, with the starting trolley already plugged in.

The groundcrew was subdued, they knew the purpose of our sortie. A wooden ladder reached into the uplifted nose and still somewhat weary we climbed aboard, settling into our accustomed places. There was the familiar wheeze of the starter motor, the slow jerky rotation of the airscrew, the blip, the wisp of vapour from the exhaust, the whorl of blue white smoke, shredded by the slipstream as the engine bellowed into powerful thrusting motion.

Minutes later and our aircraft was lumbering over the grass, the twin Pegasus growling steadily. Fifteen degrees of flap, close cooling gills then a turn into the wind. The throttles advanced steadily and the rumble became a roar and then a howl. The tail rose, our aircraft surging forward to thrust her aggressive chin and bulbous turreted nose into the air. At one thousand feet, our Wellington turned and we set course for the coast eastwards, to the cruel sage-green sea.

Butler's weak distress signal had been tracked until it finally disappeared. When the wing commander had taken off, Butler's aircraft would have been out of fuel, so they had to be down somewhere. But where? Could the searching crews rely upon the last plotted position or had the crew managed to fly on below the level of radar? Indeed had they turned back for Holland knowing that they would never make friendly landfall?

Our rear gunner and navigator watched the receding coast to gauge the horizontal visibility; it would not be possible when all about was a uniform vista of undulating water, frilled with flecks of foam. For the pilot the instrument panel held his attention. Height 800 feet, airspeed 130 knots, oil temperature 60 degrees centigrade, pressure 80lbs/sq in, cylinder heads marginally below 200 degrees centigrade. If three hours were to be spent at sea it was prudent to check that all was well before we lost sight of land.

Tiny's Wellington, now over the North Sea, flew east-south-east, 'out towards the distant estuary of the Scheldt, into the flimsy muslin mist.'

The front and rear gunners had a dual task, to scan the surface of the sea for the yellow dot of a dinghy, and to peer into the white haze as it fused into grey cloud above or dissolved the horizon into a pulsing expanse of water, watchful for fighters. Whilst the Luftwaffe was unlikely to put up a major sweep to intercept a couple of low flying aircraft safely out at sea, it could be a profitable training exercise for their own radar and novitiate interceptor crews.

Fifty miles out, and halfway to Holland, the search began, with the aircraft flying to a pattern.

The first leg was equal in length to one and a half times the visibility before a left turn through ninety degrees for another of equal length. Then a further turn of ninety degrees, the length of which would be doubled. Turning through a right angle on each occasion, extending each third leg by just less than twice the assessed visibility, a widening pattern of search would be established covering every square kilometre of sea from the starting point. After some eighty minutes, the easternmost heading would lie within less than thirty miles of the enemy coast.

And that would be close enough to hostile territory, 'the CO had already covered to within sight of the sand and mud banks of the Scheldt.' If nothing was found then there would be a move to a search area to the south west between the Thames estuary and Ostend. If they did manage to spot the dinghy then they would circle and send a signal enabling ground stations to get a good bearing; then remain in the area acting as a guide to rescue craft, but running the risk of enemy intervention.

It was agreed that two miles was the effective visibility, beyond that the prospects of seeing a ten foot in diameter yellow disc were poor. The navigator worked out a list of courses to steer and our aircraft banked and settled on a track parallel to the distant Dutch coast.

Two minutes, turn. Two minutes, turn. Four minutes, turn. Four minutes, turn. Six minutes – the pattern progressed. Six hundred feet below, grey wrinkled lips salivated with flecks of froth, pouted at us, a passive omnivorous greedy sea mouthing its insatiable appetite. Eight minutes, turn. Ten minutes, turn. Ten minutes...

'There's something away to port.' The navigator's voice in the headphones broke through the sonorous drone of the engines.

'Turn port, Skipper' came from the rear gunner, 'There's something moving in the swell.'

The wingtip was but a double span above the water as we swept round in a steep turn, losing height for clearer identification. There was something there, something yellow, something dark peeping briefly over the parapets of the restless water. Excitement gathered, ready to turn to delight. Had we found them? The wireless operator was poised over his set, eager to tap out a sighting report. Close now, suddenly we were overhead.

A lemon yellow oil drum, and two broken baulks of timber lashed or entangled with wet rope undulated at the contemptuous behest of the teasing waves. I slid open the side panel to see better, to be sure it was not some cruel trick of light, some idiot mistake. The wind howled past in a shriek of derision. I slammed the window shut. We signalled base, said what we had found. 'Noted' came the response. We picked up the pattern again. Twelve minutes, turn. Twelve minutes, turn. We set course for the second search area.

Butler, his navigator Naylor and the rest of their crew were never found. The episode remains very much embedded in Tiny's memory.

Every year I walk the cool grey cloisters of the Air Forces Memorial at Runnymede [to the missing] where I know I shall find so many friends and comrades. He is there amongst them, as are all his crew, '1940 Sergeant Naylor C'. Just six letters and an initial neatly incised in the grey stone. But I see, still clearly, a small figure kneeling beside my bed in the filtered morning sunshine; a lemon-coloured oil drum, two broken beams, a snaffle of rope, answering only to the timeless rhythm of the relentless sage-green sea.

At the time of course, there was little opportunity to lament the fate of other crews. To close out the last week of June Tiny flew on three operations to Germany. During this period Bomber Command would often be sending out around 100 aircraft a night to targets in the Reich. What is worth noting is that the bomber force would be attacking numerous targets; there was no focus on a specific one. A tactic that would be challenged as the war progressed with a move to mass attacks on one target overwhelming the defences.

But the war was now to enter a new stage. Bomber Command

would not be fighting to save an ally anymore. The RAF bomber boys were about to fight in the defence of their homeland. Within a few weeks of the evacuation of Dunkirk, France finally accepted defeat. Britain and her Commonwealth allies now stood alone. The German military, fortunately, then delayed, allowing the British forces to regroup and re-equip on home soil. RAF Fighter Command braced itself to meet the conquering Luftwaffe. RAF Bomber Command kept up strategic attacks against German industry, oil, airfields and aircraft factories. The political inclination to avoid civilian casualties was certainly waning. In July 1940 Winston Churchill wrote to Lord Beaverbrook, 'When I look round to see how we can win this war I see that there is only one sure path... and that is an absolutely devastating, exterminating attack by very heavy bombers from this country upon the Nazi homeland'. But at this stage of the war the RAF's bomber weapon just did not have the capability to carry out such attacks. That would come in a few years time. Meanwhile the men of Bomber Command were doing their best to fight back, which did provide the propagandists the opportunity to show the British public that there was still hope, although history would show that the raids were causing little material damage. In addition the bomber crews also had to be prepared to support anti-invasion operations. Most importantly trying to destroy enemy transport barges that were assembling in Channel and North Sea ports, ready for the seaborne assault on England. These attacks have been represented by historians as being of a supportive nature to the heroic feats of Fighter Command. Indeed they were but they were extremely significant. The Luftwaffe had been tasked to wrestle control of the skies over England, thereby ensuring that any crossing of the Channel would be relatively unopposed. With Fighter Command, indeed the RAF, defeated, the Luftwaffe could concentrate on keeping the Royal Navy at distance. Bomber Command's attacks on the barges were significant in that they were clear proof of how important air superiority was. Bomber Command proved that if the RAF were not defeated the crossing of the Channel would be extremely hazardous and extremely costly. The German Navy was being reminded, daily, how susceptible their flotillas were to aerial attack.

Chapter 2

From the Battle of Britain to North Africa

A variety of expectations were placed on Bomber Command during those momentous summer days and nights of 1940. The Air Ministry issued six significant directives; German industry, particularly still featured on operational orders. Added, as the Air Ministry required, would be German communications, burning of forest and crops, German shipping and attacks on the Luftwaffe – the airfields and the aircraft factories. Bomber Command would also be making one other significant contribution to persuade Adolf Hitler that the execution of Operation Sealion would be a costly mistake. Meanwhile the Luftwaffe mustered its forces within range of England, and made the first tentative probes into UK airspace. RAF Fighter Command deployed its squadrons in response and Bomber Command sent aircrews by night to the Reich.

On the night of 13/14 July 1940, Tiny Cooling flew as second pilot with Flight Lieutenant Smalley (Sergeant Douglas having been 'screened', completing a tour of duty) detailed for the Focke-Wulf aircraft factory at Bremen. Then ten nights later he took up first pilot duties attacking Gelsenkirchen. On 25/26 July he took his crew to Eshwege, and their last operation in July, on 28/29 July, was to Cologne. There had been no change in tactics, Bomber Command still spread its bombers thinly across numerous targets, 287 sorties were carried out on the nights Tiny was operational, 11 aircraft were lost, 24 airmen were killed and 15 captured. Another aspect of the bombing campaign at this stage of the war is worth noting. In addition to bombing German targets the 3 Group operation orders also asked crews to carry out the 'dropping of Nickels [leaflets] whilst causing maximum damage to targets... and creating maximum disturbance over Germany during the hours of darkness'. With respect to the Nickels, included were statements such as, 'minimum of two bundles and maximum of six bundles of Nickels one to be carried by each sortie and should be dropped in a populous area adjacent to the objectives for bombing'. Clearly this would require crews to spend longer over Germany and no doubt led to some losses. Tiny had no real feeling either way on the value of such an exercise. Sir Arthur Harris, who would later become Commander-in-Chief of Bomber Command, made clear in his post-war memoir his feelings about leafleting: 'My personal view is that the only thing achieved was largely to supply the Continent's requirements of toilet paper for the five long years of war.'

Despite the war and all the rigours of an air force operational life, Tiny had still been able to taste the finer side of life. During the month of July he became engaged to Joan Jordan, who he had met on a blind date in December 1938.

> We saw this ring, in a large jewellers in Hull. It was £14, twenty days pay! I said to the chap there, 'I tell you what, I'll give you what I have at the moment as a deposit and then the lady will come in another day, pay the balance and pick it up'. He said, 'No, no my dear sir. She'll want to wear it'. So we took it. This is during the Battle of Britain, I was wearing uniform with a pilot's wings, and he trusted me for over half the price of the ring to be paid two weeks later. Of course he had no guarantee that I would still be alive.

Tiny, naturally, felt it wise to try and avoid death for reasons other than just to pay off a debt.

Poor weather compounded by navigational difficulties lowered the odds of a crew surviving a sortie, lessened further by flak. Tiny also recollects another of the perils of flying over Germany, experienced on one of his early operations as a pilot.

> On one trip, we were coming back at about 11,000ft when the rear gunner said, 'There's balloons.' I said, 'Not at this height.' The navigator looked out and said, 'There are.' Sure enough, it was a brilliant moonlit night, we were

passing virtually over the middle of the Rhur and they had balloons flying at our height. This was some time in 1940 when the Germans realised quite rightly that really we didn't possess any offensive weapons and if they kept quiet we wouldn't know where the hell we were. The one thing to indicate that there was a target underneath was to shoot at the aircraft overhead. We didn't identify the targets by careful map reading or anything like that. We saw where all the muck and filth was coming from and thought well that must be it. So if they kept quiet we kept quiet. But on this occasion I remember seeing these balloons, doing a sharp 180 and heading back into the centre of Germany. I wanted to get away from those damn balloons. God knows where we had been, but navigation was not a fine art in 1940.

Despite all the difficulties Bomber Command pressed on with the night offensive as the summer progressed. On the night of 12 August Tiny took his crew to Diepholz and on 15 August it was to Gelsenkirchen. Two days later and there was a sense of anticipation at RAF Honington, the station diary recording:

17 August, 1300 hours: Preliminary instructions concerning the night's operations were received. The special objective turned out to be G.225 (Berlin) and a certain amount of pleasure and anticipation, in that this station was to be amongst the first to repay the attacks on London. All this enthusiasm was quelled when the target G.225 was cancelled.

As such Tiny went to Gottingen, Bomber Command sending 102 bombers out that night to attack airfields in France, Belgium and Holland, along with five German targets. Tiny was at a later date, whilst still at 9 Squadron, actually detailed for Berlin, had attended the briefing and climbed aboard his Wellington.

I had started up and we were moving out of the dispersal and another aircraft passed by blowing a coil of barbed wire right across the track in front of us. We taxied into it and it got wrapped all round the undercarriage. So we were scrubbed and I never got to Berlin.

The crews flying out of RAF Honington had to date been taking the war to the enemy. On 19 August the war came directly to them. The Luftwaffe campaign to take out the RAF's defensive capabilities was reaching crisis point with the attack now centred at the RAF itself, its infrastructure, its aircraft, pilots and airfields. Notably it wasn't only Fighter Command's stations that were under attack during the Battle of Britain.

RAF Honington Diary – 19 August 1940
0750 hours – Our anti-invasion section stood down.
0932 hours – Instructions were received to prepare ten aircraft for operations that night.
0955 hours – 3 Group asked about the unserviceability of our aerodrome and whether we were taking steps to remedy it. It was made clear by us that the aerodrome was only obstructed by a crashed aircraft and that it had been in constant use day and night.
1237 hours – Advance information of the night's operations was received.
1254 hours – An Air Raid warning 'Yellow' was received, and remained in force until 1314 hours.
1615 hours – A surprise attack by one enemy aircraft was made on the Station. The Station was taken completely unawares and the bombs dropped caused 24 casualties, of which 8 proved fatal. Structural damage consisted mainly of pierced and shattered brickwork, broken windows, concrete road and parade ground. A number of incendiary bombs were dropped, but fell in open ground and did no damage. Parts of the station were machine gunned with no effect.
1622 hours – Much ironical comment was caused when the Home Office 'Yellow' Air Raid warning was received.
1810 hours – Our 'K' site informed us that they had been attacked. Some high explosive and a number of incendiary bombs were dropped but did no more damage than to make craters.
1815 hours – The [Station] Group Captain spoke to the Air Officer Commanding-in-Chief, Headquarters Bomber Command and said that we would carry out operations as ordered.
1830 hours – A further attack was made on the Station. The approach of the raider was observed and shouts warned personnel to take cover. Only one man was injured although the bombs dropped caused the collapse of one wing of a barrack block and damaged a hangar. Our anti-

aircraft defences were able to open fire but had no success (a later report from No. 3 Group told us that this raider had been shot down).

2052 hours – Ten aircraft took off on the night's operations as instructed... at times between 2052 and 2113.

2157 hours – A delayed action bomb, dropped during the first raid on the Station, exploded. The concussion was felt through the Station, but no damage was done.

Tiny at the time of the first bombing this day was in the station mess.

There was a whistle and a bang and everybody dived. A few minutes later heads started popping up over the tables with all the food laid out, saying, 'Ooh, what was that?' One bomb fell close to my room, blew in the windows and a bomb splinter, which I kept, went right through a booklet I had.

On 24 August 1940 Tiny flew to Cologne and on 29 August to Mannheim. Bomber Command's operational tactics remained the same, numerous aircraft sent out to numerous targets, crews responsible for their own navigation to and from the target. As Tiny acknowledges, at this stage of the bomber war actually finding a target was not the easiest of tasks.

It was all by dead reckoning. We had astro-navigation but none of us were any good at it. We were grotesquely under trained. We could fly the aeroplanes, but where we flew them and what we did when we got there was in the lap of the gods. Some things you couldn't miss, places like Cologne on the river, but when somebody said go and find an oil refinery at Gelsenkirchen, which was a favourite target, it was a different matter. We went there time and time and time again. It was probably about as big as a car park in the centre of a town square, in a built-up area covered with smog and fog and filth. And you would be being shot at. You just believed what the navigator said, 'left, left, right, I think that's it. OK bombs gone.' You thought, 'Thank God for that let's get out.'

A further example of the prevailing Bomber Command tactics is the night of 1/2 September when 131 Blenheims, Hampdens, Wellingtons (one flown by Tiny Cooling) and Whitleys went to ten German targets, two Italian targets and airfields in Holland. The cost was two Wellingtons failing to return and eight further aircraft crashing on home soil. On 4/5 September Tiny flew to the Harz mountains, the operational orders requiring the attacking crews, carrying an incendiary bombload, to destroy military objectives by setting fire to certain areas of forest.

Despite the difficulties the Bomber Command crews were facing in locating and bombing targets, there was a general sense of optimism from command to group to squadron to aircrew, about the results of the raids. Bomber Command intelligence reports through the month of September are constantly reporting 'severe damage', 'great devastation'. Excerpts from two reports below are typical of the kind of propaganda that was sustaining the belief in the bomber offensive.

Bomber Command Intelligence Report – 4 September: A reliable source reports from his own observation the profound effect that recent raids have had upon the population of Berlin. The people were absolutely convinced that their AA defences could not be penetrated and the apparent ease with which the RAF reached their objectives has severely disillusioned them. Friends of the source are talking of moving to Austria and Czechoslovakia.

Considerable restrictions have been placed upon the movement in Germany of foreigners, even Italians, so that they shall not observe damaged areas.

A neutral who has been five months in Germany reports of the severe damage caused in raids and of the accuracy of the bombing so that only in a small number of cases has civilian property in the neighbourhood of military targets been hit.

A highly placed German official in a neutral country admitted that the RAF were causing great inconvenience. Production and transport arrangements had been upset and nerves were frayed. He was forced to admit to some admiration of the RAF, who, irrespective of the success or failure of individual raids never wasted themselves by attacking targets that were not really important.

Bomber Command Intelligence Report – 20 September: A reliable source has reported the great success of our razzle bombs in the attacks on forests.

The Rhine-Westphalia electricity works, the most important industrial public utility co. in Germany, serving the Rhine-Ruhr area, seems to be entirely destroyed by British bombers.

Tiny now appreciates that such appreciations were in fact wishful thinking.

We believed it at the time. But we had no means of knowing if we were bombing dummy flares or decoy fires. We didn't even know how many aircraft were going other than on our own squadron. We were novices basically and we did the best we could. Apparently we started fires but to be able to come back and say, for example, that we had hit an oil refinery in Gelsenkirchen was to say the least a bit hopeful. We weren't particularly under pressure to make optimistic reports. At debriefing they were fishing for confirmatory detail. They were debriefing other crews as well so they wanted to see if the jigsaw fit, to make a recognisable picture. But there was no pressure for great tales of, 'There was I and Germany was reeling from the shock after we left'.

Following the 'fire raising' of 4/5 September Tiny enjoyed a fortnight away from operational duties. In the meantime the Battle of Britain was at its most intense and across the English Channel the Germans were mustering an invasion armada. The Honington diary recorded on 7 September, (the day of the fateful switch in Luftwaffe tactics to the targeting of London) '1845 hours – We were warned to take certain anti-invasion precautions as an attempted invasion was believed imminent. Aircraft were bombed up, ammunitioned and fuelled and crews stood by. Parachute guards, gun crews and all defence personnel were on the alert'. The invasion would not materialise but it cannot be understated that the threat of a German landing was ever present.

Tiny next flew operationally on the night of 17/18 September 1940, detailed for the marshalling yards at Hamm. On this night his faith in the ability of the Wellington to keep him alive was strengthened.

We took off for somewhere in Germany, and climbed right out towards Orfordness. I didn't seem to be able to get

9 Squadron Wellington

above 90 knots. We were climbing desperately slowly and I realised that there was something very odd. I decided that it was no good, we couldn't get any altitude, we had no speed, so we went back. We arrived back over base and did a circuit. We still had the bombs on. By that time I had about 60 or 80 hours on Wellingtons. It was dusk, not dark, and we lined up, and started to come in. The speed fell and fell and fell and it fell off the clock. The rate of climb indicator was showing that I was climbing at about 1,000 feet a minute. The aircraft felt all right and I landed. One of the fitters, in a moment of excess, had put Kilfrost paste over the pitot-head. I had landed an aircraft with an almost full fuel load, an almost full bomb load, with an instrument which was u/s, with no reliable airspeed indicator and with no reliable rate of climb indicator. I just landed, taxied it back and took out another aeroplane.

When I think back on it, I feel I was a bloody fool. Anybody in their right senses would have jettisoned the bombs over the sea, and flown around for a couple of hours [to burn off fuel]. But to come in with the bloody bombs on board. It never crossed my mind to dump them.

To be able to return to base, find another aircraft and then go back on ops was a luxury that was possible at this stage of the war, something that could not be done later on without extreme risk, operating outside of safety in numbers.

On the night of 17/18 September 1940 Bomber Command had lost just two Hampdens, reflecting the low nighttime loss rates. Indeed during Tiny's time at 9 Squadron, his unit's attrition rate was quite low; in the period of 26 June to 14/15 October six aircraft were lost on operations (and one whilst training). An obvious result of the move to operating at night. Martin

Middlebrook and Chris Everitt in the *Bomber Command War Diaries* state that in the period 26 June to 12/13 October, 66 aircraft were lost from 1,885 sorties in daylight (3.5%), 180 aircraft lost from 8,804 sorties at night (2.0%). So the switch to nighttime operations was certainly worthwhile with respect to lowering operational loss rates, no doubt helping morale. As Tiny recalled:

> There was a peculiar security about the night. The fact that you couldn't see anything didn't necessarily mean to say there was nothing there. There were things lurking in the night which were a bit hazardous but because one personally didn't experience it, you didn't really think much about it.

Nevertheless when crews didn't return to base after an operation, their colleagues had to somehow deal with the realisation that the war claimed lives. Early on in the war the men of Bomber Command began to establish a mindset that could help them cope with the losses.

> Survival was partly due to the learning curve, partly luck. I'm not sure what else. God? People ask me if I believe in God. I say, 'I was a pilot in Bomber Command and lived.' It doesn't mean to say I believe in religion.
>
> You might talk about your next leave, but you never talked about next month. There was almost a tacit acceptance, which never was manifested, that you never looked forward because you didn't know whether there was anything to look forward to. You might talk about what you were going to do tomorrow or you reckon you might be going on leave next week, but in June you didn't say well I hope I shall be home for Christmas, or it'll be nice to do this, that and the other. It was all immediate future rather than a longer distance future. You lived from day to day.

Then there were other ways of dealing with the tension, but it was all a matter of choice.

> All this business of roistering and what have you, a lot of it was bravado. Bear in mind that a lot of us had been raised on the tales of the Royal Flying Corps and the wild

drinking parties. Initially there were thoughts of, 'Well we've got to live up to the example set us by our forebears.' There were lots of mad sods of course but there was nothing over-the-top spontaneous, not when I was there. What it was like later in 1943, at the bomber stations in Yorkshire and Lincolnshire, when things were pretty rugged and you knew that you stood about a 10% chance of finishing 30 ops, then I wouldn't know. But the people I was with both in 9 Squadron and later in 142 Squadron just quietly went along. One or two of us may have thought, 'God you know we have got to get up to four pints a night otherwise we are not men.' But after a while you thought well what's the point. You grew up, very fast. I was lucky that I got my woman early. We married in 1941 so I didn't have to go chasing skirt all over the place. A lot of the fellows had the attitude of, 'who the hell wants to die a virgin'. And that's understandable. There was bound to be that anyway and I suppose it still applies.

As September 1940 entered its final week, Tiny Cooling was approaching the end of his first tour; at this stage of the war this was set at 200 hours of operational flying. However he would, some-what unexpectedly, fly one more operational sortie, as a second dickie on the 25/26 September anti-invasion barge attack to Boulogne.

I volunteered for the trip because another of our squadron's pilots, Tommy Purdy's, second pilot went sick. I had in effect been screened already. Tommy came in the mess and said, 'Damn it! My second pilot's gone sick. I've got to find a Joe to go with me.' I said I would go with him if he liked. He did, and we went and got the OK from the CO.

The raid went without a hitch and Tiny played his small part in the Battle of the Barges; a campaign that is discussed in further detail later in this book.

Following this final effort to persuade the German Navy of the futility of a seaborne invasion, he was taken off operational duties.

They did a great big sweep, and anybody who was close to tour expired at the end of September went. We had all been through the Battle of Britain, and the invasion threat, although we didn't know it, had been lifted. They said panic was dying down a bit, let's have a complete sweep and get new fresh blood in for the winter.

As with the vast majority of tour expired airmen, the RAF required them to pass on their skills to aircrews that had yet to be tested in hostile conditions. With the first year of the war concluded Tiny left 9 Squadron and took up duties with No 15 Operational Training Unit. For the next two and a half years here and at other training units, as the air war escalated, many a fledgling aircrew had the benefit of learning from Tiny's experience before going on to operations. Tiny would actually fly once more operationally, a Nickel operation, dropping leaflets.

We dropped paper over Paris. I was married then and living out. On arriving home I came up to the bedroom to my good wife [Tiny married in October 1941], who opened one eye and said 'Alright?' I said 'Yes.' She asked, 'Where have you been?' I said 'Paris.' 'Paris!' 'Yes. We took some newspapers over to the French.'

From 15 OTU Tiny had then been posted to No 1 Air Observer Navigation School at Prestwick, then No 3 Air Observer School, Bobbington, Halfpenny Green through to 7 May 1942. Whilst at Prestwick he had to deal with one unfortunate incident. The dangers of wartime flying were not exclusive to operations.

I remember one of the Ansons being lost. It flew, in cloud, into the top of Goat Fell on the Isle of Aran. The pilot and three others were all killed. We were billeted out in local hotels and I went with two others to go through the pilot's effects and weed out anything we felt unsuitable, then send it to his next of kin.

Further training duties followed for Tiny, then in October 1942 he began to prepare for a second tour of operations, posted to No 30 OTU to begin the process of crewing up. Previously Tiny had been allocated to a crew, but now he would be part of a more haphazard procedure. At this stage of the war aircrew of the various trades were all put in the same room and told to sort themselves into crews.

I can still see Bill Holmes, a bomb aimer, standing in front of me full square, a big chap, and saying, 'You're our pilot.'

There was the rear gunner and wireless operator standing behind him. They knew I had done a tour already, so they had got together said, 'How about a pilot. Look at that long chap, he's done a tour. We'll have him.'

Tiny and his new crew prepared to enter a European air war that was certainly not being conducted in the 1940s style anymore. No longer were small forces being sent out individually, carrying out their own navigation. Now vast armadas of Allied bombers, flying common routes, were targeting built-up areas in Germany, applying air ministry policy. Tiny felt uncomfortable about the nature of the bomber offensive, his attitude influenced by a certain incident that still to this day draws an emotional response.

My home was in Hull, which seemed to be a Luftwaffe target of opportunity. There had been a number of serious raids, which terrified my mother making her cower under the stairs. My father used to go out fire watching and I used to accompany him. On one particular night I stood in the garden and he was in an adjacent field. I then heard the whistle of some bombs. They passed overhead and I shouted 'Get down!' My old man flopped onto the field. The bombs burst about two hundred yards away; you could hear the shattering of glass. The old man got up with bits of straw and god knows what in his hair.

The following morning I went down to see where the bombs had fallen. There was a drainage dyke that ran down the side of the road into which, by the grace of God, these bombs had fallen, sending the explosive force upwards. Nevertheless it seriously damaged about four houses. There was one house where they started to bring the furniture out into the garden and the woman, about my mother's age, was going round stroking it. I found it intensely moving. This was the time that we were blasting the hell out of Germany so I went back to the OTU and they were talking about postings. I said to the chief instructor that I would be much happier if there was an overseas posting where the targets I would be attacking were targets that I could identify and hit rather than just go over and clobber anything. As such I was posted to North Africa. Bill Holmes said, 'God, going overseas again, we've only just come back.' He was trained in South Africa. I said, 'Mate we're going overseas and you thank your bloody lucky stars.' I think he does now.

Tiny and his crew began their service in the Mediterranean theatre, joining 142 Squadron on 26 March 1943, as the North African campaign was approaching its climax. By this stage the German forces there were being squeezed from two sides. Montgomery pressed from the east and the Torch landing in November 1942 had placed an enemy force in the rear of the Axis troops to the west. Tiny as part of 142 Squadron at Blida, Algeria, still flying Wellingtons, set about confounding German attempts to reinforce and supply the hard pressed troops backing up into Tunisia. Prior to the end of April 1943 Tiny carried out ten night operations, four times to Decimomannu in Sardinia, once to bomb a seaplane station at Trepani, Sicily, and five times to targets in Tunis.

We used to go to the airfield of Decimomannu and our brief was to loiter. They had torpedo bombers. We couldn't stop them taking off but the idea was to stop them coming back. So we hovered over the airfields and if you saw the slightest movement, all you had to do was just drop one bomb. I remember on one occasion that we put one down and started a thumping good fire. With the last bomb we just came down to about 200ft, and shot up the fires.

In North Africa, on operations, you were on your own. You were your own commander. You decided what height you would go in at, what direction you would go in on, and it used to be my policy to see what was happening because there was a peculiar herd instinct. People would tend to go in at the same height and you could see the flak bursting say at 8/9,000 feet. If you were lying off you thought, 'fine, good' and you went in at 6,000 feet. By the time the gunners realised that there was somebody coming in at a different height, they were not going to go to all the business of re-setting their sights, and their fuses. They would stick with the swarm up above, and you could whistle through relatively unscathed.

Tiny's logbook records that most of these attacks were successful. Included against the 17 April attack to Tunis is, 'compass u/s last on target, heavy accurate flak, photo taken, bombed marshalling yards, diverted to Maison Blanche. Shaky Do!!'

We were over Tunis one night and for some reason we were late on the target. When we got over there, we were probably about the only one. This was just before Tunis fell. We were coming up to the docks and a clip of shells went off just beneath us. It really was a crack, crack, crack. I thought for a moment that we had been hit and I threw the aircraft into a very steep turn. I quite literally threw it. We got away from the area and I had lost my sense of balance. I was convinced I was flying in a steep bank with one wing lowered but my instruments told me that I was flying straight and level. I wasn't climbing, my speed was constant, my rate of climbing indicator and all the instruments were saying straight and level. I remember a flight sergeant at one of the courses saying, 'Always trust your instruments, particularly if they all tell you the same story. Never go for how you feel.' I was most unhappy and then somebody else dropped bombs just ahead of us and lit up the horizon. All of a sudden 'click' I was back in again. That was all it needed, just like switching on a light. In a trice my senses were in true orientation again, it was an eerie sensation. But if I had tried to fly by the seat of my pants, instead of by my instruments, we would have been in dead schtook. We really would have been.

Into the second week of May and the Axis troops in North Africa finally capitulated to the Allies, at a high cost in terms of men and material. Allied thoughts now switched to the follow up, crossing the Mediterranean to enter Europe through Sicily. On 5 May 1943 Tiny flew to Fontaine Chaude, Algeria, where 142 Squadron now operated in support of the next step. Interestingly Tiny, on 9 May, flew two operations, the first to Sardinia, as part of the Allied deception plan suggesting the island was next in line for an assault, and to Palermo docks, Sicily. Operations were fairly intense through May 1943, Tiny flew 13 sorties and his logbook regularly recorded 'very successful', against each raid, amidst other entries such as, 'wizard explosion', 'took wizard photo', 'started big oil fire'. Also of note is a series of attacks on Pantellaria Island, which lay between Tunisia and Sicily, at the end of May and into June. Tiny would scribe, somewhat triumphantly, in his logbook, 'June 11 – Pantellaria Island surrendered after continuous air bombardment night and day since 25 May'.

Operating from Kairouan West, in Tunisia, Tiny's operations tally moved from 54, an attack on Pantellaria docks to 60, 'hit barracks' at Cagliari. During this period luck once more held out for Tiny and his crew, on the night of 10/11 June 1943.

> We had a fitter who was desperate to fly on operations, and at that time we were doing Pantellaria, about 2½ hours off the coast of Kairouan, round trip. Someone borrowed a Mae West and parachute and stuck it on board. This fitter, of course, was there when we did all the start up and so forth. He'd come in beside me whilst we ran up the engines just to make sure they were alright. The flight sergeant, ground chief, would look in and say 'ok' and then would go on to the next aircraft.
>
> So on this particular occasion instead of throwing this fitter out when we dropped the ladder, we put him in the back. His colleagues would cover for him. So we set off and as the fitter was with us I said, 'We'll go round and come in a different direction.' As we were coming up to the island we saw a Wellington go down in flames. I thought that was a bit unfriendly. Anyhow we went round the island, came in, bombed Pantellaria, and then set course for home. Then Tex in the back said, 'There's another kite going down in flames.' The Germans had realised that everybody came in the same way at the same height and they must have had night fighters sitting up waiting. We'd come in the opposite way of course, so it was the man in front of us and the man behind us who was shot down. All because we were showing our fitter what it was all about.

Into July and a further seven operations including the support of the opening of Operation Husky, the invasion of Sicily and the first Allied step into Europe, attacking Syracuse on the night of 9 July; an operation that remains clear in Tiny's mind.

> We all knew that something was coming. When we went to briefing, it was the first time, in fact the only time that I recall, that there were armed guards outside the head-quarters, and the briefing area. I remember the groupie coming in and saying, 'This is an historic night. Tonight Allied forces will be landing on the mainland of Europe.'

The fact that Sicily was an island was irrelevant. As far as he was concerned that would do. We were briefed for Syracuse. Three of us were pathfinders, illuminators, and I was one of them. We carried 18 flares and about 2,500lb of bombs. The flares were the important things and they had to go down at 0204 precisely, from 10,000ft exactly. It was rather difficult to say what the sensation was. I stood there thinking, 'Tonight I am going to be part of history. What's going to happen who knows.' I felt privileged in a sense to be taking part in what was then the first invasion of mainland Europe.

We had a late take-off of course to get over the target at 0204. I remember coming up to the target a little early, so we had to lay off. The idea was that three aircraft would lay flares and as each lot went out somebody would add another one. We were last in the queue. The mid-mans flares went down just as we came up. When you have an old black and white negative and you hold it up to the light well that's what Syracuse looked like. The darkness of the sea and the whiteness of the buildings under the flares, and the bomb flashes. And every so often an enormous fountain of water would erupt from the harbour when someone's bombs overshot into the sea.

Then we just came round, bombed, and then lay off for another four or five minutes just to watch what was going on. In fact it wasn't very much, no different from any other occasion, but somehow you felt this really had got to be something big. But it was just another raid. A bit of an anticlimax. The only interesting thing was that we didn't do any more ops for about three days thereafter because every potential target which we had been given was then captured by the army before we could get to it.

I remember during the advance in Sicily that one of our targets was a place called Caltanissetta – a junction of roads. In effect our brief was really just to dump the bombs on the town and block the roads. That I didn't like. We went over and were down in fact to about 800 feet. It was a bright moonlit night, and oddly enough we could see there was a hospital, you could see the white with the red cross in the half light, quite close to the railway station. We did three dummy runs over the railway station before eventually Bill let three or four bombs go and hit it. We also found a bridge with a road cut in the side of a hill so we had a go at that. And the last one we tried to put into the middle of the town square which was a wide open space.

After the war I went back on a tour of Sicily and we went into Caltanissetta. I visited the town mayor and he remembered the attack and showed us some bullet holes. I could remember during the attack Tex said to me, 'There's a building in the centre and they are shooting at us.' So I said, 'Well let's shoot back.' So now here I was with the town's mayor and he told me this was the headquarters of the military police and, 'this was shot at during the war.' I said, 'Yes I can tell you the chap who did it, my rear gunner.' He took a photocopy of the page in my logbook for the town archives.

Apparently a block of flats had been hit and about 28 people killed and a chap said to me, 'Why did you bomb this place? There was nothing here.' Well there wasn't but it was a communication centre. It was the main point on a road that ran from the south to the north of Sicily. There were two other minor roads, and the idea was to stop any possible movement between north and south. They had said we might as well blow the town, 'go and create mayhem', but I'm sorry I couldn't do it. I'd have a go at the roads and the bridges and the railway station, but not the town itself. I tried to carry it out in what was an ethically responsible way.

Tiny's attack to Pomiglano aerodrome, Naples, on 14 July, would be his 67th and last operation, 'large fires, left blazing, very successful'. Following the end of his tour in the Mediter-ranean he returned to the UK and took up instructing once more. He also received news of his commission.

Whilst I was travelling back to the UK Joan had a letter saying that she would no longer be able to draw her allowance from the post office because I would be making provision for her. I came back at an ungodly hour in the morning and knocked up my parents. My father came down, opened the door, looked at me and said, 'What are you dressed like that for?' I asked him what he meant. 'You're still wearing your warrant officer uniform; you were commissioned five months ago!' I knew nothing about it.

When I went to No 15 OTU at Harwell at the beginning of October 1943 I still had the creases in my new uniform, having only just put it on. The first thing that happened when I arrived was that I was told I was going to attend a funeral [following a Wellington crash]. I remember the service, the airman's mother was there. It was all very solemn. After the service we got into a car and the padre's attitude changed completely as if it was just another job done. I felt it was insensitive but he was probably doing three or four a week.

In the month of September eight aircrew had lost their lives at 15 OTU in two separate crashes and on 2 October six further deaths occurred following a crash during a training flight. Bomber Command's attrition was not exclusive to operational squadrons. In the course of the war training would claim thousands of lives[3].

After a short period instructing, Tiny then found himself involved in the preparations for another invasion.

Somebody said, 'Well this chap knows all about invasions, post him to this unit up in Scotland where they are training for D-Day [the June 1944 Normandy landing].' The troops were carrying out exercises, landing on the beaches of Scotland from landing craft. Our job was to drop smoke and bombs on them, making life thoroughly unpleasant, so that they would get a foretaste of what they might experience on the coast of France. It was interesting work. The Blenheims carried a smoke streaming device in the bomb bay with rearward facing nozzles, and we carried these paper case bombs which were lethal at a few yards. The explosive charge of a 250lb bomb and a long firing pistol, about 18 inches long, sticking from the nose. It would explode as it struck the ground rather than penetrate. We would drop these from the Blenheims as the troops came ashore. It produced a shockwave and some nasty pieces of cardboard flying at a fair rate of knots. It could make superficial injuries; unlikely to make fatal ones.

Tiny would also fly Ansons taking officers up to show them the exercises on the ground and also to point out how tank tracks leading into woods, where tanks were thought to be hidden, would give them away. Following the launch of D-Day in June 1944, and with his job basically completed, Tiny was given another posting.

> I was posted then to Transport Command which is what I had been desperate to get into as I was looking for a future in commercial aviation. I went to Crosby-on-Eden where they had Dakotas and did two weeks of the ground course. The wing commander flying looked at me and said, 'Can you get into a Dakota?' I said, 'I don't know I have never tried.' He said, 'Right we had better try you first of all.' In a Dakota, instead of having the stick between your knees, it comes up and cranks over. When my feet were on the rudder bar straight and level was fine, but I couldn't push the stick forward to get the tail up and I couldn't bring the stick back to get the tail down for landing. So I did another OTU, would you believe it on Wellingtons.

Here Tiny would remain until the end of the European war. In recognition of the end of hostilities he was given 48 hours leave. Tiny vividly, and emotionally, still recalls the celebrations.

> Joan and I hitch-hiked home and I remember walking down the road on the evening of 8 May. There were bonfires everywhere and the streetlights were on. That was fantastic, absolutely wonderful. There was a sense of relief as much as anything else. We knew we had a future.

He was demobbed in December 1945 and his future lay in a long career with BOAC travelling world wide, and raising a family – three children and five grandchildren.

Here he gives his final reflections on his war career.

> I'm very glad that I had the experience, I'm immensely privileged in the chaps I met, and I am profoundly thankful that my sons and grandsons didn't have to do the same. I think Bomber Command has been poorly treated. There's no doubt about it, Bomber Command made a massive contribution. I think it is still being belittled for political and moral reasons. It wasn't something you'd go around saying that you took part in – laying waste to German cities. There isn't any great advantage in analysing something which is past unless it points the way forward to

avoiding the obscenities and making life better for every-body. Because war is obscene and it is one's misfortune to get caught up in it. But there was no way you could say, 'Well I am going to make a separate peace with the Germans.' Once you were in you did the best you could.

Post-war when we were living in Frankfurt, Joan and I were going through the town and coming towards us was a girl, in her thirties, about our age, on a crutch, with one leg. That hit me. She was a nice looking woman and yet she was crippled. How? Maybe it was an accident. Maybe she was a victim of the bombing campaign. I realised there were lots of people in Germany like her because of the work which I had been involved in and I hated to feel that I might have been responsible. Morality does enter into it, but you put it in a drawer right at the bottom, at the back. And it's only later when you are clearing out the drawers that you come across it. And it's inconvenient and you don't know what to do with it.

I say to my grandsons that I wish I could give them the one jewel in all the corruption of war; the sense of trust and loyalty shared, which is the essence of comradeship.

Group Captain Jack 'Benny' Goodman
DFC and Bar, AFC, AE

Chapter 3

From Defence to Attack

Mabel 'Maisie' Steel joined the Women's Auxiliary Air Force early in the war, utilising her skills as a shorthand typist. She soon moved on to serve at a Bomber Command station; RAF Mildenhall, taking up responsibilities in the operations room.

There were three of us working in the station operations room, covering the full 24 hours. Everything that happened in that room had to be logged; all the conversations and the telephoning. On an operations day we would have the instructions come through from Group and we would write up the detail on a big board; each aircraft and the names of the captains, the bombload, time of take off and estimated time of return. Later on we logged in each crew as they came back, hopefully. Sometimes we got them all back, which was wonderful. Sometimes it was a bad night and some didn't return; it was very upsetting. Breakfast the next morning was very quiet. If I had been on duty the day before and put the names up on the board, I was very anxious to get in the next morning and see what had happened.

During the war Maisie had become attached to a young Bomber Command airman, a certain Jack Goodman, (nicknamed 'Benny' in RAF circles, after the American band leader), although postings created a geographical divide.

We used to get lists of all the squadrons that were operating on a specific night and I knew if he was going out. But he was very good and he would try and ring in the early hours when he knew I was on duty.

None of us would be here if it wasn't for Bomber Command. The aircrews were wonderful, absolutely fantastic really. They worked very hard, and played hard but they needed to. Some of these men were merely 19 and captains of aircraft with six or seven men behind them and they would go out night after night and be shot at. They were marvellous.

In September 1944 Maisie Goodman's husband, Benny, received the news of further recognition of his flying abilities whilst serving with Bomber Command; the award of a Bar to the Distinguished Flying Cross he had previously won. Seventy-eight times Benny had taken an RAF weapon of war into the air battle against Germany as the award recommendation stated:

The majority of operations for which he has been detailed have been against heavily defended targets in Germany and throughout his career Flight Lieutenant Goodman has proved himself to be a cool and determined officer with a very high sense of duty. In spite of the heavy opposition which he has frequently encountered he has never failed to fulfil his allotted task with great credit.

The journey Benny experienced on the way to acknowledgement of his 'meritorious service' began, as did that of many other Bomber Command airmen, with merely a keenness to fly, set within the context of the horrors of a previous global conflict.

Jack 'Benny' Goodman was born in January 1921, and went to school in Northampton, leaving at the age of 16. He took up work as a dental mechanic, making artificial dentures.

> At the time of the 1938 Munich crisis I realised that war was coming. I felt I had to do something that I wanted to do and I didn't much fancy becoming an infantryman. With visions of the trenches in the First World War I decided that I would like to fly. I had developed an interest in flying and had read every book that I could find on the aces of the First World War. When I was about eight years old my father took me to see a display by Alan Cobham and his flying circus at a meadow outside Northampton. I greatly admired these people tearing around in their flying machines, and this really triggered me off.

Tiger Moth

Inspired, Benny joined the Air Defence Cadet Corps in 1938, number 5 Squadron based in Northampton.

> Our CO was a Squadron Leader Brown, who had flown Sopwith Camels in the First World War. Whether he was any good at flying I don't know. He didn't wear any medals that I noticed, but we thought he was God. As I neared my eighteenth birthday, I squared up to Squadron Leader Brown and asked him whether he thought I could get into the air force as a pilot. He said, 'Well the thing you want to

do my boy is to join the RAF Volunteer Reserve at Sywell.'
He told me that I could keep on doing my job and could
find out about flying. Indeed do some flying and get paid
for it as well. So it was arranged that I should go to the
town centre to sign on with the RAFVR. About 25 of us
went on this particular day and only three of us got
through. We had an oral test and a bit of a written test. Not
much, but then we had the medical test and people were
falling down on this right and left.

Benny began flying with the RAFVR early in May 1939, at No 6
Elementary & Reserve Flying Training School, Sywell, and
managed 32 hours of air time up until the end of August, 'which
was quite a lot'.

I even got a fortnight's holiday from work in order to go
and do some extra flying. Great! I was foolish enough to
think that when the balloon went up we would all be
hurled into action against the Germans, but of course that
was not to be. When the war started we were sent to
Hastings, an initial training wing, to learn drill and RAF
administration and all those important things that people
seem not to want to do.

A couple of weeks later, November 1939, Benny was posted to
No 4 EFTS at Brough near Hull, where he started to fly
Blackburn B2 aircraft.

Like de Havilland Tiger Moths except they were side-by-
side trainers; the instructor and the student sat alongside
each other. Rather like a pregnant Tiger Moth. It was fat,
with a Gypsy Major engine like the Tiger, but it was
grossly underpowered. It developed lots and lots of drag. I
recall doing everything at 70 miles an hour. It climbed at
70, flew straight and level at 70, approached to land at 70.
You had an awful job to do any aerobatics. A real pig of
an aeroplane. But the thing about the Blackburn B2 was
that you had to fly it very carefully and I learned an awful
lot. In the bad winter of 1939 there was no posting to
other places. They were all water logged or covered in
mud, so we stayed at Brough alongside the River Humber
and just flew B2s all the time. I did something like 80
hours on B2s when I was supposed to do 50, which was

very good elementary training.

In March 1940 Benny moved on to Hullavington, No 9 Service
Flying Training School, and started recording hours flying twin-
engine Avro Ansons. Benny was of the opinion however that two
engines was one too many.

> I wanted to fly Hawker Harts and Hawker Audax aircraft.
> We had a selection board presided over by a squadron
> leader and he asked, 'What do you want to do my boy?' I
> replied, 'I would like to be fighter pilot, sir,' and I told him
> my reports had been very good on aerobatics and the like.
> He agreed with me but then I put my foot in it, saying that
> in any case I didn't like the idea of bombing women and
> children. This really set him going and he told me in no
> uncertain terms that I'd better watch my Ps and Qs and
> that the RAF didn't go in for that sort of thing. And I
> blundered straight into that one saying, 'you can't tell me
> that if the war goes on any length of time we shan't be
> killing women and children.' He very coldly said to me,
> 'you had better join the bomber flight and learn what it's
> all about.' That was the end of my chances of becoming a
> fighter pilot.

In hindsight Benny reflects on this defining moment as one which
perhaps lengthened his flying career. 'It was approaching the time
of the Battle of Britain and I expect that if I had become a fighter
pilot I would have been shot to pieces. So maybe, maybe it was
a good thing.' Benny received his pilot wings on 10 May 1940, a
day he remembered well, highlighted by the change of course of
the war, the Germans attacking in the Low Countries and
beginning their devastating attack through France. From
Hullavington Benny was posted to 15 Operational Training Unit
at Harwell, with 196 hours 55 minutes flying time in his
logbook, to start to learn how to control a Wellington bomber.

> The Wimpy was an immensely tough aeroplane, with its
> geodetic construction, rather like a trellis work. It had
> radial engines, so you could get the engine peppered with
> shrapnel and it would still keep going. I never lost an
> engine in a Wellington and we were beaten up frequently,
> but you would take a tremendous amount of battle damage
> and still get home. So I have great affection for the Wimpy.

At the end of OTU Benny's flying time had risen to 265 hours 55 minutes; including just under 70 hours of approximately equally shared time, with a co-pilot, on Wellingtons. In the middle of August 1940, at the height of the Battle of Britain, Benny joined an operational unit (37 Squadron) at Feltwell. His first operation took place on 26/27 August 1940 to Stokum, as a second pilot to a Pilot Officer Nobby Clark. 'He had been a flight sergeant fitter before the war, had become a pilot and I learned more from him I think, than from anybody in the air force. Not only was he a first class fitter and a first class pilot, he was also a first class navigator and he taught me navigation and also astro-navigation. An incredible man.' On this particular raid they were unable to identify the target and did not bomb. The squadron diary recorded an additional problem for the crew.

> One aircraft, Captain P/O Clark, lost a propeller complete with reduction gear over the North Sea. This was due to the seizing of one engine, caused by lack of oil. P/O Clark showed great skill and coolness in bringing his aircraft back to base on one engine, which involved a one-engine flight of one hour 55 minutes.

Three nights later Nobby Clark and Benny went to Bottrop, then on 1/2 September to Hanover, and on 4/5 September to the Black Forest, 'with the intention of starting fires by means of incendiary bombs.' Then on 7/8 and 12/13 September Benny went with his crew to Gelsenkirchen and then the marshalling yards at Hamm respectively; whilst most of his Bomber Command colleagues were involved in the attacks on the build-up of enemy barges in the coastal ports. The squadron diary recorded difficulties on the Hamm raid, 'P/O Clark was unable to locate this target but dropped three bombs on A.A. and searchlight positions which opened on him. The remainder of the bombs were dropped in pairs against flak positions in the Ruhr'. As Benny recalled flying over Germany and locating targets was certainly not easy.

> They were all legitimate targets but we couldn't find them. Everywhere was blacked out and you couldn't see details on the ground. You could see the coast when you crossed it and the navigator could then work out a wind. This had then to carry you through hundreds of miles of enemy territory before you got to your target and then back again. Of course the wind would change, it would drop, or it

would veer, and so you could be miles and miles out. Even if you dropped a flare to find out where you were you would very often just see open fields underneath. It was very difficult to find targets unless the Germans started to fire at you and then you could turn towards where the firing came from and know you would be over a town or a city, which you might or might not be able to identify.

In those days, we used to have a primary target which might be say, Gelsenkirchen, and there would be a secondary target some distance away which would be a similar kind of target. If you couldn't find either of those you would go for something called SEMO or MOPA. SEMO were self evident military objectives and MOPA was military objective previously attacked. I do remember one night [14/15 September 1940] that we were SEMO or MOPAing and we came upon a railway line with a train puffing along it. We decided that this was a jolly good military objective, a goods train and we flew over the top of it dropping bombs, which exploded. We were at about 2,000 feet, and we turned away at the end of the bombing run. The train stopped and suddenly to our astonishment there was a most enormous explosion in the middle of the train. It was clearly an ammunition train, it blew up and went off in all directions. Of course we scuttled out of the way.

Fighter Command's defence against the waves of Luftwaffe bombers and fighters in August and early September 1940 cost the RAF dearly in terms of pilots lost. Nevertheless 'The Few' were still a potent defensive force and were still able to oppose the Luftwaffe incursions. Reichsmarschall Hermann Goering believed his command was on the verge of triumph over Fighter Command, although history would show that his opinion was founded on misinformed intelligence and overclaiming. Nevertheless, a week into September the fear of invasion hung over the defenders.

With the RAF apparently close to defeat the German Navy began the assembly of seaborne invasion craft in the Channel ports, notably barges. This build-up did not go unnoticed; Bomber Command Intelligence Report for 9 September recorded, 'All barges in the Low Countries and France especially Rhine barges of 500 tons have been seized by the Germans. It is reported that shipyards are employed altering the bows of these barges so that tanks and guns can be easily disembarked'. Measures were put in place for the RAF to go on the attack. Bomber Command's resources were needed, whilst maintaining attacks on German targets, to send bombers to the Channel ports, with some success.

On the night of 14/15 September Benny had been detailed to attack Soest and then on 20 September he went to Flushing making his first contribution to the Battle of the Barges, the squadron diary recording, 'P/O Clark delivered 3 attacks from 8,000, 7,000, and 6,000 feet respectively. The first on Inner Haven, but no results were observed, owing to the glare of the burning petrol tanks. The second and third attacks were made on Walcheren Canal with no apparent results'. Benny would be returning to the Channel ports, in the meantime it was back to Germany.

His last operation that month, on 29 September, was a 7 hour 40 minute round trip to Leipzig, 'P/O Clark also located and bombed an unidentified aerodrome from 12,000 feet, causing three large fires'. On 2 October it was a frustrated return to Hamm, 'unable to identify any target so returned with bombs on', followed two days later by a captaincy test with Wing Commander Merton. Then on 5 October Benny again took part in the crucial Battle of the Barges, still flying as second pilot to Pilot Officer Clark, to Rotterdam. When attacking the invasion barges, finding the target was relatively easy.

> We were tasked to attack them at night, and in those days you could find the target without any bother. You would find the coast, wander up and down and come across a port with docks with the barges, which we bombed. We didn't know what sort of results we were achieving; we just went on night after night doing this. The results were very good indeed. We would have been very bucked if we had known.
>
> On 5 October we were detailed for Rotterdam and were flying at about 8,000 feet. We could see it quite clearly, flares had been dropped all around the area by Wellingtons and Whitleys, and bombs were bursting in the dock bases. We homed in and Nobby opened the bomb doors. The navigator was down in the front directing him saying, 'left, left' or 'right' or 'steady'. We approached the target, 'steady, steady, steady', and Nobby was looking out

through his window on the port side. I noticed that the speed was dropping. Nobby was looking down at the ground, easing the control column back so the nose was coming up a bit and the speed was dropping. Of course a second pilot was not allowed to start telling his skipper what he should be doing. Anyway the bombs went, we could feel them all go, eighteen 250 pounders. Nobby leaned forward, closed the bomb doors and at that point there was an almighty Whomp! Underneath us an anti-aircraft shell went off and our speed was below 100 mph. The Wellington reared up and stalled, falling over on its starboard wing and into a right hand spin. Now I know that people don't believe that Wellingtons will recover from spins, and if you read the pilots notes you were forbidden to spin them, and rightly so. Anyway, our aircraft flailed down in this spin to the right.

We were looking downward ahead of us, and could see all these lights going round and round, and all the flashes of the bombs going off. I thought 'we've had it now'. Nobby blasted the engines open and closed quickly to try and shake the Wellington out of its stable attitude. It did nothing. He called, 'Jump! Jump!' the signal for everybody to bale out. My job was to pull myself forward and let the front gunner out of his turret. But I couldn't move. I was pinned in the frame at the back of the cockpit. I looked across at Nobby again and he had still got full left rudder.

He was quite a small man, and I thought that I ought to try and help him to apply the left rudder. So I lurched across the cockpit, grabbed the right rudder pedal, pulled back with all my might and felt it move a bit. Then Nobby blasted the engines open again, there was a great shudder and the Wellington came out of the spin. We were then getting down to quite a low level, there were dock lights ahead of us. Nobby eased us out of the dive, we were going like blazes, and pretty well nearly at ground level before he started to climb very gently back up again. Nobby tried the controls carefully and found that he was unable to move the control column forward or back very well so clearly there was trouble with the elevators. As soon as you tried to use the flaps the nose of the aircraft would come up and you had to push the control column forward. We couldn't do that.

Anyway we managed to get back to Feltwell and Nobby landed without the use of the flaps. When the engines were switched off we went round and looked at the back end of the aircraft, finding that the elevators had moved bodily on the rollers on the tail plane. They were within a fraction of an inch of coming adrift completely. If they had done so of course, the elevators would just have disappeared, torn off, and that would have been the end of us. We had been within an ace of death. It was a very solitary lesson for me to watch the speed, and I always did it very carefully after that, and Nobby to his eternal credit agreed that he'd let it get a bit slow. But people on the squadron were amazed, because really we should not have been able to get the aeroplane out of the spin at all. It should have flailed on into the ground and no-one would then have known what had happened to us. So that's my line shoot about Wellingtons and spinning.

When I was an instructor at 15 OTU Harwell after I had finished my tour, we had a flight commander who had been in British Overseas Airways before the war. He started one day saying, 'you know it should be possible to get a Wellington out of a spin in 8,000 feet'. Everybody said, 'Oh don't do that for goodness sake', and I was one who led the cry, 'Don't do that sir.' But sir went up, went to 8,000 feet, closed the throttles and put it into a spin. He didn't come out, just flailed on down and made a great hole in the ground outside Harwell.

As we saw in the last chapter, the general picture provided by the reports of the crews that returned from attacking barges in the latter half of September and early October 1940 is one of success. The Bomber Command intelligence narrative is full of optimistic expressions describing the scene around the respective docks following the explosive and incendiary attacks – 'saw large fires', 'large buildings appeared to be gutted', 'one building burning fiercely' and 'all bombs fell in target area'. And this optimism was well founded. Earlier on 17 September the German Navy had already recorded its concern over the regular appearance of enemy aircraft, the naval staff reporting, 'The RAF are still by no means defeated: on the contrary they are showing increasing activity in their attacks in the Channel ports and in their mounting interference with the assembly movements'. Following the night attack of 17/18 September 1940 they would report, 'very considerable losses'. William Shirer in *The Rise and Fall of the Third Reich* recorded the German Navy's summation of the night, 'At Dunkirk eighty-four barges were sunk or damaged, and from Cherbourg to Den Helder the navy reported, among other depressing items, a 500-ton ammunition store blown up, a rations depot burned out, various steamers and torpedo boats sunk and many casualties to personnel suffered. This severe bombing plus bombardment from heavy guns across the Channel made it necessary, the navy staff reported, to disperse the naval and transport vessels already concentrated on the Channel and to stop further movement of shipping to the invasion ports.' On 21 September the German Navy recorded that 21 transports and 214 barges had been lost to enemy action, which equated to twelve per cent of the invasion fleet[4]. The campaign against the barges ultimately forced Hitler to stop the further assembly of the invasion fleet and that already in the Channel ports to be dispersed, 'so that the loss of shipping space caused by enemy air attacks may be reduced to a minimum'.

Benny Goodman had played his part in what has become known as the Battle of the Barges; a definite victory for the bomber boys of 1940. The efforts of Bomber Command and men such as Benny (and Tiny Cooling) in thwarting the invasion, by attacking the build-up of barges, has alas become one of the forgotten contributions to the winning of the Battle of Britain.

On 10 October 1940 Benny flew his first operation as first pilot detailed to Eindhoven airfield, 'as there was no cloud cover at Eindhoven and fighter patrols were active, attacked Flushing docks, the results of which were not observed.' Then four nights later he took part in an attack on the dock installations at Le Havre. Two days later, detailed for operations, Benny ran into trouble shortly after take-off.

> I got airborne; all loaded up, but couldn't gain speed. The petrol filler flaps on both wings were unlocked and had risen up into the air stream becoming spoilers and destroying lift over the wing. The aircraft did not want to climb. I managed to haul it up to about 500 feet at full power, but when I throttled back a bit it started to lose height again. I did not have a clue what the matter was. I had to go round and round as I wasn't able to land because

everybody else was taking off. When they had all gone I came in and boobed somewhat; I was still a sprog and had only just become a skipper. I throttled back and sank heavily, driving the undercarriage through the wings. There was a hell of a row about it. I knew nothing about this sort of thing, that it could even happen. The flight mechanic who was responsible got 28 days in the cooler. The aircraft wasn't badly damaged. After that I was very sensitive to this sort of thing, it was certainly a hair raising experience. I might well have gone straight in and they would never have known what happened.

Benny closed out October with three operations; to oil installations at Benrath near Düsseldorf (21 October); dock installations at Emden (23 October), 'Sergeant Goodman released his bombs in the centre of a group of searchlights causing three fires which were visible through a hole in the clouds'; and Bremen (25 October), which was frustrated by cloud. As Benny reflects, with the benefit of historical hindsight, 'Most of the time we were not hitting targets because we couldn't find them. We must have wasted thousands of tonnes of bombs blowing holes in fields at the time.' Whilst Bomber Command was still finding its way during the nights of 1940, so were the German defences, in particular the nightfighters. The battle between the Luftwaffe pilots and the bomber aircrews at night would certainly escalate, but the main opposition encountered by Benny and his colleagues in 1940 was flak. Nevertheless there were encounters, Benny managing to survive one such engagement early in his operational career.

I was attacked by a fighter, and it was not very pleasant. There was a tremendous tearing noise at the back as it came in firing cannons. Then something like the crunching of enormous feet coming up the fuselage, crunch, crunch, crunch. It stopped thank god, as he broke away. I was diving like hell at the time and I really thought the aeroplane was going to fall to pieces or blow up, but it didn't. Despite the holes in it we came back safely.

The winter of 1940/41 is noted by historians of the bombing campaign as a time of decreased operational effort. The invasion threat had expired, for the time being, and Bomber Command could hope for a strategic focus. But a sizeable directive from the

Air Ministry still spread the load. Oil was kept as a priority but other targeting systems were listed; industries and railways in Germany, the minelaying campaign was to be maintained, aircrews were asked to fly to Italy and make further attacks on Channel ports to dissuade any enemy thoughts of preparing once more for invasion. In addition attacks on Luftwaffe bomber bases were called for. Bomber Command's new Commander-in-Chief Air Marshal Sir Richard Peirse was not impressed with his wide-ranging responsibilities, but he was directed to focus on oil primarily and attack the other target systems when possible. Benny Goodman would be one of the front line executors of this policy although not with the airmen he had been to war with during the previous two and a half months.

Benny's time with 37 Squadron came to an end early in November 1940, when his colleagues departed for the Middle East, 'I had an attack of flu and was in sick quarters'. For Benny the crew bond, an essential and comforting feature of a Bomber Command airman's operational service life, had been broken; a move from certainty to uncertainty.

> The squadron flew away without me and my crew went off with somebody else. I became a pilot without a crew. 3 Group headquarters decided that I should go to 99 Squadron at Newmarket because there was a crew that had done half a tour and their pilot, a New Zealander, had been posted away. They were a headless crew and I was a pilot without a crew, so we were married up together. When we met they looked at me and I looked at them. And in those days of course you were very jealous of your crew members; you didn't want to fly with anybody else. In Bomber Command, at the time, everybody was very sensitive to change; start chopping the crew round and you were heading for the hammer. The people I had flown with at Feltwell, as far as I was concerned, were the tops. And looking at this lot I wondered how we were all going to get along. I suppose they thought the same of me, and considering they had been with their former pilot for months, probably didn't like the look of me at all.

The scepticism on both Benny and his new crew's account was only temporary. The crew bond would eventually form through shared operational experience and trust in each other's abilities.

Yet to compound Benny's difficulties on arrival at 99 Squadron, Newmarket, another aspect of Bomber Command folklore sided against him.

> We flew from the Rowley mile and lived in the grandstand. Very cold it was in the winter of 1940. I was allocated an aircraft, identification letter was R – which was one of the two jinx aeroplanes of the squadron. Every squadron had a jinx aeroplane. Anything awful that was going to happen would happen to that aeroplane, and it would go missing at the drop of a hat. I was in B flight, which had R for Robert as the jinx aircraft, and A flight had B for Bertie as its jinx aircraft. B for Bertie went down the night I got to Newmarket [25/26 November 1940] with the most experienced pilot of the squadron on board; he was on almost his last trip.

Flight Sergeant Frank Swatton (Mentioned in Despatches) was lost without trace on a raid to Kiel along with his crew of five; all commemorated on the Runnymede memorial.

> Frank was a leading light on the squadron. People did not like losing such men and there was a great blow to morale when he went. Now everybody looked at me as the character that had come in to take the other jinx. Corporal Tosh Hoskins who was in charge of the aeroplane told me so to my face. I said to him very clearly that I had no intention of going down in R for Robert or any other aeroplane on 99 Squadron. Brave words but oddly prophetic. While I was on the squadron I went on leave twice with my crew. We used to have seven days leave every six weeks whether we liked it or not, and of course we liked it. Each time I went on leave and someone else took R for Robert the aircraft didn't come back. Absolutely extraordinary and the jinx was preserved.
>
> B for Bertie continued to be a very unlucky aircraft. The factory workers at Broughton, the Wellington factory up near Blackpool, presented Bomber Command with a Wellington, the Broughton Bomber, which the workers paid for themselves. It had the emblem of the works on it, and a small crowd of people came from the works to see this bomber take off on its first trip. It was allocated to one of our flight lieutenants and it took off on the Rowley mile

heading towards the south west. It got airborne, and nobody really knows how, but it hit the top of the Devil's Dyke on the south-west end of Newmarket, crashed, burst into flames and all were killed. What the people of the factory thought about it I don't know, having bought this aeroplane then seeing it go up in smoke on its first operational take-off. But that was war.

Benny Goodman's first two operations with 99 Squadron were to Düsseldorf on 28/29 November and 4/5 December. Then a raid to Bordeaux on 8/9 December. Two nights later he flew to Dunkirk, 'One exceptionally large explosion was observed and several minor explosions. Bombs seen to straddle docks... and railway sidings. Six fires were started, one of them very large.' On 16/17 December Benny flew to Antwerp and four nights later he would make the first of a number of visits to Berlin.

A second Christmas at war came and passed and the New Year suggested little more than Churchill's offer of 'blood, toil, tears and sweat'. Only a few days into 1941 and the personnel at 99 Squadron witnessed the shedding of more blood; the crash of a Wellington, onto the racecourse after two unsuccessful attempts to land from a training flight. The four crew were admitted to hospital. A few hours later a call came through for two blood donors to be sent to the hospital, but the attempts to save the lives of the two seriously injured airmen failed. On 22/23 January Benny flew to Duisburg and then on 29/30 January a raid to Wilhelmshaven, trying to hit the German battleship *Tirpitz*, which was not found and bombs were dropped in the general area. It is interesting to note that the squadron diary frequently uses the word 'believed' when referring to where bombs fell, and with crews often having to find secondary targets.

Into February 1941 and the personnel of 99 Squadron continued to experience the trials of war. On the night of 11/12 February Wellington LN-R was abandoned over England and two RAF airmen lost their lives. A week later and it was civilian lives that were lost.

99 Squadron Diary, 18 February:
1510 hours – Information received that an enemy aircraft was in the vicinity.
1520 hours – Enemy aircraft endeavoured to attack Mobile

Convoy in the Main High Street of Newmarket. Owing to bombing error all bombs fell on the side of the street. The Post Office received a direct hit from a small bomb and extensive damage was done to shops and houses in the main street. There were a number of persons killed and quite a considerable number injured. The ground defence guns on the camp opened up and believed hit the enemy aircraft, but enemy aircraft was not shot down in the vicinity of the aerodrome and disappeared from view.

Benny would actually witness the attack from the cockpit of a Wellington.

I was taking off towards the town, on a training flight, breaking in a new pilot, with a full crew on board. We were bouncing along on take-off, I was standing by the window, and all of a sudden I saw great gouts of smoke coming up from the town ahead of us. Above was a Dornier 17 'flying pencil', which had just laid a stick of bombs up one of the streets. As soon as we got off the ground I changed seats with the new second dickie and we closed on the bloody thing, underneath, the best of all places to do it. He hadn't seen us – we had seen him. We poured shot and shell into him; he was so busy turning to port to look at the damage he had done that he was unaware that we had engaged him. I expected him to catch fire and explode but he did no such thing, continued turning, shuddered a bit and then pulled up into cloud. He'd obviously realised he had been hit. I followed into the cloud but we couldn't find him. After sculling around a bit I landed and reported to the flight commander. He said he would try and find out more. Later on he sent for me and asked me to recount again what had happened. He had had a call from 3 Group HQ to say that according to the army, the Dornier that bombed New-market had been engaged by army gunners, crashing at Thetford and they claimed to have shot it down. My flight commander said to me, 'I think you ought to count it as half a victory.'

On the night of 24/25 February Benny's crew was one of 57 sent to attack shipping at Brest, then two nights later one of 126 aircraft to Cologne. Clearly Bomber Command was still having problems, on this raid Middlebrook and Everitt record in the

Bomber Command War Diaries[5] that 106 aircraft bombed reporting sizeable fires. Benny Goodman's post-raid report recorded the dropping of three 500lb bombs and three hundred 4lb incendiaries.

> One stick SE to NW. Bursts seen to straddle centre of target. Incendiaries started several fires which merged into one large red fire after a few minutes. Fire visible about 40 miles away in spite of thick haze.

Despite the optimism of the returning crews however, the city recorded just ten high explosive and 90 incendiary bombs on the edge of the city, with some bombs in villages. A total of 353 high explosive and 15,060 incendiaries had been taken to the city by the bombers.

On 1/2 March Benny was sent to Mulheim and on 11/12 March he completed his last operation with 99 Squadron to Kiel, a long seven-hour flight; although it would be far from his final operation with Bomber Command.

As Benny neared the end of his tour he came to realise the responsibility he had toward less experienced pilots.

> When you started your tour you felt very vulnerable, but as time went on you got more acclimatised to flying in Bomber Command. You didn't get over confident, you were always a bit wary, but you gained confidence all the time and you felt that you might survive. As you became more senior as a pilot you realised that the junior pilots were looking up to you. Every trip you notched up encouraged them, because the chances of completing a tour of 30 trips in those days wasn't all that good. As a senior pilot you would look at other senior pilots around you and think that as long as old Smith could keep going, you'd be alright. That was fine until suddenly old Smith didn't come back and then you realised that everybody was looking at you. This was terrible, you felt really out in front and you felt really vulnerable. But of course, if you were lucky and I was lucky, you survived and got away with it.

The course of Benny's career was to change direction once more, following a flight across the Mediterranean. He had been tasked with ferrying a Wellington to North Africa; his logbook would record that on 1 April 1941 he flew the 11 hour 30 minutes non-stop journey from Stradishall to Benghazi. Benny then expected a quick return to the UK. It was not to be. He would remain in North Africa until September 1941, once more serving with 37 Squadron.

> We weren't supposed to do any raids at all. I was told that when I took the Wellington out that would be our last trip and we would be put on the first available boat home, and I would go to Harwell as an instructor. The trip to Benghazi was a non-stop effort. They had been going to Malta and getting bombed out, so it was decided to put two overload tanks in the Wellington bomb bay, which should be able to just get you to Benghazi. It was a hell of a long trip.

When Benny arrived at Benghazi his stay was very short indeed. The British Army was retreating in the face of the Afrika Corps' recently launched offensive and German tanks were bearing down on Benghazi.

> There was a fighter squadron at the airfield and the ops officer came up to me when I landed and said, 'Get the hell out of here.' I said, 'What do you mean I have only just arrived.' He said, 'We'll put some petrol into you and get cracking.' I asked him where to? 'I don't know anywhere – get to Cairo.' I flew on to Heliopolis (Cairo) and then took the Wellington to Abu Sueir, the maintenance unit where it was made ready for operations. I was then expecting to catch the first available boat at Suez, but I was ordered to go to the Middle East HQ in Cairo where I met a very worried looking flight lieutenant. 'Look we're in big trouble in the desert', he said. 'The Army is in full retreat, some of our squadron are still out in Greece and we need more people to operate aircraft against the Germans in Libya.'

Benny agreed to his new assignment and over the course of the next month and a half he would fly eight operational sorties.

> Benghazi became the German supply base and initially we had one target only – the docks. We did score one very good trip. A couple of Focke-Wulf Condors landed at Benghazi late in the day and foolishly stood on the tarmac wing tip to wing tip. One of the reconnaissance people in the desert had found them and a couple of us were detailed

to bomb the airfield. We took off from base into the desert to refuel and then were operational that night. We flew over the top of the Condors, dropped incendiaries and burned them out. That was a triumph.

In addition to the raids to Benghazi Benny also took part in three sorties to Crete, in the latter part of May 1941, following the German airborne assault on the island.

We attacked Maleme where the German troop carriers and gliders were landing. Our job was to go and burn up as many as possible. We were armed with incendiaries and rained them down on top of the bastards, and burnt a lot out. There were only a few Wellington squadrons able to do this and it was a nine-hour trip. I don't know if we made much difference, all we could do was have a go.

As it was the island was quickly overrun by the German troops, but at a considerable cost in terms of men and material, and the German command became extremely reluctant to try such a venture again.

Following Benny's Mediterranean diversion he returned to England later that year and was posted to 15 OTU at Harwell, arriving on 4 December 1941, where he would remain until September 1943, passing on his experience and knowledge. During this time Bomber Command underwent considerable development. Of note is the impact of the Butt Report in August 1941, examining, through photographic analysis, the reported achievements of Bomber Command attacking targets in Germany. When the report was published a shock wave swept through the Air Ministry and the RAF. Basically the bombing campaign had not achieved what had been claimed. Numerous statistics proved the case, for example only one quarter of the crews reporting having bombed a target were within five miles of the aiming point. Here was proof that the shift to night bombing, necessitated by daylight losses, had led to a decline in the ability of crews to find and hit targets. A major rethink was needed for the strategic role of the bomber war.

In February 1942 the rethinking turned to policy and in the middle of the month one of the most historic directives of the Bomber Command story was issued stating, 'It has been decided that the primary objective of your operations should now be focussed on the morale of the enemy civil population and in particular of the industrial workers'. Area bombing of built-up industrial targets was now official policy. Just eight days after this directive was issued a man who would forever be associated with Bomber Command's 'morale' campaign took over as commander-in-chief. Air Chief Marshal Sir Arthur Harris quickly set about preparing for the expansion and deployment of one of the most destructive air forces in the history of warfare.

Sir Arthur Harris certainly had cause for some optimism a few months into his tenure as head of Bomber Command. Advances in technology were easing the task of his crews, plans were in place for the growth of his weaponry and the March and April 1942 attacks on Lübeck and Rostock respectively returned evidence of particularly devastating raids. But Harris still desired further appreciation of the potential of his force and this would be achieved through one of the most important attacks in the history of aerial bombardment. For his plan Harris was looking for a target whereby, 'the active and the passive defences of a vital industrial area could be similarly overcome'. He was embarking upon a considerable risk, 'committing not only the whole of my front line strength but absolutely all my reserves in a single battle'.[6] To make his statement Harris mustered a force of over 1,000 aircraft to attack the city of Cologne, stating to his crews that, 'You have an opportunity therefore to strike a blow at the enemy which will resound, not only throughout Germany, but throughout the world'. His front line squadrons were not able to meet the demand, so Harris looked to his training units for reinforcement. Previously screened pilots would fly in the bomber stream that night taking along some pupil pilots for experience. One such pilot was Benny Goodman. 'I was a screened pilot as it was called, screened from operations. That was a laugh because we all had to go on the thousand bomber raids.'

> When we bombed at Cologne, the smoke was up to our level. We flew through smoke at 8,000 feet. It had all been very unsatisfactory until then but now we could see the target. It had been marked by what we might term early pathfinders; a row of red flares laid to the east of Cologne and a row of green flares to the west. You had to bomb between them. An enormous area of Cologne was gutted, destroyed and we had never managed to do anything like that before.

The night following the raid I phoned up Maisie, at Mildenhall and asked her if she had been on duty the night before. She had. I asked her if she was listening to the news; I could hear it in the background talking about the thousand bomber raid. 'Yes' she said. I said, 'Well' and in a moment or two the penny dropped. 'No' she exclaimed. She had known Harwell was on and by then that two had been lost, but not that I had been flying.

From Harwell we sent 32 Wellingtons. The two we lost were from my flight, both friends of mine, Jack Hatton and Jack Paul, becoming prisoners of war. It was certainly hard luck on Jack Hatton. He was flying the only Wellington II we had in B Flight. I managed to fly it once, it was a beautiful aircraft. Jack said, 'I'll wave to you chaps down below.' But he didn't wave very long; a German night-fighter got him.

The propaganda opportunity provided by the Cologne raid was immense in terms of securing the future of the bomber offensive, not that Harris was satisfied. Two nights later he carried out his second thousand bomber raid (although 956 aircraft were actually dispatched) to Essen, and again he called upon his training units.

They were all training Wellingtons and had screened pilots and screened navigators and screened wireless operators, but the gunners were all student. For luck we carried a student pilot who came along just to see what was going on. It was all a bit hair-raising really. The Wellington I had wouldn't go above about 8 or 9,000 feet, it had got aileron droop. The control wires were as tight as they might have been so both ailerons dropped down a little bit. It was like putting flaps down; so you couldn't get much forward speed and nor would the wretched thing climb. However I think that may have saved us because the heavies were up at 18,000 feet and the Wellingtons were at about 10,000 feet. That's where all of the fighting was going on and we were down at 8,000 feet. I think that really we were, in an odd way, protected. We didn't see anything, we just bombed.

Throughout the second half of 1942 Harris continued the development of the bombing campaign, keeping up the pressure on the German nation, drawing in more and more German resource to the air defence of the Third Reich. His weaponry was becoming more potent. There was success, but there was failure too. Nevertheless a momentum to improve the efficiency of the bomber force and increase the striking power had been created. And Harris would still occasionally call upon his training crews to bolster this strike power; Benny Goodman flew his Wellington to Essen in a successful attack on 16/17 September 1942, 369 aircraft taking part, including some of Bomber Command's four-engine heavies, Avro Lancasters, Short Stirlings and Handley Page Halifaxes, which would be taking on more and more of the bombing responsibility as time progressed. The days of front line service for the Whitleys, Hampdens and Wellingtons were running out. It is also worth noting that Bomber Command lost 39 aircraft that night (10.6%). However, simultaneous with the development of Bomber Command was the improvement in the German nightfighter system and the evolution of the German nightfighter force into a potent defensive force. The RAF night bombing raids of 1940 compare to those of 1942 and 1943 as a skirmish to a pitch battle.

The mid-year of the war, 1942, came to a close with Sir Arthur Harris concluding, 'so ended a year of preparation, in which very little material damage had been done to the enemy, which he could not repair from his resources, but in which we had obtained or had in near prospect what was required to strike him to the ground, and learned how to use it'.[7] In 1943 Harris launched his crews into his Main Offensive, starting with the Battle of the Ruhr. Benny Goodman would not be taking part in the attrition battles of the spring and summer of 1943. That campaign is covered through the experiences of other airmen featured in this book. But as autumn approached Harris's focus switched to another main target system. Benny would once more be entering the night battle. Benny, who had married Maisie in November 1942, had been instructing for just under two years, now his second tour was just round the corner. 'I knew I had to do it.'

Chapter 4

Great Skill and Daring

If you went on heavies, the Lancaster or the Halifax, you could expect another 20 trips, taking your total to 50. Once you had done that, according to all the rules, you couldn't be called upon to operate again. That was your lot. Now there was a certain Hamish Mahaddie [who had completed two tours before joining the headquarters of the Pathfinder force], who would come round to the trainee units. As a training officer for the Pathfinder force he used to give talks on how important they were. And he was looking for people to join them. Of course some of our pilots, who had been screened for some time, responded to his blandishments. One of which was that if you were not a flight lieutenant you very soon would be, getting some more money. And if you did well you would find yourself made into an acting squadron leader.

I had a really close bosom friend, Basil Smith, with whom I had shared a room at Harwell. He went back on ops in July 1943, to a Pathfinder outfit and a few weeks later flew in to Harwell, in his Lancaster, very proud of himself. He had been made an acting flight lieutenant already and was getting more money than I was as a flying officer. I felt very envious and was thinking about volunteering as well. He flew off back to his unit, went on ops the next night and never came back. [Flight Lieutenant Basil Smith DFC and his entire 156 Squadron crew lost their lives on the Hamburg raid of 29/30 July 1943].

I was still thinking over what to do when suddenly a

> posting notice arrived, mid-August 1943 directing me to
> Marham, in 8 Group, and a Mosquito station. So whether
> I liked it or not I was going to join the Pathfinders.

The concept of some kind of lead aircraft opening raids, to aid
target finding, had been banded around since the latter months
of 1941. When Harris took over Bomber Command he was far
from keen, not wishing to establish an 'elite', but to keep
experienced airmen in their squadrons. Debate continued at high
level with Chief of the Air Staff Sir Charles Portal eventually
ordering Harris to establish a new force. Consequently, in August
1942 the Pathfinder force came into being, headed up by a most
experienced aviator, Australian Wing Commander Don Bennett.
The new Pathfinders were almost immediately into action and
over the coming months they would have to deal with both
success and failure. To aid the Pathfinders in their task
technological advances were made, most notably the
introduction of the blind bombing device Oboe, whereby an
aircraft could be controlled from stations in England. Oboe was
limited by the curvature of the earth, so the higher the Oboe
aircraft flew the greater the range. And in particular an aircraft
was found especially suitable for the task – the twin-engine de
Havilland Mosquito. Benny Goodman would soon come to
appreciate the aircraft he was about to go to war in.

> The Mosquito was a dream to fly. Powered by two Rolls-
> Royce Merlin engines, the Wooden Wonder was like a
> scalded cat. She was instantly responsive to the slightest
> control movement and had to be handled gently. Woe
> betide the pilot who pushed and pulled the controls; the
> Mossie would quickly bite him. On one engine she could be
> trimmed 'hands and feet off' and would maintain a high
> cruising speed as my navigator and I discovered one night
> when our superb steed brought us home from a spot deep
> inside Germany with one prop feathered.

When Benny arrived at RAF Marham, there were three Mosquito
units stationed there: 105 and 109 Squadrons and 1655
Mosquito Training Unit. The latter was under the command of a
distinguished pilot Wing Commander Roy Ralston, who ended
the war with a DSO and Bar, AFC and DFM. As Benny recalled,
'he had done a lot of hair-raising daylight raids on Mosquitoes in
1942-43 [including a sortie sealing a German train in a tunnel by

bombing either end]. He was a great hero of Bomber Command.'

Benny began his training at Marham on 16 September 1943 and he started to hear and learn about one of Bomber Command's most significant technological developments in target marking.

> The Mosquito squadrons at Marham were shrouded in secrecy. They had nothing to do with us, who were under training. They talked in hushed whispers in the mess and there was an odd character going around, his name was Dr R V Jones [from the intelligence section of the Air Ministry]. I remember when we were in the mess Dr Jones would be called for all the time and I wondered what sort of doctor he was. I thought for a start that he was a medical doctor, but it turned out that he wasn't a doctor of medicine at all, he was boffin. In fact he was responsible for the aids with which these Mosquitoes were fitted – Oboe; and this was a magnificent marking aid.

Benny's first flight in a dual Mosquito took place on 23 September. 'It was a flight I shall never forget. Flying the Wellington had been a push and pull affair; by contrast the Mosquito had to be tickled. As the flight commander said, "Treat her like your best girl friend – gently."' Following three hours of dual instruction Benny went solo on 25 September, 'Sheer joy. All 1,200 horses in the Merlin engine on each side neighing with delight – or so it seemed to me. Could there be anything more perfect than this?' Once deemed competent enough flying his steed, Benny paired up with his navigator: Flying Officer A J L 'Bill' Hickox, so nicknamed after the American wild west sharpshooter.

> He had already been shot down in a Wimpy and had walked back through the desert. He did not relish the idea of walking back from Germany. I assured him that his thoughts accorded closely with mine so we shook hands and became a Mosquito crew.
>
> One of the next things we did was to gather round a Mk IV Mosquito bomber for drill in abandoning aircraft. The chief ground instructor explained that if we were hit at high level we had about 45 seconds in which to get out. We had to disconnect our oxygen tubes and radio intercom plugs, release our seat belts, switch off engines if time permitted,

jettison the bottom hatch and bale out. This sounds straightforward, and indeed it was; but the Mosquito was a very small aircraft and the pilot and navigator were meant to climb in, strap in and stay put.

When Bill and I tried to do it the first time there was an unholy mix-up and after 45 seconds the CGI announced 'You're dead'. The difficulty about getting out of a Mosquito wearing parachutes was that the navigator had to clip on his chest parachute and then manoeuvre his way through the main hatch in the floor of the aircraft. This hatch was scarcely large enough to get through without a chute. If the navigator got out safely, the pilot was supposed to follow him wearing the pilot-type parachute attached to his backside. Bill and I decided that baling out was a dangerous business and we would stay with the aircraft if humanly possible.

Benny finished his Mosquito training on 21 October 1943 and there were then a number of possibilities; a posting to 105 or 109 Squadron, or being sent to 139 Squadron based at RAF Wyton. 139 Squadron it would be but not for long; just a month. Nevertheless in that month he would be over Germany five times.

In the autumn of 1943 Bomber Command's attention shifted from Harris's Battle of the Ruhr to an all-out attack on the 'black heart' of Nazism, as Harris referred to Berlin. The period from November 1943 to March 1944 is referred to by Bomber Command historians as the Battle of Berlin. Not that Bomber Command's attentions were exclusive to Berlin; that would have led to a concentration of the defences. Other targets were attacked, but Harris was after a decisive, possibly war winning, blow against the German capital. Benny Goodman, about to embark upon his second tour of duty, would be in the midst of this battle.

Benny's first operational sortie with 139 Squadron was to Cologne on the night of 3/4 November, bombing from 28,000 feet as part of a diversionary raid, whilst the main force went to Düsseldorf.

On this night, after the usual operational briefing, we returned to the officer's mess for bacon and eggs, an hour or two in which to relax, and then a leisurely stroll to the flight offices to sign the maintenance and repair document for our individual aircraft and the flight authorisation book in which each crew was named, the aircraft concerned were specified, and the 'duty' column bore the legend, 'operations as ordered'.

Our first operational take-off was only marginally longer than our take-offs from Marham in Mosquitoes without bombs – on this occasion we were carrying four 500lb high explosive bombs. The acceleration was rapid and in next to no time we were at the unstuck speed of around 100 knots and climbing smoothly away. We climbed rapidly to 28,000 feet, levelled out and settled down to an economical cruising speed of around 250 knots (true air speed).

As we neared Cologne the first of the Oboe-aimed target indicators began to cascade down ahead of us. Bill took his place at the bombing panel and began the time-honoured verbal directions, 'Left, left... steady...' and ultimately, 'bombs gone'. We then turned for home, more bacon and eggs, and bed.

The post-flight interrogation was much the same as on any operational squadron in Bomber Command, with the important exception that 139's full title was No 139 (Jamaica) Squadron and we were all offered a tot of rum on return from every operational sortie – the rum being provided by the good people of Jamaica.

On the night of 5/6 November Benny went to Hamburg, bombing from 27,000 feet, one of 26 Mosquitoes sent out that night making small attacks on five cities. He was out again the next night to Düsseldorf, bombing from 28,000 feet, one of 19 Mosquitoes again on small attacks to three cities. On 11/12 November he made his first visit to Berlin, Benny's 44th operation, bombing high again, from 29,000 feet, the attack similar in nature to the previous ones that month, as was a visit to Gelsenkirchen on 16/17 November. On the five raids Benny took part in there were no Mosquito losses; a result of height and speed in darkness. Benny's time with 139 Squadron however now came to an abrupt end.

I was with the squadron for a short time only. We had three flights A, B and C. The latter was the flight from which a new unit 627 Squadron was created. In the middle of

November 1943 we, the new crews of 627 Squadron, flew
across to RAF Oakington in our Mosquitoes. Now the
proud boast of 8 Group, and the AOC Don Bennett, was
that as soon as a squadron arrived on a station it had to be
operational. We arrived at Oakington and the whole
station was alive. There must have been a maximum effort;
the target that night was to be Berlin and we were to take
part. Six Mosquitoes were put on including mine and as the
afternoon wore on it became evident to the powers that be
that there was going to be a lot of rain coming in early over
our bases in Lincolnshire and East Anglia. So it was
decided at Bomber Command headquarters that the
heavies were not to go. It was to be an all-Mosquito effort.
Then, although we didn't know it on 627 Squadron, all the
other Mosquitoes were stood down, we were the only ones
left and we therefore had to go. So we scrambled in the
early evening and away we went. What I didn't know was
that we were now down to three aircraft and the other two
aborted with various troubles. So Bill Hickox and I set off
for the big city on our own. We didn't know that either. We
thought we were part of a combined effort. We flew to
Berlin, were not fired at, in fact nothing happened, we
didn't see anything. We dropped our bombs on the
estimated time of arrival over Berlin, and we may have hit
our target, we may have not. Then we flew back and the
worst part of the trip was getting down at Oakington
where the cloud base was about 500ft and it was pouring
with rain. As it was we got down OK.

Benny and Bill soon settled into their new environs, aided by the
'esprit de corps' of the squadron, as recalled by Benny's navigator
Bill Hickox.

It seemed to me that 627 Squadron had it from the very
start, we had everything in our favour. We were flying the
finest aeroplane in the world and lived in comfort in the
pre-war messes of a permanent station near the beautiful
city of Cambridge. Our CO, Roy Elliott was the finest
squadron commander I ever knew in a long RAF career, his
navigation leader, Bill deBoos, was a splendid Aussie
character, and even the adjutant was a good type.

Cambridge provided good entertainment for nights off,

The Bun Shop, The Baron of Beef and even Dorothy's Tea
Rooms being particularly memorable. We were a small,
close-knit community, proud of being Pathfinders and of
being part of the Light Night Striking Force, operating
practically every night, even when the main force were
stood down. We didn't even mind being known as the
'Model Aeroplane Club'.

Benny Goodman would fly regularly over Germany during the
winter of 1943/44, with a variety of tasks. On the night of 3/4
December Bomber Command sent 527 aircraft to Leipzig; the
route to the target suggesting an attack on Berlin. When the
bomber force turned for Leipzig a small force of Mosquitoes, one
piloted by Benny Goodman, carried on to Berlin, bombed and
were successful in drawing off German nightfighters. The feint
worked and losses were light, until the returning force strayed
over the Frankfurt defences and suffered accordingly; 24 aircraft
in total were lost.

Benny flew on a small raid to Derendorf on 13/14 December,
then he was part of a main force attack on Frankfurt on 20/21
December from which 41 aircraft from the 650 that took part
were lost. The Ruhr battles and the long nights of the Battle of
Berlin are noted as a period of high attrition for Bomber
Command. Harris regularly lost two, three, four hundred of his
trained and skilled aircrew. Of those who survived, most dealt
with the stresses of operational flying the best they could. Some
were able to do so. Some could not and were labelled by the RAF
as LMF – having a lack of moral fibre. These men were dealt
with swiftly by the authorities and removed from a bomber base
as quickly as possible before it 'caught' on. A modern day
perspective can make this policy appear very harsh, but in the
conditions at the time was there an alternative? Lack of moral
fibre was something that Benny Goodman only experienced
once, towards the end of 1943, brought about by a break in a
crew bond.

This squadron put up 18 aircraft on a maximum effort and
suddenly one pilot went sick, he had got a filthy cold. You
just weren't allowed to fly if you had got a bad cold
because you were liable to damage your ears. He was told
he was grounded. Nevertheless they still needed a
maximum effort, they hadn't another crew, so this

particular crew was allocated a new pilot who had just come in. I knew him personally, a very good chap. He had done one tour already on Wellingtons but hadn't done any Pathfinder trips at all. Well the crew didn't like him. They made their superiors aware but they were told they were all in it together so they might just as well get on with it. As the day wore on the navigator, a warrant officer, and the rear gunner, a flight sergeant, got together and squared up to the flight commander saying that they didn't like it at all and they would do any number of trips with their own pilot but not with this one. They were told it was out of the question, it was a maximum effort, they had got to go and that was that. They attended briefing and that was the point of no return. If you are briefed to go you have got to go. They went out to dispersal but then dug their toes in, again saying they wouldn't go. The flight commander now squared up to them saying, 'I order you to go.' They replied, 'Sir we are very sorry but we can't.' He said, 'You mean you won't.' They were both placed under close arrest, were both court martialled and reduced to the ranks, posted elsewhere to menial duties. I was very sorry, they were apparently both good chaps but they felt they couldn't go any further. Of course you couldn't allow that sort of thing to happen, if it began to spread around squadrons everybody would start to do it. You just had to make an example of people like that.

In early 1944 Benny flew on two small raids to Berlin and Kiel, his 50th and 51st, on 10/11 and 20/21 January respectively. Unbeknownst to him in the middle of January, Wing Commander Elliott submitted a recommendation for the award of a non-immediate DFC as recognition of his contribution to date.

Flying Officer Goodman has now completed 50 sorties for a total of 288.05 operational hours. The vast majority of these sorties have been carried out as a captain of the aircraft. He has, up to the present time, completed ten successful sorties on his second tour of operations.

During the whole of the period in which this officer has been engaged on operations he has shown the greatest determination to fulfil the tasks allotted to him, and as evidence, has produced successful photographic results on many occasions. He now has a long and enviable record of successful sorties to his credit, only one out of 50 sorties being unsuccessful.

His enthusiasm for all operational flying is of the very highest order and I have no hesitation whatsoever in strongly recommending him for the non-immediate award of the Distinguished Flying Cross.

To Wing Commander Elliot's recommendation the station commander added, 'I concur, strongly recommended for the DFC'. Air Vice-Marshal Don Bennett also added, 'strongly recommended'. The award was duly made, although it would be a couple of months before Benny received the news.

He flew his next operation on 1/2 February, another small raid to Berlin and one on which he came to appreciate further the aircraft he flew in.

We had been to the Big City and were on our way back, but we had been shot at and had not got all that far, I think as far as Hanover. Suddenly I noticed that the oil pressure was beginning to fall on the starboard engine and the coolant temperature was rising. A bad sign. And the oil temperature rose too. The oil pressure gauge reached rock bottom, the coolant temperature went way over and I realised that the engine was going to cease any second so I pressed the feathering button on the starboard engine. The prop would feather in just a few seconds, it was really a case of 1, 2, 3, 4, 5 and it was stopped. It didn't catch fire, and it didn't seize up. However we only had one generator and that was on the starboard engine. It drove all the electrics, so we had to turn everything off and sit in the darkness. I trimmed the aircraft as well as I could; you could trim it hands and feet off in fact. It could fly perfectly well on one engine trimmed off.

Home we came but instead of being at 25,000ft we had to lose height. We were down at 18,000ft alongside our heavy brothers, which was all right, but we were completely vulnerable if we were attacked by a nightfighter. That would be the end of us; we had nothing to defend ourselves, no guns on the bomber Mosquito at all, you just carried bombs. So we bored on through the dark until we got over Holland. Then Bill tried to turn on the electrics and the Gee set [a radio navigational aid] and fortunately, thank goodness, there was enough left in the battery to work the Gee. He calculated a fix which showed exactly where we were and then plotted a course for base. We carried on and when we were halfway across the North Sea I called up stating that we 'Pen-nib 37', were on one engine, heading for home. The most gorgeous voice you ever heard came back, and I'm sure that these girls were chosen because of their lovely voices, 'Pen-nib 37, transmit for home.' I called her up, 'Pen-nib 37 one, two, three, four, five, over.' Back she came, 'Steer 295.' And then she said, 'Friends are with you.' We looked round behind us and there was a Beaufighter, and he protected our tail all the way to the English coast. We flew on to base and landed. Fairly expertly though I say it myself. And it drew from Mr Hickox, who was imperturbable, you couldn't move him at all, just two words, 'Good show!' This was praise indeed.

During the rest of February 1944 Benny's operation sortie number would rise to 57: flying to Koblenz on the fourth day of the month, Berlin as part of a main attack on the 15th, part of the main attack to Leipzig on the 19th, a small raid to Stuttgart on the 21st and part of the main attack to Schweinfurt on the 24th. Benny recalls the stresses and strains of flying at this time, as part of the Battle of Berlin.

When we were with the heavies one of our jobs was to fly ahead of them and drop Window [metallic strips to confuse German radar]. We would have to go off at an angle to the main line of approach, say 45 degrees one side or the other and Window like hell for 50 miles. That hopefully would draw off some of the German nightfighters, but I think it's true to say that once the nightfighters had found the bomber stream they stuck to it. They did a pathfinder technique on us, flying over the top of the bomber stream dropping flares and from the subsequent lighting the nightfighters would come in and worry away at the flanks of the bombers, or look out for somebody who was on his own, a lame duck, perhaps on three engines having a heck of a job to get along. We, up at 25,000ft, would have a grandstand view of all of this.

Another job we had to do was go in at zero plus one

hour when all the bombing was over, bomb the centre of any fire seen and take a photograph of what was happening on the ground. Often these raids were quite a pushover. By then the defences had usually been overwhelmed, and they took no notice of a lone Mosquito, even if it dropped a few bombs. They weren't going to waste any shells on that, and we would get away without any bother.

It must not be assumed that Bomber Command crews sat around waiting to get the chop. Nothing could be further from the truth. When stood down we contrived to have an uproarious time. For example, the station commander at Oakington, a fierce group captain, lived in a suite of rooms at one end of the officers' mess. He used to retire to his suite at night and took no notice of the hijinx that took place in the bar.

One night a group of inebriated 7 Squadron 'toughies' decided to make the station commander a present of an ancient Austin 7 which stood outside the mess. They picked it up and carried it carefully along the corridor (with two sharp turns in it) and deposited the old vehicle outside the CO's door. It almost blocked the corridor. Next day all hell was let loose and a small army of airmen took a long time removing the offending car. Nos 7 and 627 Squadron crews were paraded by their respective COs and the 'riot act' was read, but no real attempt was made to track down the culprits. This was a good thing and raised the station commander in our estimation.

During this period, Benny also recalls that there was 'another indication that Lady Luck was on our side'.

We were briefed for yet another trip to Berlin, but during the afternoon the raid was cancelled and a short-range attack on a Ruhr target was substituted. This was to be an all-Mosquito affair, led by 105 and 109 Squadrons. Our CO decided that this was an opportunity for new crews to have a go and Bill Hickox and I were stood down in favour of a less experienced crew. We had air-tested the aircraft that morning and were satisfied that it was in all respects serviceable, yet as the Mosquito lifted off at night and entered the area of blackness just beyond the upwind end of the flare path both engines failed and there came the dreadful sound of a crash as the aircraft hit the ground. Both crew members were killed. Would this have happened if Bill and I had been on board? We shall never know.

By the end of March Benny's tally had risen to 65: a diversion to Munich on the first day of the month, small attacks on Berlin and Frankfurt on the fourth and thirteenth respectively, Stuttgart was hit by 863 aircraft on 15 March including Benny's Mosquito, and he also flew on the attack by 846 aircraft to Frankfurt three nights later. On 27 March came a small attack to Duisburg. Benny's last operation of the month was a diversion to Kassel on the night of 30/31 March. That night the diversion failed and from the 795 aircraft sent to Nuremberg 95 failed to return; Bomber Command's highest loss of the war.

By April 1944 the Battle of Berlin was over and the nature of Bomber Command's offensive took on a different aspect. Benny Goodman, and 627 Squadron, would play a significant role in this new direction. But early in the month it was really business as usual for him. On 6 April there was a small raid to Cologne and the 8th saw a trip to the Krupps works at Essen, as one of 40 Mosquitoes. It was on one of these raids that Benny and Bill had the opportunity to fly a new mark of Mosquito.

Early in the spring of 1944 a Mosquito unlike any we had seen before flew in to Oakington. It was a standard Mk IV modified to carry a 4,000lb bomb, the famous 'cookie'. To accommodate this large piece of ordnance the bomb bay had been strengthened and the bomb doors redesigned. The aircraft looked like a pregnant lady; its belly was markedly rotund. Our CO announced that we were to fly the cookie-carrier as much as possible and the most experienced crews were detailed to take her on normal operations.

The night arrived when Bill Hickox and I were ordered to try our hand with this new machine on a target in the Ruhr. Take-off was not difficult, but quite definitely she was not a scalded cat. As soon as her tail came up I pushed the throttles quickly forward to the gate (plus nine pounds boost, 3,000 rpm) and then clenched my left hand over the gate catch releases and eased the throttles to the fully open position (plus twelve pounds boost, 3,000 rpm).

In our normal aircraft this would have resulted in a glorious acceleration and a hop, skip and a jump into the air. Not so with our pregnant lady; she waddled along and took most of the runway before she deigned to unstick. Moreover, the climb was a sedate affair and we took much longer to reach 25,000 feet than with our usual steed; and when we arrived there she took a long time to settle to a steady cruise. However, we eventually sorted ourselves out and headed resolutely for the Ruhr.

In the target area I felt distinctly nervous – there we were, with the bomb doors open and Bill droning away with his 'Left, left – right – steady' and I just knew that every gunner in the Ruhr could see the enormous bomb we were carrying and was determined to explode it and blow us to smithereens. I looked at the bomb jettison handle in front of me – no delicate lever this; it was a solid bar of metal, which, if moved, would manually release the massive catch holding the 'cookie' and down the bomb would go. If the bomb doors had not been opened, that was hard luck – the cookie would still drop away and take the bomb doors with it!

However, no such inglorious thing happened. Bill suddenly announced 'Bombs gone' and as he did so the Mossie shot up like a lift. There was no delicate porpoising, as with four 500 pounders; the altimeter moved instantly through 500 feet of altitude. I had never seen anything like this before. More importantly, as soon as I closed the bomb doors our fat lady became almost a normal Mosquito and accelerated to a fast cruising speed.

On 11 April Benny flew as one of 36 Mosquitoes sent to Hanover. This raid was somewhat out of the ordinary in that during the flight the squadron's airmen would be recorded for the benefit of the BBC.

It was an all-Mosquito attack. The idea was that we were to broadcast as much as possible, because the Mosquitoes weren't easily intercepted by the German nightfighters, we tended to be in and out before they knew we were there. They'd really got to get their skates on to catch us. Now this attack was to be launched specially for the BBC to record and Stuart McPherson, one of the ace recorders and commentators of the time, came up to Oakington with his team. They would record everything – the briefing, the

Mosquitoes taking off, our chit chat in the air, on the circuit coming back and landing, and then the debriefing. For the only time in my life I was on the air on the BBC, flying down wind at Oakington calling 'Pen-nib 37 down wind', and the tower answered 'Pen-nib 37 clear to final'. Then as I got to the final turn into the approach, 'Pen-nib 37 final' and the tower said 'Pen-nib 37 clear to land'. Following the debriefing, when it was all over, everything was played back by Stuart McPherson. It appeared very successful, and Bennett who was present, was highly delighted. But Bennett could also be a very frosty individual and you could never tell whether he was really pleased or not. He had got his wintry smile on, and one of our chaps was very foolish and squared up to Bennett saying, 'Well sir that was good wasn't it.' Bennett said, 'Yes. What did you think of it?' He said "Oh. Jolly good sir and don't you think that we deserve a stand down after this.' Bennett turned on him and said, 'I'll decide when you get a stand down.' For the next seven nights our squadron was on the battle order. Normally we would have been a night on and a night off, so that punished us for having the temerity to square up to Bennett.

Benny would be one of those flying the following night, to Osnabrück, but the next time he was airborne he would be moving station.

The nature of 627 Squadron's role in the bomber offensive now changed. Air Vice-Marshal Cochrane's 5 Group was looking to develop its own methodology of target marking, notably under the direction of Wing Commander Leonard Cheshire, in particular marking at low level. Cheshire, flying in a Lancaster, proved the case for low-level marking on the night of 8/9

627 Squadron Mosquito

February 1944 in a successful twelve-Lancaster, all 617 Squadron, attack on the Gnome and Rhône aero-engine factory. But to continue marking at low level in a Lancaster was far too risky, when the task could be carried out by a less cumbersome Mosquito. And 5 Group soon sought to take this concept a stage further, requesting the allocation of a Mosquito squadron. Consequently, in April 1944 627 Squadron prepared to take up low level marking responsibilities in 5 Group.

> In the middle of the month our whole squadron journeyed by bus to RAF Coningsby and were directed to the station cinema. Here were assembled all crew members of 83 and 97 Lancaster Pathfinder squadrons, our own Squadron, the AOC and his entourage, and Leonard Cheshire.

Cochrane opened the meeting briefly describing what lay in store for the 627 Squadron airmen.

> We were to become low-level visual markers, and it did sound dangerous. Cheshire now took the stand and explained carefully how the low-level marking business was done. The Lancasters had to lay a concentrated carpet of hooded flares, the light from which would be directed downwards onto the target, making it as bright as day. A small number of Mosquitoes – four or possibly six – would orbit, find the aiming point, and then mark it in a shallow dive with 500lb spot-fires. A 'marker leader' would assess the position of the spot-fires in relation to the aiming point and would pass this information to a 'master of cere-monies' in one of the Pathfinder Lancasters. The MC would then take over and direct the main force Lancasters in their attack on the target.
>   You can imagine what a fuss this caused. We didn't really much like the idea of this marking at low-level as we had been doing all our work at high level. On returning to Woodhall, the CO called flight commanders to his office and an intensive dive-bombing practice programme was worked out.

Benny however had a mere two dive-bombing practice flights at Wainfleet Bombing Range before he was next on operations. He describes how the 627 Squadron crews developed their low-level marking methodology.

After the target area was illuminated by Lancasters we would look around for the target, a factory shall we say. Then it was bomb doors open and dive on the target. A shallow dive, about 40 degrees. You filled your windscreen with the target area and when you were at the right point of about say, 500ft, you pressed the button and released the markers to go down on top of the factory. In a very short time you could become very skilled at getting these markers right on an aiming point, or right beside it.

Such a method made the navigator redundant in one respect as Bill Hickox recalled, 'Benny was particularly chuffed, as he now had control of the bomb release.' There was also another benefit of low-level marking.

At German targets they were always much too pre-occupied with blasting away with their 88 millimetre guns at the heavies up top. They didn't bother with the Mosquitoes at low level. To some extent it was easier to go to a German target than to a French one where they had these nasty lighter anti-aircraft guns at low level specifically for aircraft like us.

The Mosquito low-level marking had yet to be tried out on a German city with all its defences, but this would be rectified on the night of 22/23 April 1944, with the marking carried out by 617 Squadron. Benny Goodman, who had received news of his DFC the day before, (as had Bill Hickox) would be flying on the raid and witness from high up if it was possible; carrying out a late reconnaissance of the target, and bombing from 25,000 feet.

We had rather wondered what the low-level marking would be like on German targets. No one quite knew. The wind as I recall it was blowing from the north east and the idea was to make an enormous great blob of red in a park on the north east side of Brunswick. This we managed. We didn't have to fly over Brunswick itself and we weren't shot at.
    The master bomber [the term master of ceremonies having been dropped] had to make allowances for the fact that this blob of red was about a mile up wind of the aiming point – the middle of Brunswick. The navigator in the master bomber's aircraft had to calculate a false wind

allowing for this difference. The attacking heavies would then put this false wind into their bomb sites, come in and bomb on the reds. Because of the false wind on their bomb sites the bombs would undershoot and hit the target area. On this occasion it was the first time we had ever tried this one and it proved outstandingly successful. Usually of course we marked the middle of a target; the middle of a town or a city. But when the bombs were dropped the markers could be blown out and you would then be faced with re-marking. Although usually what happened was that you made a great conflagration, the heavies could see it all burning, and they would come in and just bomb the middle. But this off-set technique was used to some effect.

Benny's claim of successful marking is well founded. However, the main force bombing suffered because of cloud and poor communications between those controlling the raid. Two nights later and the method was tried again on Munich, again with 617 Squadron carrying out the marking. Benny again flew high above the target, dropping Window in front of the main force and then bombing from 23,000 feet. The marking was accurate and the raid caused considerable damage. Two nights later and 627 Squadron's low-level marking abilities were called upon in an attack on Schweinfurt. Benny did not take part in the marking, bombing from 25,000 feet, but the raid by 215 Lancasters and 11 Mosquitoes, at a cost of 21 Lancasters, turned out a failure.

There now came a change in the nature of Benny's flying duties. Operation Overlord, the D-Day beach landing in Normandy and the Allied land advance into north-west France and beyond, would place its demands on all aspects of the armed services. A detailed air plan had been drawn up to support the invasion. Bomber Command, despite its commander's reluctance, would have to play its part. One of Bomber Command's key campaigns in support of Overlord was the attack on the rail communication networks that would transport German troops and armour into the battle area once the invasion was launched. In addition other targets associated with enemy transport and aircraft in friendly areas, would be attacked. These targets would be situated in built-up areas populated by friendly French and Belgian civilians. The need to stress accuracy was not lost on the Bomber Command station and squadron commanders, and this message was passed on to those responsible for finding and marking targets. This included the airmen of 627 Squadron, who were fully involved, especially with regard to marking, in the campaign against rail networks, and as Benny Goodman recalls:

> The technique was really very simple. Mosquitoes would mark each end of the marshalling yard, which were usually shaped like a lozenge, a blob of markers at each end, and the Lancaster or Halifax pilot could then steer between the two blobs of red on the ground and drop his bombs.

Benny's first operation in direct support of the invasion, the 29/30 April 1944, as part of the 5 Group attack on the Michelin tyre factory at Clermont-Ferrand, was frustrated, and he had to turn back early, bringing his four red spot-fires home, owing to extreme vibration, on climbing. Some exhaust stub studs sheared and the stub broke away into the starboard engine. A few nights later however Benny was able to complete his task, 46 Lancasters and 5 Mosquitoes being sent to the aircraft repair workshops at Tours. Benny recalls this particular attack.

> On this occasion we had examined target maps and photographs all day before we went on the trip, so we knew exactly what it all looked like. We saw what the Americans had done a few days before, or had not done. There were bomb craters in the fields all around the works and as far as we could see none on the works itself, or if there were any there might have been one or two but that's all.

Benny was the first marker on the target.

> We had two 'Pathfinder' Lancaster squadrons with us in 5 Group by then, 83 and 97. They went ahead of everybody else and dropped flares to ignite at 5,000 ft and parachute down over the target area. We would come in under the light. As we approached Tours a great carpet of light suddenly spread out in front of us. We lost more height and soon we were under the carpet at 1,500 feet and it was as bright as day. If a fighter appeared now, we would be dead ducks, and if there was light flak in the area we would certainly have a rough time. The procedure was for the first marker, we would normally have four, to call his call sign and 'tally ho'. That was a sign for all the others to get the hell out of it, and keep out of the way. On this particular night I suddenly saw the factory close by. I immediately

pressed the transmit button on my VHF and called 'Pen-nib 37', and 'tally ho'. I opened the bomb doors and dived on the works. Unfortunately I was a bit too keen. I think I got the markers bang in the middle and they went through the glass roofs of an engine repair shop and ignited inside, which meant that to some extent they were shielded from the view of the approaching main force. So the next marker who was called in was told to put his markers alongside this particular engine shop, which he did. There was a great big blob of red in the centre of these works and the Lancs came in and plastered it.

Indeed the raid was a success, with considerable damage to the workshops.

Two nights later Benny was flying his 74th operation, to the German military camp at Mailly-le-Camp. This raid takes its place in history as one of Bomber Command's fiercest air battles over French territory. 346 Lancasters and 16 Mosquitoes took part in the raid and 42 of the Lancasters failed to return that night. The initial marking on the raid was accurate, with good backing up and Wing Commander Cheshire, leading the raid, ordered the waiting main force Lancasters to come in. The order was delayed and whilst heavy bombers awaited their instructions German nightfighters arrived and took their toll. Benny Goodman witnessed what was going on above him that night, and although he avoided contact with the enemy fighters, 'It was also a night on which Bill Hickox and I very nearly got the chop because I did a very stupid thing.'

The primary object of the raid was to knock out all the tank repair facilities and kill as many Germans as possible. It was a full moon night and the nightfighters found us. We could see the developing air battle up top and as soon as a Lancaster was hit it would catch fire. First of all you would see this plume of fire streaming back and then the whole aircraft would be a huge ball of flame and it might explode. At low level we had these great flaming balls of fire heading towards us. I remember looking at them and thinking that they were going to hit me. Of course they wouldn't. They would be off a mile or two, but something coming down from 18,000ft in your general direction seems to be coming right at you believe me.

We did our bombing and then turned away at low level.

We should normally have climbed up to 25,000ft coming back at high level, but I thought I would be clever, staying low because of the mayhem in the target area. We headed low for the Pas de Calais and had not been flying many minutes before we were suddenly picked up by a searchlight and then another, until we were coned. I dived down to about 500 ft above the ground with Bill Hickox exhorting me to watch the instruments. There we were in this great glare of light and up came the light flak, towards us. Red, and green and white shells passed by exploding, it was terrible. Plop, plop, and bang, bang as they went off, but miraculously we weren't hit. And of course we were weaving this way and that but making a steady mean course towards the coast. Eventually we approached Le Tréport, and breasted a low hill with searchlights shining up behind us. Then they shone above us as we came down over the hill and towards the sea, which we could see ahead of us in the light of the full moon. Ahead was this great patch of light from the searchlights. But we couldn't be fired at by the guns. We'd got past the light flak belt. In no time at all we were going up the river estuary at Le Tréport and past the lighthouse, below the level of the light. It must have scared the daylights out of the lighthouse keeper, at least I hope it did, if he was a German.

Another member of the squadron had a lucky escape that night as related by Benny.

One of the other markers came back and somehow or other managed to run into the balloon barrage around Ipswich. The navy were there and they loved to fly these wretched balloons over their ships. Of course we were not supposed to go over Ipswich anyway but this character somehow or other managed to do so. Suddenly he felt a bump and the Mosquito slewed a bit in the air, about 10 or 20 degrees, then levelled out again and headed on. He tried the controls and she appeared a bit one wing low but otherwise she performed all right. He got back to the airfield and landed and told the groundcrew about the incident. They shone a light on the Mosquito and to their astonishment found that the starboard wing, outboard of the engine, the starboard leading edge of the wing, had been sheered off completely.

He had driven into one of these wretched balloon cables, outboard of the propeller thank god. If it had been inboard it might have come in through the cockpit and killed them both. It didn't hit the prop but hit the leading edge, slewed the aeroplane in the air, scraped along the main spar which was made of spruce, and away off the wingtip, scooping off the whole of the leading edge. Well when you do that sort of thing with an aeroplane, normally it becomes uncontrollable, but the Mosquito could take it as was demonstrated. He was a very lucky man.

627 Squadron's support to the invasion preparations continued, Benny flying to Tours on 19/20 May 1944 on an accurate raid to the rail facilities in the centre of the town, requiring considerable care not to hit the housing in the area. Not that everything went according to plan. There was an incident following the operation when the airman's wry sense of humour came to the fore.

We used to have what were called wash-ups. If anything had gone wrong after a raid we would have a debriefing in the station cinema at Coningsby. All the crews had to be there and the 'Great Ones' went into what had gone wrong. One night a good friend of mine, from 627 Squadron, had got in under the carpet of flares. We were going after a particular marshalling yard, but there was another one nearby and he went and laid markers on that. Quite wrong of course. It was heresy; you mustn't do a thing like that. It was before we had developed a technique whereby if a marker was in the wrong place another Mosquito was detailed to go in and drop in a yellow alongside it. The rule was that if you saw a red marker on the ground with a yellow alongside it you did not bomb. But if you saw markers with greens alongside them you did. But at the beginning we only had reds. So my friend had got this marker down in the wrong yard and the other Mosquitoes had got them down in the right yard. The master bomber was trying to explain to the crews coming along behind that they were to bomb between the two markers that they could see in one yard. Unfortunately some of them decided that the two markers were my friend's. So to some extent the raid went adrift. There was one heck of a row in the station cinema and Cochrane did not like it at all. The base commander, in charge of Coningsby and Woodhall Spa, eventually summed it up by saying my friend was, 'only too willing to admit he boobed. He had dropped the markers on the right place in the wrong yard.' That of course brought the house down, and even Cochrane permitted himself one of his wry smiles.

Three nights later and it was a return to Brunswick for Benny and his squadron colleagues, but the raid failed, owing in the main to unpredicted cloud cover. As May drew to a close the actual launch day of the Normandy invasion neared and targeting became more tactical in nature, including attacks on the enemy coastal batteries that would threaten the invasion fleets. Benny flew to St Martin de Varreville on 28/29 May, one of three coastal gun emplacements targeted by Bomber Command that night. As the month closed his logbook now had the record of 77 operational flights serving with Bomber Command. On the first day of June 1944 Benny and Bill were tasked with marking the Saumur marshalling yards.

> We weren't to know it but this was to be our final trip. It sounds very strange that we should stop at that point when the invasion was only five days away. But you did a tour of duty and when you reached your requisite number of trips you stopped. The fact of the matter was that by then the chop rate in Bomber Command had reduced greatly, although there were the odd exceptions like the bad casualties on the Mailly-le-Camp raid. It was mine and Bill's 38th Mosquito trip; we were supposed to do 30. Usually if you did a second tour on heavies it would be 20 trips, whereas a second tour on Mosquitoes was 30 trips. This trip took me to 78 in all. Way over the top, but that was the way the cookie crumbled at times. We were detailed for this particular raid and as usual it turned out a copy book 5 Group attack.
>
> We were briefed in the morning and then went to the AOC's briefing in the afternoon, as was usual for the marker pilots that were on the raid. This meant that when you went into the briefing room, your squadron commander was there, as was the squadron commander of 617, Leonard Cheshire, and all the marker pilots, and our station commander, and the station commanders of all the

stations in the group, and the squadron commanders of all
the stations in the group. Quite a gathering. The AOC
would say a few words about what he thought of this
particular raid and any special things he wished to be
attended to. Very often he would say, 'Now tonight we
have really got to make sure of getting this one and I want
everybody to come down to shall we say 8,000 feet', which
would create a fuss among the squadron command. They
didn't like that, they liked the Lancasters to be up at 18,000
feet or perhaps they would come down to 12,000 feet but
they didn't like the idea of coming down that low. But
obviously the lower they got the more accurate they would
become. On some of these marshalling yard trips that's
what they had to do and the AOC would tell them so. And
I will never forget on one particular trip he said, 'and
tonight you must get this target and if you don't get it
tonight then you will go tomorrow night and you will go
the night after that and every night until you do get it.' So
at the squadron commander's briefing to their crews they
would pass this on making it clear that they had got to get
this target, no argument, the AOC wants us to do it, get
cracking. Marker pilots never said anything, and on this
particular occasion, after briefing, we prepared for our task
of marking the Saumur yards. The heavies had got away
first, of course, they were in the air usually a couple of
hours before we ever took off. We would catch them up
and pass them.

On this particular night I remember that an ENSA
concert party was on the station. They had a piano
mounted up on the back of a three tonner and went round
to the dispersals. There was a very good pianist and a very
good girl soprano. She was a dish, she really was. When
they came to our dispersal the Lancs had all gone and it
was made clear to these rough tough Mosquito people that
this girl was going to sing a song. We all looked bleakly at
her, the poor soul. The pianist started up and it was to be
Dream o'Day Jill, one of Edward German's songs. She sang
it beautifully and we did clap in a sort of half hearted way.
Away she went, blushing crimson, round the perimeter
track to do the same thing at some of the other dispersals
where the groundcrews were all assembled. Away we went

with the tune of the song Dream o'Day Jill ringing in our ears.

We flew over to Saumur, catching up the Lancasters and getting ahead of them. The Lanc Pathfinders were ahead of them dropping their flares [starting at 0107 hours]. We flew in underneath, arriving over the target at zero minus five minutes. We had five minutes in which to mark and get out of the area. This we proceeded to do in the time-honoured fashion. The marker leader flew in and announced to the controller up top that the markers were all in place so it was safe to go ahead. The controller then gave the all clear for the heavies to come in and bomb.

The first markers were dropped by Flight Lieutenant Bartley at 0108 hours and the marker leader Flight Lieutenant Devigne claimed the markers were within ten yards of the aiming point. As the bombing progressed the red spot-fires became obscured, the bombing was halted and Flight Lieutenant Bartley was again called in, placing a green, assessed at 150 yards south east of the aiming point. The bombing then restarted. Benny Goodman had arrived at the target at 0104 hours ready to mark the target if needs be, but he was not called upon and having spent 34 minutes over the target he was ordered to leave. Benny and the returning bomber force left considerable destruction behind them.

> The yard was destroyed. The Bomber Command war diaries announced triumphantly that the bombers were led by four Mosquitoes and all aircraft returned safely, which I think was really quite superb. As far as I was concerned, it was something I didn't often encounter. Almost always somebody was lost. This time everyone returned safely. A good point at which to end I think.

The raid to Saumur was one of many successful attacks, using low-level marking, in the run-up to D-Day and in the weeks following. 5 Group's Air Vice-Marshal Cochrane was certainly appreciative of the work of his airmen, writing in the 30 June 1944 5 Group News.

> The Group carried out more attacks than in previous months this year and each attack was more efficient than in the past. Throughout the month the centre of pattern of

bombs dropped averaged only 100 yards from the aiming point.

This improvement has been brought about mainly by the system of marking used and I wish to pay tribute to those pilots of No 627 Squadron who have gone in low to mark the target and have not allowed their aim to be spoilt by the light flak defences.

Their accuracy has been consistently of a very high order, far exceeding any other system tried.

Benny had completed his last flight. He had to his name an extraordinary list of operations completed, starting in the days of navigation and bombing by dead reckoning to the use of sophisticated electronic aids to locate, illuminate, mark and bomb targets. Unsurprisingly Benny was to receive further recognition of his contribution to the bomber war. The opening of his recommendation of a Bar to his DFC is recorded at the start of this account of his career; it went on to further state:

This officer has recently been employed as one of the Initial Markers for the precision bombing operations of No 5 Group. In this highly skilled and vital role, which has demanded great daring, Flight Lieutenant Goodman has shown the same steady determination to bring each sortie to a successful conclusion. Although this officer has only carried out nine sorties since the receipt of his previous award he has in actual fact completed twenty-nine sorties since the recommendation was forwarded to higher authority. In view of his long and highly successful record of operations I recommend him for the award of a first Bar to the Distinguished Flying Cross.

The recommendation met with approval from the higher authorities and the award was duly made.

After operations Benny took up training duties until the end of the war. He was soon to receive a permanent commission and set about further instruction. His training abilities were soon recognised with the award of the Air Force Cross, gazetted on 14 June 1945, the citation noting that Benny had flown 1,078 instructional hours.

As an A.2 Instructor, this officer has maintained a high

standard of efficiency. He is employed as a Flight
Commander in one of the Dual Conversion Flights and, by
his fine example and devotion to duty, he has contributed
much to the successful training of the pupils. The number
of flying hours he has completed during the last six months
is unusually high and is indicative of the zeal and interest
with which Squadron Leader Goodman undertakes his
duties.

Benny would go on to serve a distinguished career with the RAF
although his flying days were cut short owing to a problem with
his eyes. He took up administration and intelligence
responsibilities, becoming secretary to the Joint Intelligence
Committee in the Middle East and promoted to group captain.
He completed his final two years service at HQ Support
Command Andover, retiring in 1976. In 2007 Benny and Maisie
Goodman will be celebrating their 65th wedding anniversary.

When looking back on his wartime career with Bomber
Command Benny holds the opinion that, 'we were done down
and people have been less than kind to us.'

What we did was decisive. Leonard Cheshire summed it up
well before he died. If when the bomber offensive and the
whole war is analysed, it is decided that we had lifted the
lid on Fortress Europe just enough to let the Allied armies
in then by God that was enough. And that is what we did
do. The bomber offensive was absolutely necessary and we
could never have won without it. I think people are
beginning to come round to the idea that perhaps we did
have to do what we did.

Flight Lieutenant Joe Petrie-Andrews DFC, DFM

Chapter 5

The Reluctant Bomber

Betty Haywood was 17 years old when she signed up with the Women's Auxiliary Air Force, in 1940, taking up responsibilities as a driver. After some time at RAF Finningley she was sent to Castle Donington.

> *I was the first WAAF there. There were 600 airmen building an aerodrome and I was the only qualified driver to start with. There were men drivers, but they were doing*

other jobs. A few days later two more girls arrived and they became my best friends. At the dinner dances around Christmas and New Year the men were queuing up for a dance as the females were in such short supply. I was spoiled rotten!

I then got engaged to my first love... a navigator and he was shot down (all crew lost) two nights before our wedding. They were coming back from one of the first bombing raids over Italy and went down over the Pyrenees. The Pope sent out people to search for the wreck and it was found 18 months later complete with the skeletons of the crew. I later had a letter from the Papal Office confirming the aeroplane number.

By now I was driving a 'crew bus' taking the lads out to the 'kites'. The planes were the mighty Lancasters. They flew to Berlin every night – and returned in full what the German bombers had done to us at home. God Bless Bomber Command – we won the war. I am proud to have helped.

Joe Petrie-Andrews's first run-in with RAF authority came the day he tried to join up. Not that he should have been there anyway. He was underage, but Joe clearly did not consider that an impediment. He wanted to fly. In his teens interest had grown watching RAF cadets get to grips with de Havilland Tiger Moths at Hamworth airport, near to his Hampton home. A few enquiries later and he was able to leave school and start up with Tipsey Aviation. There was little objection from his school. On 12 March 1940 the headmaster of Hampton grammar school wrote to Joe's single mother; an early indication of Joe's unwillingness to follow other people's agendas and a desire to take his own path.

Dear Mrs Andrews
Thank you for your letter of 20 February saying that J.C. had taken a job with an aircraft factory at Feltham.

I did recommend him to take the opening. I did so only because he seemed keen about it and he was not keen to carry on with the humdrum grind of school life in an examination form.

He has been a great problem, as you probably know even better than we do. He has certain assets to an outstanding degree – physique, appearance, manners, speech, charm. But he has never yet learnt to work and until he does his assets will prove liabilities. We have, I am sorry to say, failed, but not for lack of many good attempts to make a man and a worker out of him.

I was extremely sorry to find that he celebrated his departure by cutting his initials and the date on one of the new classroom doors. No one else, so far as I know, has so far thought it right to disfigure any part of this magnificent building. I shall have the damage made good but it will be done at private expense.

Joe's foray into working life had begun, and, whilst living with his mother at Sunbury-on-Thames, he took up another duty. Despite being too young, he managed to join the Local Defence Volunteers, (Home Guard), guarding Shepperton Lock. Meantime he witnessed the historic events taking place in the skies above, watching keenly as the Battle of Britain was fought during the summer of 1940, and the aerial mêlées over London. 'We had a lot of bombs fall around Sunbury and there were a tremendous number of anti-aircraft guns. When at Shepperton, the Vickers factory was only just across the way at Weybridge and they were always getting bombed. It was certainly noisy.' But being a spectator was not enough for Joe, he wanted to be part of the excitement above, 'how I would have liked to have been involved.'

One day I went into the local recruiting office at Hounslow with a friend. In due course we were sent, with a railway warrant, to Cardington near Bedford. I felt I was doing fairly well but I didn't seem to be getting on with a squadron leader wearing First World War medals and an observers badge. I felt I knew a bit about the air force and that he was just a crew member really and that they didn't have observers badges in the first war. I questioned him on that – he wasn't best pleased. He asked me what I had observed on the bus from Bedford to Cardington. Having left the house at 6.00am I confessed I was asleep. I don't think he was impressed and he said that he would recommend me for wireless operator/air gunner. I thanked him and told him I didn't want to be an air gunner.

Joe's passion to fly remained undiminished and a month later he tried another recruiting office.

> I was sent to Uxbridge, where a charming squadron leader with a DFC led the interview board. He thought I would be a likely lad but then asked how old I was. I told him 18. He replied that I needed to be 19 to start pilot training. I thought, 'Oh hell. Why didn't I just tell him I was 19, he wouldn't know.' I'm sure he noticed my disappointment. He said, 'well you are pretty big for your age. I'll recommend you for immediate training.' I was delighted. I was in! He added that I probably wouldn't be called up for six months and by that time I would be 19. Well as it turned out I was called up in 1940, still only 16, and was sent to ITW (Initial Training Wing) at Scarborough, spending three months chasing around and saluting everything in sight. One day we had to fall in with our kit and they put us on a train. We had no idea where we were going. We set off north, to Scotland.

Unlike pilots such as Tiny Cooling and Benny Goodman, who had learned their trade in the UK, Joe's ongoing training was to take place overseas away from the now crowded and dangerous home skies. In Greenock Joe and other raw recruits boarded the luxury liner *Britannic*, 'all stripped out with about 7,000 potential pilots, crowded into every part. I was in a single cabin, with four others.'

> We left the following morning with the HMS *Rodney* and HMS *Renown* and two destroyers. It seemed great. The next morning however the two battleships had gone and the morning after the two destroyers had disappeared. They had all gone to chase the *Bismarck* and we were being shaken to pieces as the ship's engines went flat out.

On arrival in Canada the recruits were entrained to Toronto. They were told there they would be going south, to the United States.

> They issued us with tropical kit, khaki shorts and trousers. We asked where we were going but nobody would ever tell. Three days in a very old train, real rattley old thing, nowhere to sleep, and we were in Camden, South Carolina [9 June 1941]. We arrived at about 4 o'clock in the morning and there was no transport. As it was the whole

town had turned out in their cars to meet us. It was quite emotional. They were lovely people and drove us to the camp.

Joe's training was now to come under the Arnold Scheme (named after General 'Hap' Arnold) and the United States Army Air Corps. In fact he was to be in the first intake of 549 cadets, from which 302 would go on to graduate. In total 7,885 trainees would enter the scheme between 1941 and 1943, but many would not meet the standards of the training – 4,493 would pass out as pilots.[8]

Setting out on the primary training Joe began honing his flying skills on Boeing PT17 Stearmans, 'nice aeroplane, twice the power of a Tiger Moth. I loved flying, it was magic really.'

The only problem was the American training scheme had upper classmen and lower classmen. When we arrived there were American cadets with upper classmen status, and they had come straight out of civvy street. If they said 'pop to' you had to stand to attention and sound out name, rank and number. It did not go down at all well, these blokes knew nothing about the services at all, six weeks as lower classmen and now they were ordering us around.

There were a lot of civilian instructors. Mine was a crop duster. A wonderful old boy but the laziest man you ever saw. I was quite slight, a bit over six foot tall, but long and thin. I had to carry his parachute everywhere and the weather was steaming hot. One day we were up flying around and he'd asked me to do some lefts and rights, which I did for a while. Into the intercom, which was a tube, I said, 'Was that alright then?' No reply. He was sort of sliding down in the cockpit, getting lower and lower. I said, 'Carry on shall I?' No reply, so I carried on. 'You alright?' No reply. He was quite an old man and I thought he had passed out, or perhaps had a heart attack, I hadn't solo'd and we had no radio to the ground. 'Oh Christ', I thought, 'I had better land. How do I do this?' He had shown me two or three landings, but I was quite nervous. I started making an approach to the airfield, nearing the edge, levelling out, when suddenly up he came, 'God! What the heck!' A rattle of the engine and off we went. He had fallen asleep. I was expecting to get a DFC or something.

Following three months of primary training Joe passed on to basic training on Vultee BT13As at Macon, Georgia. After another three months he progressed on to No 1 Pursuit School at Selma, Alabama, for advanced training, to fly North American AT6A Harvards. Here Joe had his second run in with the higher echelons of service life.

Vultee BT-13

We were the first cadets to be trained by the US Air Corps, class 42A, which meant we were the first class to graduate in 42. It was a good flying training course. We did 200 hours as opposed to the 120 that we would have had in the RAF, but we knew more about navigation and meteorology than the instructors. All went well until the very end of the course. We had to fill in one hour before we went on a cross country flight. Four of us went up and set about a chase me Charlie, someone would do a roll, and we would follow. We did get down fairly low at one time but it was no problem really. When we came back someone came along and told us that we had to report to the chief flying instructor. When we presented ourselves to him he said, 'Why were you low flying?' Our response was that we weren't really low flying, we were lost and went down to have a look at a railway station to see where we were. Of course he was having none of it. While we had been fooling around somebody else had joined in, an instructor, and he had returned and reported us for doing unauthorised aerobatics. We had really finished our training at that point, now this was a disaster; we were all 'washed out'. Fortunately an ex Battle of Britain pilot Wing Commander Rampling was over there and he explained how much we were needed in the UK; punish us as much as possible but no 'wash out'. We all got below average assessments. Grading was from A to F, which was a fail. We got graded E. When we got onto the next course they really gave us the run around, check flight every month, which was tough.

With training completed at Selma, Joe went to Nova Scotia by train and then on board the *Vollendam*, in a convoy, back to England. Accommodation was basic, in the hold and sleeping in hammocks. U-boat attacks added to the discomfort.

By the time Joe got back to the UK 'the Battle of Britain was long gone'. Initially his future was to be on nightfighters, training on Oxfords and then on Blenheims at No 13 OTU, Bicester. Here Joe began to assemble a crew, which of course began in the usual fairly arbitrary way. 'We were put into a big room and told that we needed a navigator and a wireless operator. I had a look round and I was lucky.' John Backhouse took up responsibilities as Joe's navigator, 'he seemed quite laid back while we were chatting about crewing up.' John Backhouse recalls, 'It was haphazard, really was. Joe always said he picked me, but I'm not sure if he was pulling my leg.' As Joe and John were looking around Joe recalled seeing, 'quite a smart looking guy, bit older.' Jim Berwick became Joe's wireless operator. Training continued and on one flight Joe decided to acquaint himself further with the father of one of his new crew. John Backhouse's father, a former naval officer had retired to the Isle of Man, and felt it necessary to telephone the Air Ministry and complain one day following a low pass by a Blenheim; unbeknownst to him it was flown by his son's pilot. Nothing came of the complaint and nothing more was said, although a wireless mechanic had been silenced with half a crown; the aircraft's trailing wireless aerial had been 'deposited' around a church spire.

Joe finished flying Blenheims on 18 August, and was assessed as an average pilot, and above average in bombing and formation flying. 'Having done OTU, and having some good results, we thought Mitchells, or Bostons, or maybe some intruder work. That fell through; our destiny lay with heavy bombers.' Demand for Bomber Command pilots now meant Joe, reluctantly, ended up at 24 OTU Honeybourne on 18 September, flying Whitleys.

This was really the pits. 120 mph, flat out or cruising. Dreadful aeroplane really. Going to Bomber Command, I thought that was the end, which it wasn't at all really. Flying nightfighters was bad enough, bombers were awful and flying a Whitley was really depressing. The sooner I could get out of Bomber Command the better. The first thing I did when I got to the Heavy Conversion Unit at Pocklington was volunteer for Pathfinders, with the belief that if you did two tours with Pathfinders you could then pick your next posting. But what I didn't realise though was that by this time bombers were quite exciting really. It was fairly quiet except for Bomber Command.

Following his time at Honeybourne Joe then transferred to 1652 Heavy Conversion Unit at Pocklington, also the home of 102 Squadron. He began flying on 20 December and gaining experience on a four-engine Halifax. Through OTU and HCU new members also came in to team up with Joe, John and Jim.

I asked a likely looking bloke, a gunner by the name of George Dale, if he was crewed up. On being told no I asked if he would like to join us and if he knew of any other gunners. 'No, not really.' He looked across at someone, 'He's a funny fella, doesn't say much.' I asked if he was a good gunner. 'Oh yeh he's a very good gunner.' That's how we got Darky Barnett. He had joined the RAF as a boy entrant and had actually flown with Butch Harris pre-war. A quiet man but when it came to guns he was magic. In his rear turret he'd often test his guns, and come back with something like, 'Oh, number 3 is not working.' I'd ask if he could do anything about it. 'I'll strip it down and have a look.' This is in a turret at night, with no lights, whilst on ops. He'd then ask if he could try it, I'd say, 'Yep help yourself', and off it went.

The crew set about forming a bond in the time-honoured way. 'We used to go out and have a few drinks, although Darky didn't drink at all really. He'd married a WAAF and she'd shaken a fist in his face.' The five-man crew became seven when flying Halifaxes. A Sergeant Jackson came in as Joe's navigator (Backhouse took up the bomb-aimer role). 'Happy Jackson as we called him; a good navigator, but a terribly serious man.'

Taffy Morgan came in as the flight engineer. A quiet fellow, been to university, well educated. He had originally signed up for aircrew but he wasn't needed at the time so they put him in an aircraft factory whilst awaiting his call up. As time got on he became fed up, so he volunteered as a flight engineer. He was a brilliant engineer.

By 4 February 1943 Joe and his crew had completed their conversion on to four engines and were ready for operational duties. Joe managed to get one operation under his belt before the rest of his crew, flying as a second dickie with 102 Squadron, a minelaying trip to the Kattegat, which he felt was 'a very easy trip'. The crew were then posted to operations with 158 Squadron, currently based at Rufforth, Yorkshire. On 13 February Joe took his crew to Lorient as part of the Bomber Command campaign against the French U-boat bases. The entry against the crew's name in the squadron diary records the lack of difficulty on the raid.

> Target – Lorient. Primary Load 4 x 1,000 lb G.P. [General Purpose] T.D. [Time Delay] 0.025, 720 x 4lb: 90 x 4lb: 16 x 30lb incends.
>
> Good visibility and clear over target. River, docks and isle of Groix seen and own bursts identified. Fires all over the town and on both sides of the river. Big explosions in target area seen after leaving.
>
> Captain states: 'Extensive fires in target area. Good visibility and inaccurate flak make the operation 'A Piece of Cake'.

A fortunate opener, which was not always the case for novice crews. Often the newer crews would be given 'easier' trips to break them into operations – such as minelaying. However, many a crew found that their first operation took them to the Ruhr or even Berlin, and many a crew would not even survive their first trip.

The night following the Lorient raid, Joe Petrie-Andrews's crew were detailed to attack Cologne, their first experience of a German target.

> Defences were something we hadn't experienced before. There was quite heavy flak, but we weren't hit, and we weren't coned by searchlights. But it was a difficult operation as were the next ones to Munich [9 March], Stuttgart [11 March], and Essen [12 March]. All heavily

defended and you just had to keep your head down and hope for the best. The searchlights were more frightening than the guns actually. Once the gun had gone off and you saw the flash of the shell burst you knew that they hadn't hit you. The thing to do was change position every half minute or so and occasionally you would see that if you had continued on a course, that's where the bursts and explosions were. But searchlights were worrying, they would float about and if one caught you you'd get coned as others came in. We were coned more than once and I would struggle to get out of it by turning. But most of the time you couldn't get out. It was important not to panic. You would increase speed, losing a bit of height, to try and get away from the danger. With more than one searchlight on you though, you'd be able to turn out of one but be still in another.

Joe's crew survived the first three trips to German targets; 42 other crews would not be returning. One of these was the 158 Squadron all-sergeant crew of Sergeant Witham, lost on the raid to Stuttgart with a total loss of life. Joe's next operation was to St Nazaire on 22 March, on which he had his first experience of being coned, followed by a trip to Duisburg on 26 March. This was his, and most of his crew's, seventh operation with 158 Squadron. But during this time he had had four different navigators. Jackson had been having trouble with his ears and replacements had come in. One of these was Jack Armitage who had flown with the crew on 22 March. But Jack was now to become a 'full' member of the crew. Joe fully acknowledges the benefits of having highly competent navigators in his crew.

> Jack Armitage was very good, bit older than we were. He was an officer and the rest of us were sergeants. Backhouse, who should have had a commission, was also a wonderful navigator, but he was also a brilliant set operator [H2S – a rotating radar, scanning underneath the aircraft providing an image of the terrain below on a cathode ray tube]. He therefore became the bomb aimer. Jack and Backy were ideally suited for both jobs.

Joe's crew had been achieving good results on their operations to date. As such they were given the opportunity to transfer to 8 Group, Pathfinders (following Joe's previous request) under the command of Air Commodore, and later Air Vice-Marshal Don Bennett.

The Butt Report of August 1941, examining the accuracy of night bombing by Bomber Command, had highlighted that there needed to be considerable improvement in bombing accuracy and in the ability of crews to find targets. The Air Ministry responded and, as described earlier, the concept of a specialised target locating and marking force developed. Don Bennett, who would eventually head up this force, had been given the opportunity to make his views known on improved bombing in 1941.

> They interviewed me with a couple of these wing commanders and roughly speaking, I heard the sad story of bomber aircraft going out claiming they had wonderful results, all the place destroyed, the whole place burnt down and so on, and the next day the photographic reconnaissance proved that not a slate was damaged, not a single windowpane broken. What was going on?
>
> And I simply put it to them – this was a year before Pathfinders – I said 'If you were, as a general duties officer, highly specialised and well trained, given a bomber aircraft in pitch black darkness, with a compass, an altimeter and an air speed indicator, and told to go out in that little aeroplane into the heart of Germany in the middle of everything you could think of and hit a pin point target, could you do it?' And their reaction was the same in all cases, 'Oh no we're not navigators.' So I said 'Well there you are, the word is navigators. You've put you finger on the mark. You must have navigators. They must be good navigators and they must have a lot more than an air speed indicator to get them there.' And that's what started it.

In April 1942 Sir Arthur Harris was presented with the idea of establishing this new force. He was by no means in favour, as he stated in his post-war memoir *Bomber Offensive*, 'the formation of a corps d'elite seemed likely to lead to a good deal of trouble and might be thoroughly bad for morale.' Despite Harris's protestations, Sir Charles Portal finally stepped in with instructions to Harris to establish this new force. Harris complied and Bennett was appointed to command; Harris stating that Bennett was, 'the obvious man at this time available for the job of head of the Pathfinder Force.' In August 1942 five squadrons – 7, 35, 83, 109 and 156 – duly came under the Australian's command.

Through the winter of 1942/43 the Pathfinder force (which was designated 8 [PFF] Group on 8 January 1943) developed tactics and methodology. Various pyrotechnics evolved, flares to light up targets, TI (target indicators) of various hues for marking targets in the air or with pools of colour on the ground. In addition the employment of the blind bombing device Oboe was developed along with H2S. The initial use of these devices encountered teething troubles but they were soon to enhance greatly the ability of Bomber Command crews to find and mark targets. In Bennett's book *Pathfinder* he tells of the optimism he held at the start of 1943. 'We had the crews, we had Oboe and H2S, we had pyrotechnics and we had a little experience... we had already made a tremendous difference to the effectiveness of the Command... The mighty sword of Bomber Command was veritably poised for the attack.' The thrust came in the spring of 1943, with a considerable escalation in Bomber Command's offensive when Harris opened his attack on the Ruhr. Bennett's Pathfinders, with targets in the range of Oboe, would certainly be stretched in support of the battle. He was certainly pleased that Lancasters came in to replace his Wellingtons and Stirlings (35 Squadron keeping its Halifaxes for the time being owing to its connections with 4 Group). In addition throughout the spring and summer period new squadrons would come along, with new crews, including that of Joe Petrie-Andrews.

> We had been getting good target photographs, which meant more or less that we were doing the right sort of thing. We had said previously that we were interested in Pathfinders and we were given the opportunity to volunteer [which Joe had actually done back in November 1942 whilst still at the operational training unit]. Instead of 30 trips we were volunteering for 45. I had sought the crew's approval, which was given, perhaps with some caution. Previously I truly had not wanted to be in Bomber Command, that's because I did not know anything about it. A four-engine aircraft was not the thing I was looking for. However as I became more involved I was really very happy as a bomber pilot. There was an awful lot to it. I had always fancied myself as a fighter pilot, being on my own

and looking after myself. But that of course wasn't the way things were. Usually you were in a formation, following the leader. As a bomber pilot you were more of an individual than you would have been in a Fighter Command squadron.

Joe and his crew made their move to 35 Squadron, still on Halifaxes, early in April 1943. New crews at a Bomber Command squadron were rarely given the opportunity of flying the best aircraft available. They had to take what they were given. The first cause for concern for him and his crew when they came across their 'new' weapon of war, was the lack of a front or mid-upper turret; George Dale would be spending the first part of his operational career on a mattress peering through a Perspex blister on the underside of the bomber. The patchwork appearance of the wings of the Halifax, added to their concern; although the new Pathfinders were assured that this was owing to small cracks due to wing flexing, and not flak damage.

On 14 April the Petrie-Andrews crew flew their first 35 Squadron operation to Stuttgart, bombing as part of the main force. Two nights later and they were part of the attack on Pilsen, again as part of the main force It was another long flight of 8 hours and 41 minutes and a considerable effort of concentration was required of the crew.

> You had a lot of things to consider. I don't think I really did any forward thinking. It was all about staying on track, getting there and getting home. You were pretty busy. If you weren't looking at the instruments you were searching the skies.

'Getting home' in an operational context, did not mean merely reaching friendly airspace, it meant landing and coming to a safe standstill. Weather conditions could have deteriorated during the flight out and an aircraft may well be damaged. Joe came to appreciate such a situation early in his operational days with 35 Squadron. 'Returning from one raid, we could see the fog moving towards the airfield.' The fog dispersal equipment, FIDO, in place at Graveley had been damaged and was out of action.

> We were preparing to land but then somebody else called up and asked for an emergency landing, and took ages to get down. The fog continued to move in and I voiced my

concern to those below, my worries centring on our shortage of fuel. They told us to go and bale out. I informed the crew that they were telling us to jump and leave the aircraft, but that I wanted to land it. The reply came back, 'We're with you!'

Joe managed to get the aircraft down safely but his actions did not meet with the approval of his superiors. Although he explained that he had not heard the bale out order, alas the crew's discussions had been transmitted on the radio.

The night of 20/21 April would certainly be a pretty busy one for Joe – indeed a busy one for many Bomber Command airmen. A large force of 339 heavy bombers set off for Stettin that night with a mixed load of high explosive and incendiaries; 86 Stirlings were sent to attack the Heinkel works at Rostock, 11 Mosquitoes to Berlin, with 18 Wellingtons minelaying, and three Wellingtons dropping leaflets in the Lille area.

Of the force sent to Stettin, 46 aircraft were provided by Pathfinder squadrons including the Halifax of Joe Petrie-Andrews. What happened on this raid would forever remain in his memory. Joe lifted W7779 (U) from the Graveley runway at 2112 hours and course was set for Denmark and the long crossing of the North Sea.

> It was a long one and a nasty one. We went in low level across Denmark, and it really was very low. It was supposed to be a surprise attack. There had been a fair amount of minelaying in the Skattegat and Kattegat. We hoped we would surprise them by suggesting minelaying then suddenly switching off low level across Denmark. Whether it worked or not, I don't know, but I doubt it. We were attacked by a lot of light flak going across Denmark and they would have reported aircraft on a course going east. So clearly we weren't minelaying.
>
> As it was we flew across a flak position, coming under heavy fire and lost an engine.

The shell exploded in the nose of the aircraft, just before midnight and whilst at 1,000 feet. The bombsight, the airspeed indicator, the DR compass and the intercom were all taken out. John Backhouse and Jim Berwick were also wounded.

We continued on and when we reached the sea the other

side of Denmark, we turned and climbed, managing about 14/15,000 feet. Nevertheless, we were able to get to Stettin on time, on the three engines and climbing.

At 0103 hours the four 1,000lb bombs were dropped, the crew's post-raid report recording: 'Lake and rivers identified and bombed on green target indicators. Burst not seen. High explosives were observed falling in town and docks. A big fire started in the dock area near the aiming point and several other fires were seen together with a large explosion in the middle of the town.'

Other bomber crews recorded similar sights on their return to England. The Bomber Command intelligence summary reported that, 'the visibility was excellent, with no cloud, and though most crew were able to identify the river and other ground features the PFF route and target-indicating markers were found very helpful.' The attack had opened at 0102 hours and the aircrews had watched as fires broke out over the whole town, and a column of smoke, to 10,000 feet, was reported. 'The glow of fires could be seen over 100 miles on the way home.' Returning crews also noted that searchlights were ineffective, with the flak defences, 'only moderate'. *The Bomber Command War Diaries* note that the operation, 'proved to be the most successful attack beyond the range of Oboe during the Battle of the Ruhr... approximately 100 acres in the centre of the town were claimed as devastated; much of this area comprised industrial buildings... A large chemical factory was among the places where production was completely halted. 586 people were killed in Stettin.'[9] The cost for the success of the raid was 22 RAF bombers, with 154 airmen from these aircraft unable to add their experiences to the collection of post-raid intelligence. Other raids that night had also met opposition, eight Stirlings failing to return from the Rostock raid, and one Mosquito from the Berlin attack. A total of 31 aircraft lost and 212 trained airmen. In addition two men from 35 Squadron would also not be returning that night, although the rest of their crew did. Their aircraft had been struck by falling incendiaries, whilst over the target, and with the Halifax out of control, they decided to bale out. Shortly after, control was regained and the remaining crew of five nursed the damaged bomber back to Graveley.

Joe Petrie-Andrews's crew was one of those that reported what they had seen over Stettin; Joe having managed to bring his aircraft and crew back across the North Sea with an engine down. Unsurprisingly they were a little late returning home, landing at 0521 hours.

> We were given a priority landing on the main runway, which was a little bit downhill. Putting the aircraft down was not easy. For one thing we didn't have an airspeed indicator and then I found when we landed that I hadn't got any brakes. Fortunately I had landed virtually at the start of the runway. I chose not to go back to our dispersal point, which would have meant turning left and I had only the one engine that side. I knew that they wanted the aircraft to go to a servicing hangar, so I tried to turn the aircraft round. Anyway three quarters of the way along the runway I turned right for the maintenance hangar. I asked one of the crew to stand by the fuselage exit with his parachute. As we came up a bit of a slope I got him to jump out and put his parachute in front of the wheel, which worked well enough.
>
> Having been debriefed and gone to bed I was woken up a few hours later by the warrant officer from the maintenance hangar saying, 'We have your aircraft in the hangar but we didn't realise you hadn't any brakes. When we started it up to taxi it, we couldn't control it and it got stuck in the mud, going off the taxi way.' He then asked me if I would mind saying that I had got it stuck in the mud. I replied, 'Oh yeh sure'. It wasn't important to me really.

Joe's efforts that night, bringing home his damaged aircraft, would eventually lead to recognition at a higher level.

Sir Arthur Harris was now throwing his bomber crews, indeed everything he had, into the Battle of the Ruhr. The German industrial heartland was the focus, but there would be the occasional operation outside this target system. Joe Petrie-Andrews found himself regularly en route to the Ruhr, flying amidst the aerial battles over the targets and bringing his crew home as best he could. On 26 April he flew to Duisburg (561 aircraft, 17 losses), then in May came two trips to Dortmund (596 aircraft, 31 losses and 826 aircraft, 38 losses), another to Duisburg (572 aircraft, 34 losses), one to Pilsen (168 aircraft, 9 losses) and one to Düsseldorf (759 aircraft, 27 losses). On the 4/5

May operation to Dortmund the post-raid report recorded, 'aircraft coned for five minutes... being passed from cone to cone'.

The trip to Pilsen is of note as the crew were tasked as blind illuminators; to use H2S to find the target and then drop flares, illuminating the target for visual markers. However on this occasion the H2S failed and no bombs or flares were dropped. There could be no guess work here, as marking errors would of course jeopardise the whole success of the raid.

Throughout the summer months Joe and his crew would regularly be amidst a bomber stream in hostile night skies; a period in which the night air battle was escalating to an unprecedented scale. During this time Joe found a familiar way to deal with the stresses and strains of operations.

As a crew we weren't stand offish but generally speaking it was your crew that you stuck with. And we were pretty close as a crew. If I was going out for a drink I would see if any of the others wanted to come. Some enjoyed a drink, some didn't, but most of us liked to go to the pub. Not to get screaming, just for relaxation. Into the local town and perhaps finish up at a dance.

Sometimes we would go into St Neots for a few drinks or a dance. On one occasion I had agreed to give anyone who needed it a lift in my Hillman 10, and they were to be outside the pub at 11.15 p.m. I was a bit late and some of the lads had waited in someone else's car. As I was driving back to camp, with two of the lads sitting in the back I noticed them messing about with something. I turned round and there was a Lewis gun. 'Where did you get that?' I asked. 'Oh it was in the back of some bloke's car.' I told them to get rid of it and they threw it in a pond. The next morning a policeman came to the station asking if anything was known about a missing gun, making it clear that he didn't want any fuss, he just wanted the gun back. I suggested that he have a look in a certain pond. I was in St Neots a few days later and asked the policeman if he had found it. He had. We gave him one of our navigation watches and were best of friends after that.

Such was the nature of the Bomber Command war. One night airmen could be above a boiling cauldron of fire, their lives on the line. The following night they could be standing in a bar, singing, drinking, flirting. And the next night they could be back in a rear turret scanning the sky for enemy fighters, or peering through the front blister on their bomber, aiming their bombs on the conflagrations below. In the middle of 1943 Joe and his crew were often in the heat of battle.

> Most of the Ruhr targets were short but the defences were very good and you could reckon on a lot of fighter activity. If you were coned by the searchlights, the German fighters would come in, risking their own flak, to attack. If one of my gunners told us there was a fighter out of range but following I would ask him to keep an eye on it. Of course if he was going to attack, and we had been able to see him, I could take evasive action. But we wouldn't unless he was menacing us. The rear gunner or mid-upper would let me know that they could see one and I'd move out, away from him. Not turning because the glow from our exhaust pipes would then show up and give you away. Just gently move away. Never do anything too quickly or in haste – it used to upset the crew.

Joe's tactic was common to most bomber crews when encountering an enemy fighter; if possible avoid combat and try and lose the enemy in the dark of the night. He did however, on one occasion early in his operational career, seek to engage a nightfighter.

> One of my gunners reported a nightfighter at distance wing tip to wing tip. I eased towards it ensuring I didn't get too far in front, which would expose the exhaust pipe glow. I could only see an outline. We gave it a long squirt from the mid-upper turret and then cleared off.
>
> I was quite disgusted when we got back. We were making our report to the intelligence officer and he called the CO over, who told him to take the encounter out of the report. He thought it might have been one of ours – a Mosquito. I was bloody furious; my gunner would never have made a mistake like that. It was ridiculous. The Mosquitoes would have been thousands of feet above us anyway; and the gunners would know the difference, quite clear by engine type, between a Mossie and a Ju88.

Following participation in the raid to Le Creusot on 19/20 June, Joe and his crew flew to Krefeld on 21/22 June, one of 705 aircraft. This was typical of the many intense air battles that he and his comrades were involved in. They were detailed as markers that night but they would return with their TI as they were not required. Indeed the marking that night was described as almost perfect; 2,306 tons of bombs fell and the centre of the city was claimed by fire. The *Bomber Command War Diaries* record 5,517 houses destroyed, 1,056 people killed, 4,550 injured, 72,000 people made homeless. An extraordinary demonstration of the destructive potential of Bomber Command. But the RAF's heavy bomber crews also paid a high price, 44 aircraft lost, with 35 Squadron losing six of the 19 Halifaxes sent from which 20 men were killed, 16 became POWs and one crew survived a ditching in the North Sea. The attrition for both sides in the night battle over Germany continued into Joe's next operation to Wuppertal on 24/25 June. There was extensive carnage and suffering on the ground and Bomber Command lost 34 aircraft from the 630 sent.

The 35 Squadron diary recorded simply the loss of each of the crews on the night of 21/22 June in what had become a standard way; 'This aircraft is missing and nothing was heard from it after take-off.' Indeed most Bomber Command squadron diaries are very much matter of fact when reporting on operational activity. Fighter squadron diaries are often written from a much more human angle, describing living conditions, aircraft characteristics, lamenting the loss of aircrew, celebrating acts of derring-do. Bomber Command diarists in the main appeared unable to do this. Quite possibly this is a further example that camaraderie, developed through shared experience, is common within an entire fighter squadron, whereas it lies within the confines of a crew on a bomber base. And the author of the diary may simply not have had enough time to get to know new crews before their beds were taken over by replacements.

Joe, having just turned 19 years old, next flew operationally to Aachen on 13/14 July, acting as a backer-up. The attack unfolded in a similar way to his previous two operations, 'A *Terrorangriff* of the most severe scale was delivered', is how it was reported in Aachen. Bomber Command lost 20 of the 374 aircraft that took part. Joe then flew to attack the Peugot motor factory at Montbéliard, a suburb of Sochaux near the

France/Switzerland border, on 15/16 July 1943. The raid caused only minor damage and some of the bombing fell in the town with resultant loss of life.

At the end of July and early in August Joe took part in one of the most devastating attacks in the history of aerial warfare. On 27 and 29 July, and 2 August he piloted his crew to Europe's largest port – Hamburg – for an attack on a city in which U-boats and shipping were constructed. Not that the operation appeared to be anything special to him. 'It was just another operation really. Not a bad one, about four hours so not a long night.' But the massive loss of civilian life shook the German High Command to its foundation.

On 9 August Joe flew to Mannheim, acting as a blind illuminator, and although the bombing was reported as scattered there was considerable devastation. He was also detailed for operations the next night; another one to remember.

> Nuremberg was a long one. The winds were against us. But I was fortunate that I had two very good navigators and we worked out that the winds were much stronger than we were told, and behind us. So we lost time on track, whereas a lot of the guys did not realise this and they were way ahead of themselves. As Pathfinders we would not drop our markers until the time detailed. So there were a lot of aircraft milling around over Nuremberg waiting, before the markers went down. Unfortunately somebody in Sunbury, where I lived, had a son who got shot down that night. A report had got back that they had arrived at the target before the Pathfinders and were losing time, and she was adamant that it was my fault. That report had come back to her from her son's squadron, but it just was not true. They had arrived long before they should have done; they just had not worked out the wind accurately enough.

On 12 and 16 August Joe took part in two attacks on Turin, part of the bombing campaign against Italian cities, his crew, one of many, attempting to demonstrate further, as the Allied land forces in the Mediterranean theatre of operations overran Sicily and looked to the Italian mainland, that being allied to Germany came at a price. Italy was not prepared to pay this price and surrendered on 8 September. On these raids Joe's crew would be acting as visual markers.

Tiny Cooling

Top: A Blackburn B2, at Brough, late 1938/early 1939.

Bottom: Summer 1939, four men who trained with Tiny, all of whom would lose their lives during the war. From left to right: Basil Tree – killed 28 August 1942, Bob Wilson – lost flying a 4 Squadron Lysander over Dunkirk 1 June 1940, Lionel Pilkington (also well known to Tony Iveson) – lost flying with 111 Squadron over the Irish Sea 20 September 1941, Frank Lorrimer – lost flying a 101 Squadron Blenheim on a shipping strike 25 September 1940.

NB: All photographs are from the relevant pilots' collections except where stated.

Top left: A Hawker Hind crashed at Brough by Ben Johnson who would become Tiny's best man. Johnson would later lose his life in a mid-air collision at a beam approach school.

Top right: Tiny in front of his Miles Magister at Brough May/June 1938.

Middle: Tiny's Miles Magister at Brough, 1938.

Bottom: A 9 Squadron Wellington on its return from the fateful daylight operation to Wilhelmshaven, 18 December 1939.

Top: Squadron Leader Hinks's 9 Squadron Wellington, pranged on return from a raid.

Middle left: Sergeant 'Dougie' Douglas – captain whilst Tiny was operational as 2nd pilot.

Middle right: Tiny's crew.

Bottom: Damage at Honington follow\ing the Luftwaffe attack in the summer of 1940.

Top left: Jock Gilmour – navigator.

Top right: Stand down.

Middle left: 9 Squadron Wellington Ic WS-Y.

Middle right Tiny and Arnost Zabrs of the Czech Air Force
– 311 Squadron, at Honington.

Bottom left: Tiny in North Africa –
Fontaine Chaude.

Bottom right: Tiny's Wellington at Blida,
North Africa.

Jack 'Benny' Goodman

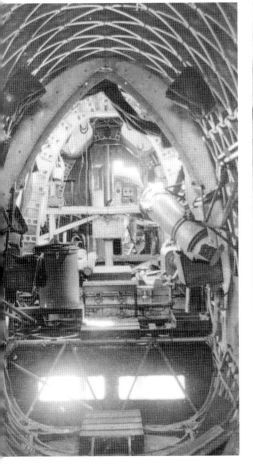

Top left: Jack Goodman on the day of his first solo flight in a Tiger Moth, at Sywell 7 June 1938.

Top right: Wellington R-Robert, late 1940, Jack to the left in his sidcot suit.

Bottom left: Interior of Wellington R-Robert.

Bottom right: Side view of the Newmarket grandstand from the cockpit of Goodman's Wellington.

Top left: Jack Goodman in front of his 37 Squadron Wellington Ic, Shallufa, Egypt, May 1941, at the end of the Battle of Crete. 'We had survived yet again.'

Top right: 37 Squadron Wellingtons – Mark Ic.

Middle: Jack Goodman stands between Flight Lieutenant Willatt (left) and Flight Lieutenant Berry at 15 OTU Harwell, May 1942.

Bottom: Jack with Bill Hickox to his right, in front of their 627 Squadron Mosquito at Oakington, December 1943.

Top: Artist's impression of Jack Goodman on a low level marking operation.

Bottom left: Damage at the Tours aircraft-repair workshops marked by Jack Goodman on the night of 1/2 May 1944.

Bottom right: Group Captain Goodman, DFC and Bar, AFC, Headquarters Strike Command.

Joe Petrie-Andrews

Top: Joe Petrie-Andrews second from right, during training in the USA.

Middle: Vultee BT-13s, on which Joe learnt the art of flying. *(ww2images.com)*

Bottom: Bristol Blenheim IV flying from 13 OTU. *(ww2images.com)*

Top: The crew at Graveley, 35 Squadron. From left to right, Taffy Morgan, Jim Berwick, John Backhouse, Joe, Jack Armitage. George Dale, Darky Barnett.

Middle: The Joe Petrie-Andrews crew on the ladder in front of their 35 Squadron Halifax. From left to right, George Dale, Taffy Morgan, Jack Armitage, Joe, John Backhouse, Jim Berwick, Darky Barnett. In front and in the inverted V of the ladder are the groundcrew. *(John Backhouse)*

Bottom: Joe in a Spitfire XXIV, flying with 615 Auxiliary Squadron, 1958.

Harry Hughes

Top: Harry Hughes (left) in Quebec January 1942.

Middle: A 102 Squadron Halifax gets clearance for take-off on the raid to Le Creusot, June 1943. *(ww2images.com)*

Bottom: 102 Squadron debriefing – summer 1943. Fourth from the left is Wing Commander Coventry. Possibly at the front, with his back to the camera is Harry Hughes. *(ww2images.com)*

Top: 692 Squadron Mosquito DZ637 and 4,000lb cookie, April 1944.

Bottom: Harry Hughes (right) and Roy Montrowe in front of their 692 Squadron Mosquito, Graveley, August 1944.

ww2images.com)

Tony Iveson

Top: Tony Iveson (right) at Brough E&R FTS in front of a Blackburn B2, December 1938.

Bottom: Tony Iveson flying a Hawker Hind at Brough in the summer of 1939.

Top: No 5 FTS at Sealand, December 1939. Tony is on the back row third from the right. Many of the men in this picture would not survive the Battle of Britain.

Middle: Tony Iveson in a Tiger Moth at 27 EFTS Induna, Rhodesia, 1942.

Bottom: A Miles Master flown by Tony at 5 FTS, Sealand, March 1940.

Top: Drew Wyness's Lancaster – crash-landed at Kegostrov, following the flight to Russia in preparation for the first attack on the *Tirpitz. (Steve Darlow)*

Middle left: A khaki-clad Tony in Southern Rhodesia, 1942.

Middle right: 617 Squadron Lancaster KC-F at Woodhall Spa, 1944.

Bottom: The 617 Squadron rugby team late 1944, with Tony Iveson in the middle at the back.

Top: Groundcrew loading a Tallboy into the bomb bay of a 617 Squadron Lancaster, 1944. *(ww2images.com)*

Middle: Tony Iveson, second from right, at Sumburgh in front of his damaged Lancaster following the Bergen raid. From left to right, Jack Harrison – navigator, Des Philips – flight engineer, Tony, Frank Chance – bomb aimer. The other three members of Tony's crew had baled out.

Bottom: From right to left, Tony Iveson, James Tait, Leonard Cheshire and Cliff Caple (the engineering officer at 617 Squadron), 1966.

Top: Tony, Sir Arthur Harris and fellow former 617 Squadron pilot Ken Brown at the 617 Squadron reunion dinner, 1966.

Bottom: Tony Iveson and James Tait in the cockpit of the RAF Museum Hendon's Lancaster.

There was more responsibility because if, as a visual marker, *you* dropped a marker then that took priority. It had to be right. We were in the happy position that at that time we were also blind markers so we used to carry both colours. Visual markers had number one priority and it was no disgrace to bring them back if you weren't sure. If you had blind marking TIs with you and you dropped them they would get second priority. The better visual markers would go in first, as would the better blind markers in case the visual markers were not available, and they would support right the way through the raid.

On the 16 August raid his post-raid report recorded, 'First red target indicators and stick of flares seen at 0012 hours, a little to south of central railway station, which was identified in the light of flares, but too late to drop yellow target indicators. Aircraft orbited and came in again but smoke was then too thick to identify aiming point positively so bombs only dropped onto green target indicator.' Of note is Joe's decision to orbit and carry out a second bomb run, over the defences, something he would do a number of times in future operations. John Backhouse recalled, 'I don't think anyone other than Joe, Jack and myself had much say in the matter really. We quickly decided and that was that, without any long discussion. This was wartime, we were trying to do the best we could and if this seemed the best way of doing it we did. Joe's captaincy style was laid back really. There was a discipline but it was at a pleasant level, not severe.'

The 16 August raid was Joe's 29th (28 as captain). His superior flying abilities were now to be recognised, with the recommendation for a Distinguished Flying Medal; in part owing to his record to date, in part owing to his commitment and skill on the Stettin raid.

> *Particulars of meritorious service for which recommendation is made.*
> Flight Sergeant Petrie-Andrews is captain of an outstandingly successful crew. On many occasions he has been detailed to attack in the most responsible role, and the exceptional result he and his crew have achieved is proved by the photographs they have taken. This crew's reliability has become a feature of the squadron and an inspiration to their fellow aircrews.

On one occasion his aircraft was hit by a light anti-aircraft shell, which, when exploding in the cockpit, rendered his blind flying panel, DR compass, inter-communication system and brakes unserviceable. Nevertheless, he continued to the target and carried out a successful attack, subsequently returning to base and making a safe landing under these difficult conditions.

Fight Sergeant Petrie-Andrews has now completed 28 night bombing attacks on Germany, Italy and the Occupied countries. He continues to show the greatest keenness to attack the enemy and it is considered that his fine record of tenacity and reliability fully merits the immediate award of the Distinguished Flying Medal.

The station commander backed up 35 Squadron's CO; 'Flight Sergeant Petrie-Andrews is an exceptional captain of aircraft and by his example has extracted the utmost effort from his crew. Strongly recommended for the DFM.' Air Commodore Bennett added, 'Strongly recommended'.

On 23 August Joe made his first flight to Berlin, 'a long one and tiring'. Harris had sent 727 aircraft to the German capital, from which 56 would not be returning; 35 Squadron contributing four Halifaxes to the loss statistics. On one of these aircraft the highly respected Graveley station commander Group Captain Basil Robinson DSO, DFC & Bar, AFC, lost his life. He should not have been flying, as Joe recalled, 'He was always flying and constantly being told to cut it down. But he wanted to be there. His loss did upset us greatly.'

On 16 September 1943 Joe flew his bomber south to target the railyards at Modane, through which German reinforcement could reach Italy. He then took part in two attacks on Hanover on 22 and 27 September, split with a raid on Mannheim on 23 September. Joe attacked Kassel on 3 October, Frankfurt the night after, Bremen on 8 October and Kassel again on 22 October. This last raid, on which Joe's crew were visual markers, is described in the *Bomber Command War Diaries* as exceptionally accurate and concentrated and as 'the most devastating attack on a German city since the firestorm raid on Hamburg in July'. The initial blind marking was inaccurate but the visual markers were more successful. Joe's post-raid report recorded, 'Weather clear – visibility good. Identified visually. Saw ornamental gardens and bridges right in the sights. Bombed visually with aiming point in bomb sight. Attack had not started properly when aircraft arrived. Red target indicator seen on aiming point and greens going down on reds. No fires seen.' But as the raid developed fire did take hold, and an estimated 5,599 lives were reported claimed by a firestorm. There was severe damage to the Kassel rail system and industry. The raid also had a significant impact on factories involved in the production of flying bombs – the V1 German secret reprisal weapon that would inflict damage and misery on London and places like Antwerp in the latter half of 1944. The Bomber Command raid earlier in October had resulted in the Fiesler works at Kassel, involved in the V1 production, moving to nearby Rothwesten. Following the 22/23 October raid many of the workers failed to show up for work and at the start of November the work's senior engineer informed Field Marshal Erhard Milch that, 'Because Kassel has been lost, Rothwesten is to all intents and purposes lost as well. The men live in Kassel and their homes and transport are wrecked. In consequence, the final trials of the weapon's power unit, control-gear, diving mechanism, compass and air log were held up.'[10] The destruction and loss of life at Kassel, inflicted by the blunt weapon of Bomber Command, may well have stopped the Germans launching the V1 offensive prior to D-Day, and without doubt it saved the lives of numerous Londoners.

Chapter 6

Leading the Way

After the 22/23 October 1943 operation to Kassel Joe Petrie-Andrews spent a few weeks away from operational duties, then on 11 November 1943 he and his crew, with a Flight Sergeant Henry Stroud replacing a sick Jim Berwick, prepared for a long journey south to Cannes, detailed as a visual marker, lifting their Halifax from the Graveley runway at 1831 hours; one of 124 Halifaxes and 10 Lancasters despatched by Bomber Command. All was going well for Joe's crew until they neared Cannes. 'We lost an engine near the target and would have been unable to gain enough height to fly home over the Pyrenees.' Then matters worsened.

> We dropped our markers and then, on the second run to drop the bomb load, we were shot up by a ship in the harbour and lost another engine. All we could do was to make for Sardinia on the remaining two engines. After fifty minutes a third engine quit. I had to pull back power on the remaining starboard motor to retain direction and down we went towards the sea. The crew had only just got into the rest position, between the main spars, before we hit the water. After nearly a kilometre of screaming engines, everything was deathly quiet. I then had a great deal of trouble opening my cockpit hatch, and then finally from the cockpit roof I could see that the crew hadn't been able to release the dinghy. I went back into the cockpit and got my parachute which had a small dinghy in it.

As the aircraft began to sink Taffy Morgan then took hold of the

emergency axe and was trying to release the crew dinghy –
housed in the wing, which was now underwater. In the meantime
John Backhouse re-entered the submerging aircraft in an effort to
find some of the parachute dinghies. All this was taking place, it
must be remembered, in the darkness of night.

> In the fuselage John lost consciousness, overcome by petrol
> fumes, and was floating on his back. I had to re-enter the
> fuselage, which was now almost half full of water and
> petrol from the 1,000-gallon overload tank that had split in
> the front bay on ditching. I pushed John up through the
> small escape hatch. After a struggle the dinghy popped out
> and we all climbed in. Seconds later up came the tail and
> the aircraft slid under water, it was so quiet! I don't know
> how long it was before we started talking. Backhouse was
> still unconscious and somebody was smacking his face.
> Somebody said loosen his tie, and when this was done he
> coughed and came round.
>   It was so quiet and peaceful. Then somebody said,
> 'what's that floating near by?' Next time it was on the other
> side. Taffy the engineer had received quite a nasty cut on his
> hand when releasing the dinghy. I didn't think anybody
> knew there were sharks in the Med! We wound away on
> the radio many times but it was only a transmitter, and we
> rigged my parachute up on the radio aerial. The wind was
> light south east, which was taking us towards Sardinia.
> Then the weather deteriorated, large waves tipped us over
> twice and two of the crew were unwell, but we kept
> together. We lost the radio and some of the water cans but
> it was raining heavily so we didn't miss the water.

For two seemingly interminable days Joe's crew clung to their
dinghy, buffeted by the sea and drenched by the rain. On the
morning of the third day the weather cleared and they could see
land in the distance, and in the direction they were drifting.

> By mid-day we were close, a mile or so, but then the current
> started taking us east between Sardinia and Corsica. I
> thought about swimming but was not really up to it, then
> in the afternoon a huge ship appeared, we guessed it was a
> cruiser. We could see sailors on deck so we waved and as it
> neared we fired a distress flare. I told the crew they
> probably couldn't stop and would send somebody back,

but obviously they hadn't seen us. Later that afternoon we neared Sardinia and could see a light on a headland. We fired our last red flare and paddled like crazy with our hand held canvas paddles. It was dark when we finally reached the shore, squeezing between some huge rocks.

We could see a light coming down from above, but had no idea of the nationality of the bearer. At briefing we had been told that Sardinia was in our hands but there were still patches of resistance. I told the crew to take cover behind the rocks, as I was the only one with a 45mm automatic. When the light bearers neared I decided that they were not unfriendly, although I did not recognise the language. I stepped out from behind the rock and said, 'Hello'. Well they ran! I called out, 'Amigo, Comrad', and all the men joined in, but they wouldn't stop and ran straight back up the cliffs. We had a hell of a job following them in the dark, all unsteady on our feet, and one fellow had to be carried all the way.

At the top of the cliffs Joe and his crew found a captain from the Italian merchant navy, accompanied by four of his crew. 'They had lost their ship previously and were wonderfully helpful. They produced an enormous pot of stew! At least their week's ration, but it was so greasy no one could eat it. Strangely enough nobody was hungry just thirsty.'

For at least a week we spent all day winding away on the telephone. As soon as we got a reply we called one of the Italians but they were unable to give us any news. Once or twice someone spoke English but they seemed to be cut off immediately.

Then one day we saw two cars coming across the field. Two naval ratings got out, asked if we were the survivors, and gave us seven lots of survivor's kit! Wellingtons, white socks, roll neck sweaters and boiler suits. We were instructed to be at the small local port the following morning. We waited from early morning to about midday, then a fishing boat anchored off shore and a dinghy approached. We were being saved! After several trips we were aboard a fishing vessel originally from the Bristol Channel, commandeered as part of the R(AUX)N and the owner was captain. It was quite small, very little room on deck, and we were asked to stay in the cabin as much as possible. They had lots of gin and tinned potatoes and we were told to help ourselves. In due course we arrived at Ajaccio port, Corsica, and the first thing we saw was an RAF air/sea rescue unit. We asked them why they hadn't been looking for us and they replied they knew nothing about us. As far as we knew our radio distress signal to UK had been acknowledged.

The Navy gave us a great welcome and we all dined in the officer's mess, despite the fact that some of the crew were NCOs; much appreciated from the senior service. A few days later we were transported to the local airfield where an American Dakota was due to land at 9am and take us to North Africa. It didn't turn up due to the presence of three Me109s, but next day another one took us to Blida.

Joe now spent some time in a hotel in Algiers and set about rekitting. 'As we were going to fly an aircraft, we were given a complete set of flying gear including electrically heated Irvin suits, boots, gloves, the lot! I had never seen them before.' After a few days they went to the airfield at Blida and Joe took advantage of the generosity of the station commander, 'A lovely man, a group captain with MC & Bar, and he allowed me to fly his personal Hurricane – an aircraft put together from bits in the desert.'

A Halifax was found at a French base about 50 miles away. We had a very interesting week there trying, without assistance, to get this aircraft serviceable. We spent a week cleaning filters and tanks, charging batteries etc, and eventually we managed to start all four engines. It was time to go. After clearing all the crowds and sheep away by turning the aircraft and blowing sand at them, we took off. The undercarriage would not retract. Our engines would not give power and we could do little better than 130 knots. If an engine cut we would have to land immediately. There was a range of hills at about 3,000ft and we had to go out to sea to get around them. Ditching is bad enough, but with wheels down impossible. We were very relieved to reach Blida and gave them a long list of problems.

The station commander then asked if I could fly a Lancaster. I was prepared to fly anything to get home. They had an ex 44 Squadron Lancaster flown by Wing Commander Nettleton who had been doing a shuttle exercise, bombing targets around the Med, bombing up again at Blida and then bombing on the way home. I wondered if the station commander would ask us to do the same, but he had better things in mind – he had a few parcels! It was near Christmas and the bomb bay, and that is big, was filled with baskets and hampers, it seemed one to every senior officer in the RAF. We had to hoist them manually into the bomb bay and then gently close the doors pushing the hampers in. On top of this we had to transport three very senior officers from Army, Navy and RAF.

Our plan was to take off at night and cross the Spanish/French border at about 10,000ft then do a fast run home. At about 7,000ft we iced up and lost 3-4,000ft. That meant a return to Blida – and only my second landing in a Lanc! It went well enough, but we had to find another way home and all aboard were asking how and when? On 13 December we flew from Blida to Rabat on the west coast of North Africa and the following night we set off for St Mawgan. We flew across the Bay of Biscay at 1,000ft during day-light without interference.

At St Mawgan I was surprised to find what I thought was a naval officer trying to board the aircraft. I hadn't heard of customs officers. He was most indignant and went off to see the station commander. We rapidly set off for RAF Graveley. I heard nothing more.

It was now time for Joe to have another of his run-ins with RAF seniority. John Backhouse recalled that on return to Graveley it was, 'typical Joe, he wanted everyone to see that we were back.' Joe had decided to 'show the lads' his new Lancaster.

I did a low pass close to the flying control tower. In the summary of evidence for my court martial, the met officer stated he had seen the aircraft fly below his window. He was on the first floor! Unfortunately my arrival had exactly coincided with the departure of an air marshal who was just leaving the briefing room with the area station commander and others. They had all ducked, and the instruction went out, 'Arrest that man'.

Two weeks later I was instructed to report to the station commander who kept me waiting 45 minutes and then he drove me, without a word between us, to Huntingdon and 8 Group's HQ. We arrived at Don Bennett's office where I was told to enter, and the station commander was to wait outside. Bennett seemed friendly and I had to describe in detail our adventure. He congratulated me and asked how long I had been under open arrest. After a short consideration he said that the charge was changed from low flying, a court martial offence, to careless flying. Fourteen days confined to camp. I was quite unprepared for this and speechless for a minute or two. He asked me if that was OK! I thanked him very much. The station commander was not asked in, and on the way home he asked what had happened. I told him that Bennett would be making a report to him in due course, but when I got back to base I told the lads the story and my bar book, which had been closed for two weeks, took quite a bashing.

Despite Joe's 'careless flying' on return to Graveley, the CO of 35 Squadron, Wing Commander Daniels sought recognition of Joe's recent activities.

Particular of meritorious service for which the recommendation is made.
On the night of 11 November 1943, Pilot Officer Petrie-Andrews was captain of a Halifax detailed to attack Cannes. Before reaching the target one engine failed, but in view of the importance of his mission, Pilot Officer Petrie-Andrews decided to continue to his objective on three engines. The target was reached and bombed successfully, but a second engine became unserviceable whilst he was over the target.

Rather than risk the crew falling into enemy hands, Pilot Officer Petrie-Andrew decided to set course for Sardinia although he had two engines feathered and useless. Unfortunately before land was reached at Sardinia a third engine failed, so he was compelled to ditch the aircraft. The ditching was carried out successfully and all the crew boarded the dinghy safely. They paddled for 70 hours before finally reaching land on the Sardinian coast.

Throughout this operation, Pilot Officer Petrie-Andrews displayed courageous determination and fine airmanship. This officer has completed many operations in a most important role and he frequently presses home his attack from a low level despite heavy defences.

In recognition of an outstanding record of service, Pilot Officer Petrie-Andrews is recommended for an immediate award of the Distinguished Flying Cross.

The station commander backed up Daniels. 'A very courageous and capable pilot who has taken part in a large number of sorties with outstanding success.' Joe, in due course, received his DFC.

The Petrie-Andrews crew next flew operationally to Berlin on 2 January 1944, but Joe was unable to reach the target having to contend with another of the many adversities facing bomber crews.

Icing was a funny thing. At night, in cloud, you couldn't tell if you were in icing conditions or not. We were unlucky on the Berlin operation. We flew through a super-cooled cloud and got iced up. I couldn't maintain height, the weight of the ice brought us down and the engines were not as good as they could have been with a free flow of air. Everything was working against us and we did not complete that one.

On 5 January Joe piloted another long operation to Stettin, and on 14 January a raid to Brunswick; on both operations having responsibility as a visual marker. On 27 January as part of a small attack on Heligoland, acting primarily as a diversion to a main force raid, the crew were tasked as primary blind markers, a reward for their recent good results. The next night Joe's crew had the responsibility of again trying to fool the German nightfighters, acting as route-markers, carrying out a 'spoof attack' – 63 Stirlings and four Pathfinder Halifaxes minelaying in Kiel Bay. 'We were trying to draw the fighters off from the main attack on Berlin, part of a small number of aircraft, dropping all sorts of colours, to confuse their controllers.' The minelaying was to take place five hours before the main attack on Berlin. In addition Mosquitoes would also be feigning attacks and targeting nightfighter airfields. The various ruses did have some success drawing the attention of some nightfighters, however from the 677 aircraft sent to Berlin, 46 failed to return, many falling when the German controller did manage to concentrate some nightfighters over the city.

Two further attacks on Berlin followed on 30/31 January and 15/16 February. On both raids Joe's crew were acting as primary blind markers, carrying flares, TI and bombs. On both occasions there was complete cloud cover and Joe's post-raid reports record, 'Target identified by special equipment [H2S] and bombed by same'. On both nights the population of Berlin suffered and on both nights Bomber Command lost men and machines; a total of 76 aircraft. The 15/16 February operation was Joe's 46th, his 45th as first pilot. Along with his crew, he had now reached the end of a Pathfinder tour.

We celebrated; although we generally didn't need much excuse. I had originally volunteered to do 60 operations, so I was prepared to carry on. A few of the crew decided that they had had enough, which was fair dos. As such I lost my navigator and bomb aimer, and the mid-upper gunner retired because the others were retiring. Backhouse, who was a navigator as well as being a bomb aimer, was offered the navigation leader's job by the CO, if he would fly with him as a bomb aimer. I was really quite pleased when he turned him down.

So to continue I had to get half a new crew. Good blokes but not as good as my original crew. The biggest problem was that I was given two navigators, so didn't have a bomb aimer; Jack Plank, a New Zealand welterweight boxing champion, a good man and a good navigator, and Tommy Cooper, also a good man and good navigator. Neither wanted to be a bomb aimer, they both wanted to navigate and weren't interested in dropping bombs or were any good at it. We even used to go out with the flight engineer dropping bombs. Taffy was a wonderful engineer but he wasn't really a bomb aimer. I don't know why but I wasn't given the crew I deserved really. I consider that my efforts were wasted.

Of course his efforts had not been wasted. He had taken part in some of the most important bombing operations of the war. Quite possibly Joe's run-ins with seniority had a part to play in all this.

Joe's next operation was in fact with his original crew, with the exception of John Backhouse, to Stuttgart on 1/2 March, then the nature of his operational targeting was to change. His next flight over enemy territory was over one month later, 'I had a new crew so we did a fair amount of practice bombing.' In addition Joe had to accustom himself to a new aircraft, the Lancaster III, 'good aeroplane, lightweight compared with a Halifax, but they were both very good. I couldn't say I preferred one or the other. Although I always felt the Halifax was a much stronger aeroplane.'

On the night of 6/7 March 1944 Bomber Command sent 261 Halifaxes and six Mosquitoes to the railyards in the French town of Trappes. The raid was a success, with massive destruction resulting. This attack was the first in a considerable commitment made by the RAF's heavy bombers in the run-up to D-Day. Through the early months of 1944 plans had been drawn up outlining the expected role of the air forces in support of Overlord. The heavy bomber support in the lead up to, on the day itself, and in the follow-up would be key to the success of the operation. In particular the Normandy battle area had to be isolated from German reinforcement, which would come in the main through the rail networks. Bomber Command would have the responsibility of creating a ring of destruction in the railyards around Normandy. And not only those directly feeding the proposed battle area, indeed as part of an Allied deception plan, suggesting a seaborne invasion in the Pas de Calais area, the rail network in the north of France and Belgium would also be blasted. Sir Arthur Harris, for one, was certainly not keen on the idea of diverting his force from the all-out attack on Germany, but he resigned himself to the direction his force had to take describing it as an 'inescapable commitment'. As such the campaign against the rail network began with the raid on Trappes and over the next six weeks further attacks were made on railyards. Bomber Command was actually undergoing a test in the initial stages of the campaign; the railyards were in built-up areas and friendly casualties had to be minimised. Indeed there was extensive debate throughout the command chain, right up to the War Cabinet, as to the acceptable scale of friendly casualties. Eventually such 'sacrifice' was deemed unavoidable and necessary to ensure success on the Normandy beaches.

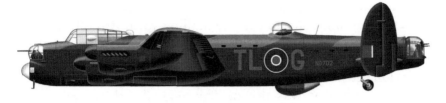

35 Squadron Lancaster

On 10 April Joe Petrie-Andrews's new crew began to make their contribution during the build-up to D-Day. 'We had no idea when D-Day would be but we realised there had to be an invasion.' That night Joe, now a flight lieutenant, flew his first Lancaster operation, acting as a supporter, to the railyards at Lâon, but inaccurate marking resulted in damage to just part of the target area. The next night it was back to Germany in a very successful attack on Aachen; Joe unhappy on his first run, coming round for a second, 'to endeavour to get below cloud and see target indicators.' The Rouen railyards were blasted by Joe's crew, one of 273 Lancasters accompanied by six Mosquitoes (with no losses) on 18/19 April, and two nights later it was back to Germany again; Cologne suffering from accurate bombing. The concentration of bombers over the target that night led to an unpleasant experience for the crew. Some 4lb incendiaries dropped from above hit their Lancaster putting a hole in the roof, one rib was hit and the starboard ammunition trap was buckled. The flight became a little more uncomfortable when the 4,000lb bomb failed to release, Joe no doubt taking a little more care when he returned to base. Two nights later it was back to Lâon, Joe detailed to act as an illuminator. His post-raid report, his 51st operation, is detailed below providing a good example of the nature of operations against the French rail targets and the emphasis on accuracy.

Target – Lâon
Load: 5 x 4 hooded flares, 9 x 1,000lb MC [Medium Capacity bombs]
[Three runs] 23.25 hrs, 6,000 feet 168M, 170 knots; 23.27 hrs, 6,000 feet, 098M, 170 knots; 23.29 hrs, 6,000 feet 098M, 170 knots.
Weather – very clear. Target identified initially by yellow target indicator and visually by whole of marshalling yards,

which were very clear. On run-up it was possible to identify actual aiming point in the marshalling yard. Aircraft made three runs. On first run yellow target indicator slightly undershot aiming point and aircraft bombed to overshoot it. On second run bombs did not go. On third run a green target indicator was down. This was slightly to port of aiming point and as instructed by Master Bomber bombs were aimed, using bomb sight, sharply to starboard of it. One big red/yellow explosion seen at 23.26 hours. Actual aiming point in marshalling yards seen, in bomb sight, in all three attacks. Very successful attack.

April closed out for Joe Petrie-Andrews with two returns to Germany, Karlsruhe and Friedrichshaven on 24 and 27 April respectively. In between there was a visit to the Villeneuve St George railyards. Joe had new responsibilities on this raid, acting as deputy master bomber. With accuracy paramount on these raids the use of a master bomber, to communicate with and control and direct the main force, was essential. A highly important function for the airmen who took on that role and also one in which the respective crews were often at greater risk, spending more time over the target. Indeed on the 22/23 April raid to Lâon the master bomber Wing Commander A G S Cousens, from 635 Squadron, was shot down and lost his life. Joe's task on the raid to Villeneuve St George was in part to step in should the master bomber be lost or be unable to communicate. The planning and execution of the raid is detailed below. It is worth contrasting with some of the earlier bombing operations detailed in this book – the 1940 raids carried out by Benny Goodman and Tiny Cooling – providing a clear example of the considerable advance in weaponry and tactics since the early years of the war. The plan of attack was as follows.

Oboe groundmarking on both aiming points under the direction of a Master Bomber. The south aiming point was to be marked first and the north 30 minutes later. In each instance 4 Mosquitoes were to drop yellow, green and red TI and red spot-fires. Illuminators were to drop flares and bombs at the TI. The Master Bomber and his deputy were to direct the bombing and drop other markers if necessary. If the Mosquitoes had dropped no TI by zero hour, the Master Bomber was to release white TI visually. The main force were to bomb as directed by the Master Bomber.

Timing
Zero hour: south aiming point – 0005 hours; north aiming
point – 0035 hours
Duration of attack: south aiming point – 2359 to 0015
hours; north aiming point – 0029 to 0045 hours

4 Mosquitoes at z-6, z-4, z-2 and z-1
Master Bomber and Deputy at z-5
6 Illuminators at z-5
2 Illuminators at z+2
29 main force aircraft from z to z+4
32 main force aircraft from z+4 to z+7
29 main force aircraft from z+7 to z+10
(The same timing was to be followed for both attacks)

So for each aiming point 104 aircraft were expected to pass over
the target in the space of 16 minutes (as it was 181 aircraft in
total took part in the two attacks). Joe's post-raid report noted
his work with the master bomber during the attack on the south
aiming point.

Target – Villeneuve St. George
Load – 1 TI white, 3 x 1,000 MC
00.10 hrs, 7,000 feet, 007M, 170 knots.
Weather – clear, good visibility. Target identified by target
indicator white seen in bomb sight. Red target indicators
[dropped by the Oboe Mosquitoes] went down
approximately 2 miles east-north-east of aiming point but
did not attract any bombing. Master Bomber told main
force not to bomb until he had dropped his white target
indicators. These were dropped on aiming point at 0005
hours approximately and own aircraft was asked to back
up a few minutes later. Bombing in early stages was
somewhat scattered but later a good concentration was
believed within the marshalling yard. A large blue
explosion was seen at 0015 hours approximately. Master
Bomber's instructions were clearly heard throughout.

For the attack on the north aiming point the main force were
unable to hear the master bomber, assumed to be the result of
German jamming. The main force therefore divided the bombing
between two sets of groundmarkers. The raid was followed up

the next day with a reconnaissance sortie, which revealed the following:

> The main weight of the attack fell on the southern end of the railyards. Extensive damage was caused to wagon construction shops, carriage workshops, rolling stock and railroad tracks. One direct hit was scored on a train at the end of a bridge. Some damage was caused to residential property south east of the target.

An outstanding attack in terms of its military objective, but as was feared, yet accepted, there had been a price to pay. There was little aerial opposition. A few fighters were seen, there were a couple of engagements and a Me109 was claimed as damaged. In addition, 'a third combat took place between two Halifaxes, without serious consequence'. There was one aircraft loss, 'seen to blow up over the target'; Flight Sergeant Wilkinson's entire 78 Squadron crew lost their lives.

Into May and the first few days of June, the support to the invasion preparations continued. Joe entered enemy airspace on eight separate occasions.

> **8/9 May** – Haine St Pierre as part of the main force; 'Saw yellow target indicator at 0325 hours and made run on it. That disappeared into smoke as about to bomb. Second run on south of green as instructed by master bomber which fell at 0326 hours – this seen in bomb sight.
> **10/11 May** – Lens; 'Target identified by target indicator yellow. Red spot-fires went down at 2320 hours. Master bomber told us to wait for a few minutes. Then heard instruction to bomb white target indicator and the yellow target indicator, seen in bomb sight, with three seconds overshoot.'
> **11/12 May** – Louvain as a supporter; 'Own bombs seen to straddle row of big sheds near marshalling yards.'
> **19/20 May** – Boulogne as a supporter; 'White target indicator went down at 0059.30 hours which was seen in bombsight bang on aiming point and master bomber instructed main force to bomb it.' This raid is also noted by Joe as one in which his aircraft was hit by 'friendly' flak after crossing the English coast on the return.
> **22/23 May** – Dortmund again as a supporter; 'Centre of two red target indicators seen in bombsight.'

24/25 May – Aachen yet again as a supporter (Joe's 60th operation); 'One red target indicator on ground seen in bombsight.'

27/28 May – Bourg Leopold as a backer-up carrying 12 white TIs and a 4,000lb bomb; 'Target identified by red target indicators... seen to cascade at 0155 hours when aircraft 20 miles away. On arrival yellow target indicator was on the ground and master bomber was heard instructing backers-up to bomb the yellow target indicator. Our own white target indicator fell slightly to the north of it but close to the two yellow.'

2/3 June – Trappes railyards, as an illuminator; 'Aircraft retained flares because master bomber was not heard at the time detailed. When he did ask for them the R/T was not on because crew were talking at time for making bomb run.'

Late on 5 June 1944 Joe and his crew attended a briefing for operations. 'We were just not aware that we were actually going to be involved in D-Day until we were at the briefing.' Joe was detailed to attack the enemy gun batteries at Longues-sur-Mer, threatening a seaborne approach to the Normandy beaches.

It was a very interesting trip. We were told that we had to fly between 8,000 and 10,000 feet because we had aircraft with gliders below us and slower aircraft, troop carriers, above. On the way to the target the navigator said, 'come and have a look at this Joe.' I replied, 'What are you talking about?' He responded, 'Just come and have a look.' On the radar set there were masses of double blips – tug aircraft towing gliders. We had to maintain height until we got some distance from the coast and then come down quickly as we were visually marking the target. We had been given a particular gun to take out and to do that we had to put one through the window more or less. We couldn't reduce height until we were very close to the French coast, but we had to give the bomb aimer and navigator some sort of chance to get on to the guns. We found it, but missed it the first time and had to come round again, but the bomb aimer reckoned he put one through the window.

The aircraft dropped its bombs at 0420 hours that morning and a few hours later the momentous events on the Normandy beaches unfolded. As night fell a beachhead had been fought for and won, and in the following days the Allied armies looked to press on inland. Key to the outcome now the beachhead was attained, was to win the battle of the build-up. Bomber Command's campaign against the railyards prior to D-Day had been highly significant in ensuring success in the early stages of the invasion, but the job was far from over, and hindering the deployment of German reinforcement was now crucial.

Joe had now passed the 60 trip mark but, 'things were hotting up a bit so we carried on for a few more.' On 8/9 and 12/13 June the crew attacked the railyards at Mayenne and Arras respectively, acting as backers-up. On 15/16 June the ammunition dump at Fouillard was targetted, and on 16/17 June a trip to Sterkade Duisburg, Germany, in response to a call to Bomber Command to carry out attacks on German oil production. A few nights later the Petrie-Andrews crew went on a successful raid to Lâon as a backer-up. Operation number 68 for Joe. However his morale was not high.

> I was getting rather disheartened really because apart from Longues when we, 'stuck one through the window' our results were not good, nowhere near the results I had been getting previously. I felt that I was rather wasted on the squadron, I hadn't got a proper bomb aimer. That's really why I retired shortly after D-Day. I thought I was wasting my time and I was very disappointed really – in the leadership.

The raid to Lâon was Joe's last and he left the squadron on 11 July 1944, his twentieth birthday, his logbook recording his CO's assessment of ability as 'exceptional'. His operational days were over. He had completed his operations as pilot showing great skill and courage and been awarded an immediate DFM and DFC in the main due to specific incidents respectively. Possibly it may have been due to his disagreements with seniority, but why Joe did not receive at least a Bar to his DFC is beyond this author's comprehension.

Joe now spent some time training as a flying instructor and a posting to 85 OTU Husbands Bosworth. But he did not settle in to the monotony that this entailed and he regularly applied to go back on operations. All were turned down, the European war ended and Joe left the OTU. The war against Japan still raged however and he prepared for a trip to India to fly Avro Lincolns; this was cancelled, however, following the dropping of the atomic bombs.

Although his operational days were over Joe still sought further excitement through flying. 'I wanted to be a test pilot, put in for it but they said my education wasn't good enough. I think somebody was standing in my way quite honestly. I was actually put in the King's Flight and we were going to go all over the world.' Whilst training for this task he made a further demonstration of his flying ability; a green endorsement in his logbook reading:

> Good airmanship, in that he on Friday 8 February 1946 when Student Pilot in the port seat undergoing instruction in Lancastrian I VM.730 by great presence of mind and skilful handling of his aircraft under the direction of his Instructor landed it at RAF Carnaby without damage in spite of the fact that the aileron control was locked over to port for half of its travel, thereby saving one of His Majesty's valuable aircraft.

What actually happened is lost somewhat in the official use of words, and perhaps with a view to save reputations.

> I was being checked out and had a special helmet on, through which I could only see the instruments of the flying panel. The instructor was throwing the aircraft around and he toppled the gyroscopic instruments, losing the artificial horizon. Of course without that he couldn't tell what position the aircraft was in. He then said I had control. When I took over, the aileron was straight up and down, whereas normally flying straight and level it was horizontal. I couldn't move them, they were locked solid. I fiddled with them and then said, 'I give up. What have you done with them?' He said 'Get on with it.' I considered him a very officious, nasty piece of work. I took my helmet off and said, 'You try it.' It was locked solid and we were in almost a ninety degree turn. His response was, 'Oh crikey' and he jumped out of the seat and went off. I got Taffy my engineer to come and sit with me; it was bloody hard trying to control the elevators, never mind the ailerons. I pulled back two engines on one side, got the thing more or less level, but lost lift. Kicking full rudder we were sort of

crabbing along. I did not know what the instructor had
done and he had disappeared. With the Lancastrian the
crew didn't have parachutes, although I had still taken
mine, to sit on as they were still the original seats. Anyway
all the escape hatches had been sealed off and the door they
had put in faced forward so it was impossible to open when
flying. I called up for an emergency landing, telling them of
our problem. Emergency airfields were close by, with
3,000-yard runways but I couldn't get to them. We
managed to get the aircraft round on an approach and I
prepared to land on the grass wheels up. When we were at
200 feet, I was easing off two engines, suddenly the aileron
control came back. I banged the wheels down and we
almost touched down immediately.

Despite his new role on the King's Flight, Joe was frustrated with
the lack of flying, 'always cancelled. I got so fed up with the RAF
that I came out.' Joe left in the autumn of 1946 and took up
commercial flying. In 1948, whilst working with Westminster
airways, Joe's flying experience was utilised during the Berlin
Airlift; flying in supplies from Hamburg, over two hundred trips,
to the blockaded western Berlin. 'Bloody hard work. I never
worked so hard in my life. Three trips a night.' Joe was staying
in Hamburg at the time, 'Parts of it were in a dreadful state and
I was almost ashamed to go round them. The Germans were
lovely; I wore a uniform, with my decorations up and I was asked
if I ever bombed Hamburg. I didn't hesitate to say yes yet never
did get a punch in the face.'

In September 1948 Joe travelled to Ireland with his new wife
Fay, to celebrate their honeymoon. 'Whilst there I got a telegram
thanking me for my "very valuable service" but I wasn't needed
anymore for the airlifts. And at this stage there were loads of
spare crew and my wife didn't want me to go on flying.' Joe then
settled into a career in the construction industry, starting with the
Marley tile company, going on to airfield runway construction
and resurfacing, and road construction. In the post-war years Joe
was given his long desired opportunity to fly fighters. 'It was
what I always wanted to do', joining 615 County of Surrey
Squadron of the Auxiliary Air Force, flying Spitfires and jets –
Meteors and Vampires. Joe, a father of two daughters and
grandfather of five, retired in the mid 1980s. He lost Fay in 1995
and now lives in Somerset.

Joe Petrie-Andrews DFM, DFC had left the RAF in 1946 somewhat disillusioned but his record shows that not only was he a talented flyer, he also flew on some of the most intense and significant air battles in the history of the Second World War. As his DFC citation recorded 'courageous determination and fine airmanship' were a feature of his operational flying career. Looking back after 62 years, Joe reflects on the contribution Bomber Command made to the war.

> It was superb. I am sure it broke the Germans, broke their hearts. They really got pasted. Everywhere they went or whatever they did Bomber Command would go and spike it really. The criticism is not justified. Absolutely not. Germany started it and were slinging bombs everywhere in the south east of England at the beginning of the war. I used to come home on leave through London and see people in the underground stations. It was awful, it really was. The Londoners really had a tough time. I was already in the air force by then so it didn't motivate me as such to take up the fight, but it made me bitter and gave me a purpose. Without Bomber Command we would either have lost the war or it would have lasted twice as long.

And how should the men of Bomber Command be remembered? 'With a lot of gratitude really. For much of the war there was nothing else to stop the Germans.'

Flight Lieutenant W Harry Hughes DFC, DFM, AE

Chapter 7

Glad to be There

Hilda Burston (née Jones) was 16 when the war broke out. She was soon having to come to terms with the news of family members lost, and then endure many nights in an air raid shelter as bombs fell around her house in Birmingham. 'My own war story really began in earnest in 1942 when, impatient to do my bit in the struggle against Nazism, I enlisted for the Womens Auxiliary Air Force.' Following basic training, Eileen, (known by her middle name) took up a number of postings, as a telephonist, at various Bomber Command stations.

Being women on an airfield miles from anywhere, which was staffed mostly by men, it is suffice to say that some of our most endearing friendships were those we soon established with the aircrews, many of which turned to romance. Looking back, the most dazzling loves of my life were those that blossomed amongst those brave lads whose Lancasters and Wellingtons we would wave off on missions over Germany. They were real dashing gentlemen – our heroes! Yet the joy of such friendship so often turned to grief when news filtered back that a pilot we knew had been posted as missing, or that a gunner or navigator boyfriend of one of my fellow WAAFs had returned back so badly shot-up and maimed that he was unrecognisable as the handsome young man that she had strolled hand-in-hand with a mere twenty-four hours earlier.

Being a telephonist, it was often my dubious privilege to find out before most who had and who hadn't returned from a mission. On nightshift, at about 3.00am or 4.00am, the first returning aircraft would arrive and the lines would go busy as reports were filed backwards and forwards between airfields. Then, at daybreak, wives or sweethearts would also call in, anxious for news of their loved ones. Procedure dictated that all we could do was wipe away any stray tears and advise them that there was no firm news of such-and-such an aircraft yet; though of course we knew that their commanding officer was, even as we spoke, preparing to summon up a form of words that would explain how their husband or boyfriend had courageously made the ultimate sacrifice for his country.

I still shed a tear when I watch a Remembrance Day ceremony; when I see those fields of poppies, each one symbolising a promising young life so cruelly snuffed out in its prime. Those poppies are real to me – friends I once had who never came back, or the last sight of whom I had glimpsed was of the orderlies lifting their burned and mutilated bodies down from a wrecked aircraft; people whose smiles can now only ever be a memory and whose laughter I can never share again.

So while occasionally I still yearn to transport myself back to the comradeship and solidarity of those far-off wartime days, I quickly snap out of it and give thanks instead that – unlike my fallen comrades – my own grown-up son has never had to spill his precious blood upon a nameless field in order to defy one man's evil megalomania.

Flak burst all around and searchlights sought out bombers laden with high explosives and fuel. German nightfighters prowled intent on sending enemy airmen and aircraft burning to the ground. And every now and then the sky was lit as a flaming bomber plunged or another exploded. Rear and mid-upper gunners in their cold turrets stared into the dark, watching for danger, avoiding bright lights and a loss of night vision. Bomb aimers peered through bombsights at brightly coloured pyrotechnics below, poised to release their explosives. Navigators, flight engineers and wireless operators tensed, listening, as the bomb aimers guided their focused pilots over the burning target. At any moment death could rip through the aircraft and seize each and every one of them. In one such bomber sat navigator Harry Hughes and his recollection of the raid 64 years on was simply – 'I was so glad to be there.'

As a youth in the 1930s William Henry 'Harry' Hughes had developed an interest in flying, reading the aviation magazines, 'and I became more interested in flying when the war started.'

My father had a friend who was a captain in the Royal Navy, and this seemed to influence him. They had spoken and decided that the best job for me was a career in the Navy, signing on for a full term. With that in mind I had to go to Portsmouth and sit an exam. Twenty columns and twelve rows of figures – add the columns, add the rows, then add the totals at the bottom and add these totals at the end. They should have agreed. Mine didn't. My maths was good, but not this kind.

I recall that we had lunch in the galley. It was a rather steamy, warm day, humid and I remember the green and yellow tiles and the smell of cabbage. It did not impress me. On the way back to Sherborne, in Dorset, the next day, I had to change trains in Salisbury. There was a two-hour wait so I walked into town, saw an RAF recruiting office, went in and joined up, down for a pilot or navigator.

When I got home my father wanted to know how I had got on. 'Alright,' I replied. He asked, 'Do you think you passed?' 'No.' 'So why say you got on well?' I told him I had joined the air force and he asked me what as. I said, 'pilot or navigator'. His face fell, he was really quite upset. It was 1940 and he had the feeling, even at that time, that it wasn't going to be the safest of jobs.

Harry left school in July 1940, and spent some time working as a wages clerk with a large company building army camps in Dorset and whilst waiting to enter the air force the drama of the Battle of Britain 'was quite evident' to the aspiring airman. Harry went to Oxford for his attestation and was chosen for pilot duties. 'I was then on four months deferred service while they fitted me into the training programme.' Harry's flying training was to take place in the USA and Canada and he soon found himself setting out across the Atlantic – not before being issued with some civilian suits; the USA was neutral at the time. 'A man from Montague Burtons came and walked past each one of us in line. He gave us three figures, chest, height, inside leg. We took these figures to the store and we all had perfect fits.'

> On the journey to Canada I remember that there was a bit of a panic. We were part of a convoy going to South Africa, which would split half way across the Atlantic. Just before we separated a Focke-Wulf Condor appeared flying all the way round the horizon. As such we expected an attack. I volunteered for submarine watch and spent a lot of time on the bridge seeing the destroyers dashing around dropping depth charges. I figured it was the safest place to be. At one point we hit a terrific storm. I had never seen sea like it. Just horrific. But we felt safe as no submarine could attack in those conditions.

On arrival in Canada the recruits went from Halifax to Toronto, 'billeted in the Bull Run, massive place, double bunks'. From here the young airmen went by train to Maxwell Field, Montgomery, Alabama, to train as part of the Arnold Scheme.

> We were the first to have the benefit of a period of acclimatisation. We were 42 E. Courses A, B, C and D had come before us and we were due to pass out May/June

1942. On arrival, having pulled into a siding at Maxwell, and as soon as we had stowed our kit, we then changed into our RAF uniform. It was terrible, so called tropical kit. If we ever left the station however we had to wear civilian clothes.

Whilst undergoing training the trainees were kept well aware of developments in Europe. 'We used to listen to Ed Murrow broadcasting from Europe, it would start off our classes in the morning.' The recruits were subject to quite a strict disciplinary regime. Harry's experience was similar to his predecessor in the scheme, Joe Petrie-Andrews.

It was terrible. We had been used to discipline, but having left school you did not expect to find worse discipline, almost childish. The one thing I could not stand was that there was an American course just ahead of us, only a few weeks; we had been in our service longer than they had but they could ask us to do stupid things.

Harry would occasionally find himself subject to punishment. Although sometimes this had its benefits.

There was a demerit system. Any transgression and you could usually get one to three demerits or even more. On one occasion I got five. For every demerit over three in a week you had to walk up and down with your rifle whilst everybody else was out in the town. Once when I was walking off some demerits I went into one of the blocks and got myself a coke; it was such a hot day. I was reported by one of the so called upper classmen, an American. One thing you did not do was tell on your fellow pupils; well certainly not if you were British.

The local young ladies used to be at the fence watching us, they preferred the bad boys. I used to make dates with some of these girls, go out to the wire at night and meet them. I had spent seven years in boarding school, where you learn how to get away with things.

Despite the occasional run-in with his 'seniors', Harry remained focused on the reason he was there; aspiring to be the pilot of any aircraft he flew. After he had completed a solo flight on a Boeing PT17 Stearman he was sent for the chief instructors test. His hopes were dashed.

I did not pass and was sent back to Canada washed out. I enjoyed flying, and it was a very big disappointment. What we didn't realise at the time was that the Air Ministry had pretty well given instructions to the Americans to wash out 80/90 per cent of us as they needed to fill other crew positions. The four-engine heavy bombers were coming and they required navigators, bomb aimers, gunners, flight engineers. Bomber Command was going to build up at a rapid pace.

Harry, tongue in cheek, has always felt that his flying training was subject to sabotage.

I was trained by a man called Schmidt; he had a German background. I always say that was why I was washed out. They had clearly figured out that Hitler could not win the war if I got through.

On the aircraft we had a Gosport tube for communication and I could not hear a damn word he said. He used to tell me to tighten up my 'Goddamn' strap. I would but he still wouldn't hear. He would ask me to do a rate 2 left turn; I wouldn't hear and just carry on straight and level. You'd have thought they would have had a system whereby you could hold your hands up indicating that you couldn't hear. I think a good instructor who spoke clearly made all the difference.

Harry was to be sent back to Canada, and just before he was due to leave the USA news came through of one of the most significant turning points in the war.

We were giving an exhibition rugby match in Albany, Georgia. Half way through, the announcement was made that Pearl Harbor had been attacked. We had to scrub the match and go home. The following day we were to be on our way back to Canada. There was a little Scotsman and he found where the air raid siren was on the station. He decided to let it off. Panic!

Harry ended up at Moncton, New Brunswick, a new holding centre for trainee aircrew from the UK. 'When we arrived we had no money as we had not been paid. Officially I didn't get paid for two and a half months.' Harry then set about a money-making scheme. 'I had a parker pen and pencil and we raffled it, 10 cents a time. I made about 40 dollars. So we then bought anything anyone wanted to get rid of, such as cameras. We had a raffle a day and it was quite remunerative.'

The world of commerce then had to wait. 'I was sent down to Trenton, Ontario to remuster. My interviewer was a Group Captain Massey, the brother of Raymond Massey, the film star. He could have been his twin, they were so alike.' Harry's navigator training soon got underway, from 19 January 1942 to 27 April 1942, learning new skills at No 8 Air Observer School, Ancienne Lorette. From here he went to the No 9 Bombing and Gunnery School, Mont-Joli, on the Saint Lawrence river.

> Where we were subject to strict prohibition – it was a dry town. But just up river was the timber port at Rimouski. It wasn't dry there and only about 20 miles in a taxi. We went into a bar and asked for three whiskies. It came out like gin, a clear liquid. After three of these we decided to go back to camp, it was a pretty dead town. On the way back we had to stop the taxi and were quite sick. And it was lucky that we were. On our return we saw a note on our notice board warning of a spirit which had been fortified with wood alcohol and no way should we drink it. We had, and it could have made us blind.

On 8 June 1942 Harry went 'to a very good course, mainly astro-navigation' at 1 Central Navigation School, Rivers, Manitoba, then in late July 1942 he was sent back to the UK, arriving in Bournemouth, then travelling to No 2 Observers Advanced Flying Unit at Millom, Cumberland. Here he continued his training on Ansons, 'to get us used to flying in wartime conditions, such as where the balloon barrages were.' Harry at this point was still unaware of his final destination with regard to operations. 'I had no aspirations. I would just go where they sent me but the chances of it not being Bomber Command were very slim.'

Avro Anson

Indeed it was to be the RAF's heavies for Harry and he was sent to 15 Operational Training Unit at Harwell, arriving on 22 September, continuing on Ansons and Wellingtons, also flying from the satellite aerodrome at Hampstead Norris. 'When we arrived we were on tenterhooks. Crews from the unit had been on the thousand bomber raids and we wondered whether such a requirement would be placed on us. It was not to be.'

Harry now began the all-important process of crewing up. 'Initially I crewed up with a wireless operator, Tommy Thompson, and got used to flying with him.' Then he met his pilot, and they subsequently picked up a gunner and a bomb aimer.

> Sam Hartley was the pilot. A big man. He had been an instructor on Tiger Moths and had quite a few hours behind him. He could throw a Halifax around like a Spitfire. He was very strong. He had come up to me in the crew room and asked, 'Are you Sergeant Hughes?' 'Yep.' He said, 'Right you are my navigator. Are you alright with that?' 'Yep. Why not?' How he picked me I don't know. As captain Sam treated us as if we were one entity and he didn't throw his weight around; although it wouldn't have done him any good anyway.
>
> Jackie Myers, from Leeds, came in as rear gunner, although he would eventually become mid-upper gunner. He seldom came out with us.
>
> Harry Hooper, the bomb aimer, had completed a full navigation course out in South Africa. He had been told, on return to the UK, that he was to be a bomb aimer, as indeed a lot were. I think he was always a little peeved though he never showed it and we were always good friends.
>
> When we went to the heavy conversion unit at Riccall [28 January 1943] we picked up our flight engineer Canadian 'Red' Flannery (with red hair). I always got on well with all the 'colonials' but I was particularly fond of the Aussies and New Zealanders. As it was 'Red' fitted in very well with us and we had a great respect for each other.
>
> When we arrived at the operational squadron we had to fly with a number of different rear gunners before eventually getting a permanent one, Ken Lazenby.

Whilst at 15 OTU Harry began to appreciate more that flying in wartime conditions, even though it was in a training environment, was a dangerous business. On non-operational duties an extraordinary 8,090 Bomber Command men were killed and 4,203[11] were wounded during the war. The operational training units contributed to the grim statistic. In November and December 1942 the diary of 15 OTU recorded 15 crashes, fortunately with no fatalities. But there were deaths in the next two months. The 15 OTU diary records reveal the following.

5 December 1942: At 2112 hours a Wellington crashed on take-off for cross-country training. Three of the four crew were all killed, the man who survived the crash would die several hours later.

6 December 1942: A Wellington from No. 12 OTU developed engine trouble, overshot Harwell and crashed one mile to the east. The navigator was killed and two of the crew received slight injuries.

16 December 1942: A Wellington on local flying flew into wispy cloud and then dived steeply into the ground, shattering on impact and burning out. The crew of five lost their lives.

30 December 1942: A Wellington on a training cross-country flight crash-landed at Beckington. The navigator was killed and two other men were injured.

8/9 January 1943: A Wellington on circuits and landings crashed on a hill and was burnt out. One man was killed, the pilot was seriously injured with concussion, two men received cuts, and another man was seriously injured with a badly burnt left leg and left hand.

23 January 1943: A Wellington on a training cross-country flight developed technical trouble in an engine and attempted to land at Yeovilton. Following an approach one engine faltered on overshoot and the aircraft crashed 1,000 yards ahead, striking the far bank of a small stream and bursting into flames. Four of the crew were killed. The rear gunner was seriously injured and placed on the dangerous casualty list. He subsequently had his left leg amputated below the knee.

25/26 January 1943: A Wellington on a training cross-country flight was reported to have burst into flames and it finally crashed into a farm house, Llansilin, near Oswestry.

The farm house was set on fire and two of the occupants were killed. Only two of the crew were identified, the remaining three were not recovered or identified and were classed as missing believed killed.

Merely surviving training, before a crew had even reached an operational unit, was an achievement in itself. Harry had carried out his last flight at Harwell on 4 January 1943, then following some leave the crew were sent on a battle course.

> We went to Driffield to receive some training from the RAF regiment and the army. We finished up with an escape and evasion exercise. They took us out in a blacked-out van and we were dropped off somewhere in the Yorkshire Wolds. That night a Heinkel had been shot down and the crew were unaccounted for. We had no idea. We went to a farm, where we were given something to eat and then we heard the farmer on the phone calling the police. We escaped out the back door, eventually making our way back without being caught.

On 28 January Harry and his colleagues arrived at 1658 Heavy Conversion Unit, to familiarise themselves with four-engine bombers. Whilst there they had to do another escape exercise, 'to which we had become somewhat acclimatised to.'

> We were dropped off to the north of Harrogate, right out in the wilds. We saw a car on a road, ran down, stopped it and asked where the nearest town was. He told us Harrogate and when we asked if he could take us there he said, 'Yes. I'm a taxi.' We had managed to take some money by putting it in our socks and we spent a night in a hotel. It was an escape exercise and we were using our initiative after all.

The following day the 'escapees' made their way south, their luck eventually running out when they were picked up by the home guard, then returning to base.

> We got back too early, we had been given three days, so we were given four days leave. The intelligence officer insisted that we had slept in a barn. Our response was, 'Oh yeh, yeh we did.' He said, 'I thought so. I could smell the hay.'

Harry spent a month at the heavy conversion unit before it was time to move on, to a front line squadron.

In February 1943 Harry Hughes and his crew were to take up operational duties, just prior to the opening up of Sir Arthur Harris's Battle of the Ruhr. Harris described the series of attacks in 1942 as, 'commercial travellers' samples which I could show to the War Cabinet' – referring to the attacks on Lübeck and Rostock and the thousand bomber raids. But he knew that these attacks in isolation would not be enough to have a major impact on the course of the war, 'not one or two such strokes, but the cumulative effect of hundreds of them would be needed before the enemy felt the pinch'.

The Battle of the Ruhr was an extraordinary period in air war history during which the belief in the destructive power of the RAF bomber force was put to the test; a time in which thousands of Bomber Command airmen would lose their lives, become wounded or bale out over enemy territory to end the war as 'guests' of the Third Reich. Harris's main campaign against the Ruhr began on the night of 5/6 March 1943. He called upon 442 aircrews to man the bombers he sent to Essen that night; fourteen would not be returning. The die was cast, as Harris would state, 'at last we were ready and equipped' and into the forthcoming battle would enter Harry Hughes and his inexperienced crew. 'We arrived at Pocklington in Yorkshire to join 102 Squadron. Of course I did not know then that 102 Squadron was destined to sustain the second highest loss rate in Bomber Command although the losses were running high at that time.' In the weeks preceding their arrival, the aircrews of the squadron had been in the midst of the bomber battle of Germany and had suffered accordingly. On the night of 14/15 February seven 102 Squadron men lost their lives when their Halifax fell to the guns of a nightfighter. But engagements with the enemy were not the only cause of loss. Earlier that day another Halifax had been destroyed by fire at its dispersal pen, fortunately without loss of life, although two men were injured. On 25 February, whilst en-route to Nuremberg one crew of seven men lost their lives, falling victim to severe weather conditions and crashing in Essex. On the night of 26/27 February two crews failed to return from an attack on Cologne, fifteen trained airmen losing their lives, and another aircraft was written off that night when the undercarriage collapsed on take-off fortunately without injury. On 8 March a 102 Squadron Halifax was claimed by a German nightfighter pilot, who crippled his prey, setting fire to one of the bomber's engine; fortunately the crew had time to escape the burning aircraft, two men would evade capture, the other five were not so lucky.

But despite these losses any drop in morale did not seem apparent to Harry Hughes on his arrival at the squadron. 'I liked the feel of the place. A good atmosphere. I had trained for this, 18 months by that time. It was great to see these big black Halifaxes at dispersal.' Harry certainly took to the Halifax, one feature appealing to him in particular. 'It was a very good aircraft to get out of, especially for the navigator who sat right on top of the escape hatch!' However another feature of the squadron's Halifaxes, BIIs, did not appeal to mid-upper gunner Jackie Myers.

> There was no mid-upper turret [and the nose turret had been removed to improve performance] so the mid-upper gunner had to lie near the Elsan toilet and look through a Perspex blister – no guns. Jackie was absolutely disgusted at this. He had wanted to be the rear gunner but we had picked up someone more experienced in that position. Jackie wouldn't put in his logbook 'duty – mid-upper gunner', he would put 'duty – rear gunner's mate'.

Tension built up in anticipation of their first operation as a crew; Harry recalls thinking, 'Here it comes and we might not be around next week.' He and his crewmates dealt with the stress in a familiar way.

> We went out and had a few pints. We went to York and saw *Road to Morocco* – one of the Bob Hope and Bing Crosby road films. Dorothy Lamour and Bing sang *Moonlight Becomes You*, which will always move me. It was the night before our first operation.
>
> We were expecting a nice easy trip like minelaying. Sam had already completed two operations as a second pilot. We were hanging around on tenterhooks until he had completed these.

The minelaying trip Harry had expected did not materialise. In fact his first trip was to be to one of the most fiercely protected targets in Germany. As Harry recalled, 'I nearly went LMF on my first trip', but it was not because of a lack of courage, or the presence of fear; it was because of frustration concerning the ability to do his job. Indeed many bomber airmen felt relatively comfortable on operations despite the threat of flak, and nightfighters, and having seen other aircraft go down. An inability to do their job often created fear; the uncertainty of no longer being in control.

> On 12 March 1943 we were briefed to go to Essen, and of course we were aware it was one of the most heavily defended cities in Germany and you had to fly over the Ruhr to get to it. We had the Mk I Gee navigational aid at that time, which had to be tuned. It was imperative to me that I got the Gee working, so as soon as we were airborne I had to tune it in. On this night as soon as we got a signal the aircraft would shake and it would go off. We arrived at the English coast and I was supposed to alter course, as per my flight plan, but I was still fiddling with the Gee trying to get it to work. Sooner or later I thought it would work, I could get a fix and start my air plot from there. We achieved operational height and I was still trying to get the damn Gee to work. Luckily Harry Hooper was also a navigator and had done some astral navigation. All through OTU Hooper used to take the star shots and I would work them out and plot them. So on this occasion I said to Hooper, 'We'll have to go on astro.' He got a couple of star fixes as we went across the North Sea; we were still heading for Denmark. I calculated new winds and altered course for Egmond on the Dutch coast, which we hit right on the button. The rest of the crew thought I was a genius, and come to think of it I thought I was a genius too at that time.

Harry then managed to direct his crew to the designated target. But the city defences were desperately trying to oppose the bomber force.

> When I saw the flak I just could not believe that you could possibly get through it. But I was so glad to be there after all the frustration. We had managed to get to the target area despite the difficulties but the danger never occurred to me. We had got there the hardest possible way from a

navigational point of view. I wasn't scared of the flak, I was truly thrilled to be there. I knew there was a good possibility of me going LMF if we had turned back. I would have felt that I had let my crew down.

The crew's post-raid report recorded what they saw beneath them:

Attacked primary target at 16,000 feet heading 189M, IAS 170. No cloud, good visibility. Red TI markers at target area seen falling. Red and green TI markers in bomb sights. On arrival whole target area covered in fires. At 2135 enormous explosion occurred in target area with red flame shooting up to 4/5,000 feet. Smoke and glow seen when crossing Dutch coast on homeward journey.

Sam Hartley managed to pilot his aircraft over the burning city without damage from flak. But the aircraft would not come through unscathed.

We had five incendiaries drop on us from an aircraft above, right through our aircraft's skin. Luckily they didn't ignite. The flight engineer and I had to put on oxygen bottles, and we went back to kick them out of the door.

Harry navigated his crew back to base, but not all 102 Squadron aircrews returned. As Sergeant Charlebois approached the target flak smashed into his Halifax and Charlebois ordered his crew to bale out. He then held the aircraft steady so his crew had plenty of opportunity to escape. His bravery cost him his life, and his rear gunner also died. Sergeant Newland's Halifax was also hit by flak, he lost his life along with five others from his crew, one man surviving and being captured. What happened to Flying Officer Barnes's Halifax is not known; the names of the pilot and his crew are etched on the Runnymede Memorial to the missing.

Harry Hughes recalls, 'It was always a great relief to get back of course. As we were being debriefed we would look at the board and see who hadn't returned.' Bomber crews were virtually always a close knit unit. And whilst there was fraternisation, the airmen did not really establish that many long lasting friendships with other crew members. The attrition rate played its part according to Harry, 'You just didn't get time to meet them.' Initially Harry did not notice a decline in morale at the squadron but he believed that it did come into play later on as the turning back early rates increased.

It would be just over a month before Harry was next on operations, the crew enjoying some early leave. 'We had about ten days leave officially every eight weeks, but it used to come up in about five weeks. You were on a roster and as people got the chop ahead of you, you went up the list.' During this period one more aircraft failed to return from operations, seven men killed and from a raid to Essen Squadron Leader Marshall's Halifax returned with a dead gunner.

On 14 April the crew took part in the attack on Stuttgart and two nights later they were detailed to go to Pilsen. Harry's navigational skills were, once more, to be put to the test.

> It was our third trip and it was a moonlit night; we were flying at about 10,000ft. My bomb aimer, Harry Hooper gave me a pinpoint on the Moselle which put us six miles north of track. After about eight minutes we were coned and got some flak.
>
> The best thing to do if you were coned was to go into a dive and then turn 180 degrees, come out of it and go back the way you came. Then climb up again. This was where experience came in. You could see some crews just carrying on when coned and you could imagine someone saying, 'We've only got two minutes to go skipper.' By that time they were all dead.
>
> There was nothing north of our track, but Saarbrucken was south so I drew a track from the pinpoint and extended it beyond Saarbrucken to find that we would go over Karlsruhe, which we did. On extending it further I found that we would hit Stuttgart. I told Sam Hartley our pilot that as soon as we saw the first searchlights to go on to a north-west course until I calculated that we were back on our original track. By this time I was able to calculate the wind velocity. It must be borne in mind that I was still new to operations (a sprog) and as a navigator the most important thing was to know where you were. Well we carried on to our next turning point which was to the south of Pilsen but about seven minutes before my ETA the Pathfinder flares went down and Harry insisted that he could see the Skoda works so we bombed along with everyone else despite my protestations.

On the way home we were routed north of Mannheim which was also being bombed that night. We could see the fires but we were to the south which confirmed that I was right. We had to land at Harwell and did not get back to base until 1330 hours the following day having had to repair the flak holes in the ailerons and the tailplane. We finally got to bed but I was awoken after two hours to go to the operations room where I found everyone pouring over my log and chart. It had been confirmed by the photo-reconnaissance Spitfire that we had not bombed Pilsen and I was told that I was the only navigator to have insisted that we had not.

102 Squadron lost one Halifax; the aircraft of Squadron Leader Lashbrook DFC, DFM being shot from the sky by a nightfighter, and with the port wing and both engines in flames the crew baled out. The rear gunner lost his life; Lashbrook and three others evaded capture, two men ended up in a prison camp.

Harry's next flight took him to Stettin on the night of 20/21 April. (Also flying in the bomber stream that night was Joe Petrie-Andrews.)

We had to come in over Denmark. We checked very carefully that there were no flak ships and dropped down to the deck, about 50 feet. I remember that that night we went under high tension cables. As we went over Denmark the Danes were putting their bedroom lights on. It must be one hell of sight for them, about 300 plus aircraft going across at 50 feet. We climbed to 13,000 feet to bomb, and on the way back we dropped down again. We picked up one bullet, a .303, which sliced right through our elevator control. Likely to be some guard with a rifle. So now we were at 50 feet with no elevator control. Sam managed to hold it on the trimmer tabs. Then our flight engineer went back to have a look. He had a hammer in his tool kit, and he tied the handle to the controls with copper wire. It held and got us back.

Two aircraft failed to return from the raid. The entire crew of eight on Sergeant Griffiths's Halifax lost their lives. Flak claimed Sergeant Olliver's Halifax, only the pilot and one other man surviving from the crew of seven.

Harry's crew now had some experience under their belt. The

first few operations were often the most dangerous, as a crew set out on their tour. On every flight new lessons could be learned, then applied and crews often came to their own conclusions to improve the odds of their survival.

> A lot of pilots liked to weave. I said no way are we going to be able to navigate accurately if weaving so let's fly straight and level. Lazenby was in agreement because he wanted a steady platform adding that he could watch for fighters so we needn't worry about it. And we had the blister underneath, so the general consensus was why weave? It's only a personal opinion and there are a lot of very well known pilots who used to weave on every trip.

But the risks an operational bomber crew had to deal with were not always of the enemy's making. Harry recalls one occasion when fortune played a part in preserving his life.

> Another crew took our aircraft out one night when we were on leave. The pilot was a great one for saving fuel and he came back at about 1,850 revs, not much boost. This subsequently caused one of the engines to vibrate. The following day we were in the aircraft preparing to take off for a test. We were revving the engine up and the propeller flew off. It came straight through my navigator position, where I would have been sitting. Fortunately I was back in the rest position. Then we got a new aircraft.

They were now to fly in a Halifax with a mid-upper turret and a Perspex fairing on the nose. A change of aircraft would usually be accepted reluctantly by a bomber crew, but not in this case, one person at least was happy. 'Jackie Myers was delighted – we had a mid-upper turret. His Christmas had come.'

Following the Stettin raid Harry found his crew's name regularly down as detailed for operations; 26/27 April – Duisburg (one 102 Squadron aircraft lost, seven airmen killed), 28/29 April – Kattegat, minelaying, and two nights later another trip to Essen. Into May and an attack on Dortmund on the night of the 4th/5th of the month (two 102 Squadron crews lost, eleven killed, three captured, and one Halifax ditched in the sea, the crew rescued by air-sea-rescue launch). Harry would not be operational again until 23 May, by which time two further squadron aircraft had been lost, 13 dead, one captured; and a

Halifax had been lost ditching in the sea, the crew fortunately rescued. On the night of 23/24 May Harry once more went to Dortmund; he would return, but one crew did not, four men killed, three captured. Two nights later, Sam Hartley took his crew to Düsseldorf. On their return it was necessary to fill out some extra paperwork, detailing their encounter with enemy airmen.

102 Squadron Halifax

From Gunnery Leader, No. 102 Squadron, Pocklington
To: Headquarters No. 4 Group
Date: 26 May 1943
Combat Report – night of 25/26 May 1943
Halifax II W7920 'D' Donald of 102 Squadron
Raid on Düsseldorf, height 15,000 feet, speed 180 IAS, course 315 degree M
Visibility: Clear above 10/10 cloud – no moon
No searchlights, flak or fighter indicators

At 0207 hours Halifax 'D' of 102 Squadron was returning from a raid on Düsseldorf, position 5131N 0532E, two single-engine enemy aircraft were seen by rear gunner on the port quarter up – no lights, range about 600 and 800 yards. One enemy aircraft turned in to attack Halifax and rear gunner instructed pilot to turn and dive to port.

Enemy aircraft opened fire with 4 machine guns and rear gunner replied with 3 bursts at 300 yards approx. Enemy aircraft broke away to starboard, down at 200 yards. Rear gunner was unable to see any strikes and Halifax was undamaged. Enemy aircraft did not return to attack and the second one was also lost by the evasive action taken.

Approximately 400 rounds fired from rear turret. Enemy aircraft identified as Me109s.

On 27/28 May it was time for Harry and his crew to go back to

Essen and run the gauntlet of flak once more; 23 aircraft were lost from the attacking force of 518. Their post-raid report recorded, 'TI flares seen. Remnants of a steady white marker in bomb sight. 1 x 1,000lb hung up and was jettisoned 8 miles NE of target. Glycol leak in port outer. Flak holes near w/ops position.' Ground defences weren't the only opposition encountered that night, Ken Lazenby claiming a Me110 probable. There was little Harry could do in such situations except sit and listen to the gunners reporting the movements of the fighters, and hear the sound of the guns.

> Combats were quite scary. Ken Lazenby would say, 'We have a 110 coming up behind us. I don't think he has seen us. I don't think so. No. No. Sam as soon as I give you the go, do it – diving turn to port. But hold it, steady now, hold it, nice and steady.' Here's me trying to work out the next course and trying to ignore the fact that at any second we were going to be blown out of the sky. Especially as we believed they operated in pairs and maybe Ken hadn't seen the other aircraft. And then all of sudden Ken's 303s were firing. 'Think I've got it. Yes it's gone down, take a note of the time.'

Yet more attrition sapped the morale of the squadron that night, Pilot Officer Jeffrey killed with his entire crew, victims of a nightfighter attack.

On 29/30 May the crew was sent to Wuppertal; another journey to the Ruhr and another flight over heavy defences. And again, not all the danger was of the enemy's making.

> It was a narrow valley, which we had to fly up for maximum effect. Suddenly a 1,000lb bomb took our port rudder and tail plane away. The rear gunner was certainly surprised but you couldn't worry him. And about eight incendiaries dropped in, two of which ignited. We managed to kick them out. We had already had the practice on a previous raid. We had to get back to base by crabbing. I worked out that we were at an angle of about 10/15 degrees, which I just added to the course.

102 Squadron lost one crew this night, seven lives extinguished. Bomber Command lost 33 crews from the attacking force of 719 aircraft.

Harry and his crew were now approaching the mid point of their tour, and they had all by now gained valuable experience. There would be no let up as Harris maintained the intensity of his attacks on the Ruhr. On the night of 12/13 June 102 Squadron detailed 22 aircraft for an attack on Bochum, but Sam Hartley's crew were on leave. One aircraft failed to return, crashing into the sea; eight telegrams informing families that their sons/brothers were missing; indeed they had all died. On 19/20 June the crew were part of a 290-aircraft attack on the Schneider armaments factory and Breuil steelworks at Le Creusot, 'Buildings of works seen, identification assisted by surrounding water. Saw stick of 4 bombs burst right across works.' Unfortunately not all crews had been quite so accurate, the *Bomber Command War Diaries* recording that 'only about one fifth managed to hit the factories. Many bombs fell on nearby residential property'.[12]

It was operation number fourteen for Harry three nights later, to Mulheim, Harry inscribing in his logbook, 'Home on 2 engines, returned early 40 miles inside enemy territory.' Then a return to Wuppertal on 24/25 June, one of 630 aircraft; carrying out a particularly destructive and devastating attack. On his return from the raid Harry recorded in his logbook, 'Good show'. His gunners also recorded another encounter with an enemy nightfighter.

From: No. 102 Squadron, Pocklington
To: Headquarters No. 4 Group
Date: 25 June 1943
Combat report – night of 24 June 1943, Halifax II W7920 'D' No. 102 Squadron
Target – Wuppertal
Position – 5038N 0712E, course 193M, time 0126 hours, height 18,000 feet, Speed 180 IAS

Me110 first sighted at 1,300 yards port quarter down by blister gunner. Enemy aircraft tipped nose towards Halifax and at 1,000 yards opened fire. The blister gunner gave instructions for a diving turn to port, and this evasive action caused the enemy aircraft to go out and disappear on starboard.

The Halifax was not damaged and the rear gunner was unable to bring his guns to bear on the fighter.

Sam Hartley's crew had survived this encounter, avoiding combat. Bomber Command lost 34 aircraft including two 102 Squadron crews that would not return from the raid; twelve airmen dead and two captured. The team work between Harry's pilot and gunners had been crucial in avoiding combat. Experienced enemy nightfighter pilots preferred to creep up on the RAF bombers. Unseen and unopposed they could take up position, fire their weapons and peel away. Why attempt to fight a turning, diving bomber, which was spitting back bullets when there were other unalerted bombers nearby? Many an RAF bomber crew suddenly felt their aircraft shudder as enemy fire tore into it. Some had time to escape, many did not either losing their lives when the aircraft exploded or when trapped amidst the flames, plummeting to the ground.

On their return from the Wuppertal raid Harry's crew managed some sleep before awakening to the news that they were back on operations that night. The station was already alive with the preparations for the raid. Once more Harry spent his day going through the pre-operational motions. Once more he would be going to the Ruhr. Once more 102 Squadron would be entering a night battle.

Chapter 8

Battle

Sam Hartley's crew were detailed for an attack on Gelsenkirchen on the night of 25/26 June 1943; a night on which they and many other crews would again have to fight for survival. Using reports from returning crews, and from details concerning some of the losses, a feel for the air battle that night can be formed from the RAF perspective. At briefing the crews were informed of the flight path, which took the bomber stream across the North Sea to the Dutch coast, then to the north of Amsterdam, continuing east-south-east for just over 100 miles before turning south to Gelsenkirchen. After bombing the navigators were briefed to tell their pilots to turn right and then fly to the north of Amsterdam once more and head out home across the sea. A fairly direct route, almost an in and out with as little time as possible over enemy territory.

In the last hour of 25 June, 473 RAF bombers, crewed by approximately 3,300 airmen took off, climbed over England and set course for the Dutch coast. Shortly after midnight the vanguard of a bomber stream, which would stretch over 100 miles of night sky, began the flight across the North Sea. Soon the enemy coast passed below. The airspace then became hostile and Luftwaffe nightfighters soon found the bomber stream.

0045 to 0100 hours
A twin-engine enemy aircraft closes on a Stirling from port and the pilot throws the bomber into evasive action. The Luftwaffe pilot follows, to the rear, then to starboard. The mid-upper gunner opens fire, which is followed by the rear gunner's, and their enemy breaks away.

A Lancaster pilot throws his aircraft into a corkscrew as two enemy aircraft, with amber lights in their nose, approach. One fires off a one-second burst and the rear gunner replies from 400 yards believing his bullets hit home. The amber light goes out. The nightfighter dives into cloud and a flash is reflected on the cloud; the enemy aircraft is claimed probably destroyed.

Bullets fly into the belly of a Ju88, which had appeared from cloud and approached a bomber. The rear and mid-upper gunner fired at their enemy who turned and exposed his underside.

A Lancaster crew see white flares burst above some cloud and the subsequent silhouetting of other bombers. Then a Me109 moves from port above to starboard quarter and the Lancaster gunners fire. The bomber dives to starboard and loses contact.

The pilot of a 78 Squadron Halifax is killed following a nightfighter attack. The rest of his crew manage to escape the aircraft, and are subsequently captured.

Seven 100 Squadron aircrew are killed when their Lancaster is sent to the ground by a nightfighter.

0101 to 0115 hours
A Ju88 breaks from in front of a bomber and the mid-upper gunner manages to get a short burst away.

The two gunners in an RAF bomber fire upon what they believe is a Me109, which breaks away.

A 106 Squadron Lancaster falls and plummets into the sea off the coast of Holland with a total loss of life.

A twin-engine enemy aircraft fires from 800 yards on a RAF bomber. The rear gunner replies and contact is lost.

A five-man Wellington crew are killed following an attack by a nightfighter.

Seven lives are lost when a 427 Squadron Halifax falls victim to the guns of a German nightfighter.

A Lancaster turns into the attack of a Me109, following the rear gunner's four second burst. Then contact is lost.

0116 to 0130 hours (The front of the bomber stream begins to pass over the target.)
Six members of a 218 Squadron Stirling crew are killed

following a nightfighter attack, the surviving airman becoming a POW.

A Stirling's gunners, as their pilot puts the aircraft into a corkscrew, open up on an enemy aircraft, which dives and then a fire and flash are seen. The nightfighter is claimed as destroyed.

A Lancaster, with the front guns jammed, weaves to lose an enemy aircraft, which had managed to unload five seconds worth of bullets at the bomber.

The entire crew of a 218 Squadron Stirling survive a nightfighter attack, managing to bale out of their doomed aircraft, but all are subsequently captured.

A Stirling is thrown into a corkscrew as a Me110 approaches and opens fire. The rear gunner's machine guns spit their bullets into the enemy aircraft's nose, setting the port engine alight. The Me110 peels away and is lost.

A Lancaster turns into the approach of a Ju88 and the rear gunner manages to get off a short burst before contact is lost.

A Ju88 comes into the range of a Wellington rear gunner, who takes exception and opens up, the tracer streaming below the enemy's wing. The Ju88 turns to attack, fires and misses, then swings to starboard, then down, and then on a parallel course to port, and is finally lost.

A Ju88, with a yellow light in its nose, closes on a Lancaster behind and slightly above. The German nightfighter continues its approach despite the opposition from the rear gunner, and at 300 yards his crewmate in the mid-upper turret also unloads his weapon. Sparks fly off the Ju88, which passes below, still under fire from the rear gunner. The nightfighter bursts into flames and explodes.

On the bombing run a Lancaster is approached by a Ju88; the rear and mid-upper gunner fire and a violent turn to starboard shakes off the unwelcome company.

A twin-engine enemy aircraft, which had opened fire, is lost owing to evasive action.

A FW190 from the starboard quarter down opens fire on a Lancaster and the bomber's gunners respond. The enemy nightfighter breaks off the attack, passes over the starboard wing and makes for cloud cover.

Seven from a crew of eight are killed when their 408

Squadron Halifax falls prey to a nightfighter.

A weaving corkscrew and a rear gunner's fire ward off the unwanted company of a nightfighter.

A rear gunner fires a three second burst as a twin-engine enemy aircraft approaches, which banks and then disappears.

A Ju88 approaches a bomber head-on and then to starboard. The rear and mid-upper machine guns open up and the nightfighter turns away.

0131 to 0145 hours

A FW190, above and to the starboard, follows a bomber for thirty seconds. The rear gunner lets off a three second burst at 300 yards and the enemy aircraft replies at 250 yards closing to 150 yards, and then breaks off in a slipping dive.

A Me109, on the port beam, turns tightly trying to attack a bomber from astern, but comes in on the starboard. The mid-upper gunner fires and the Lancaster dives to starboard. Thirty seconds later a light is seen flickering to starboard of the bomber, which grows to a ball of flame, against which the gunners can see the enemy aircraft's outline. They watch as the flames descend.

300 rounds from a rear gunner and a five second burst from the mid-upper turret sets the engines of a Ju88 alight as it dives away and is lost.

A twin-engine nightfighter appears out of cloud, a rear gunner fires and his enemy breaks away.

Two single-engine enemy aircraft come into the range of a Lancaster's gunners, are fired upon and then disappear.

A Luftwaffe nightfighter pilot is able to claim the shooting down of a four-engine bomber. Only two men survive from the 214 Squadron Stirling, becoming prisoners.

A Lancaster's violent corkscrew and short burst from an alert rear gunner see off a Me110.

0146 to 0210 hours

A rear gunner fires a burst at a FW190 just below and above, which peels away.

Seven aircrew from 51 Squadron are killed when their Halifax is shot from the sky by a nightfighter.

A mid-upper gunner fires at a Me210 and when the Lancaster pilot turns into the attack the enemy aircraft is lost.

A 51 Squadron Halifax plunges to earth and crashes, with the loss of seven lives, following a nightfighter attack.

A Lancaster rear gunner and Me110 open up on each other. The Lancaster dives steeply and the enemy aircraft passes below starboard to port, giving the front gunner the opportunity to let off 40 rounds, and tracer is seen to strike home.

A mid-upper gunner and enemy aircraft exchange bullets to no effect and contact is lost.

Harry Hughes's crew had, so far that night, avoided any contact with the enemy. Although the occasional sight of a burning aircraft kept them aware that the sky was by no means friendly. Then at 0210 hours, to the east of Amsterdam, Ken Lazenby made Sam Hartley, Harry Hughes and the rest of the crew aware that they had unwelcome company.

Combat report – night of 25 June 1943, Halifax II W7920 'D' No. 102 Squadron
Position – 5220N 0540E, course 306M, time 0210 hours, height 16,000 feet, speed 190 IAS

The rear gunner first sighted a number of yellow fighter flares astern of the Halifax and then a Ju88 appeared dead astern and at the same height as the Halifax. As the enemy aircraft came in the gunner told the pilot to stand by for a corkscrew. At 800 yards the rear gunner gave the executive word 'go' and at the same time opened fire with a long burst, which required no deflection allowance. At 600 yards range the starboard engine of the Ju88 caught fire and it went into a fairly steep dive. The Halifax gunner then gave another burst and the enemy aircraft's starboard wing caught fire and the dive became steeper. The Ju88 did not open fire. The whole of the encounter was seen and confirmed by the engineer watching from the astro hatch.

The engineer, blister gunner and rear gunner all saw the enemy aircraft pass into cloud still in flames and shortly after there was seen the reflection on the clouds of what was probably the explosion of the Junkers as it hit the ground.

Visibility good. There was no moon but the Northern Lights were of assistance.

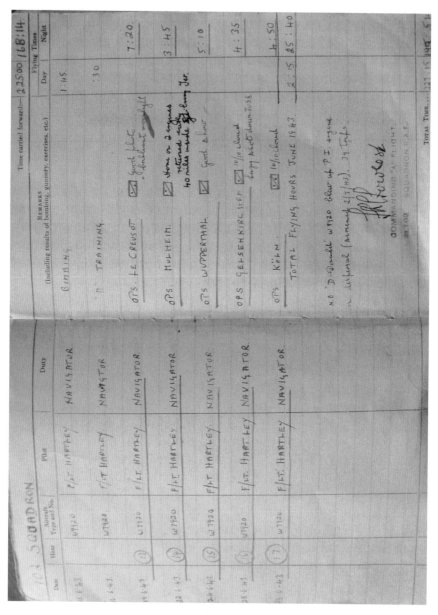

Harry's logbook, second half of June 1943, briefly recording the shooting down of Ju88.

There was of course little time to relax following the encounter. The skies were still dangerous and the air battle continued.

0211 to 0230 hours

Two Ju88s close on a Halifax from head on and below, pulling up their noses and firing. Tracer streams past the bomber. Then four Ju88s dive from the port and starboard beam. The Halifax is thrown into a corkscrew, managing to lose all but one adversary, which follows the bomber out across the sea before contact is finally lost.

A Lancaster dives steeply and the rear gunner fires in a successful attempt to shake off a Me110 and FW190.

A five second burst from a rear gunner appears to see off a twin-engine enemy aircraft.

A rear gunner fires on a Me109 as it flashes by.

A nightfighter attack ends the lives of four members of the five-man crew of a 196 Squadron Wellington.

A Ju88 and two RAF gunners fire at each other without result.

A 9 Squadron Lancaster falls to the ground following a nightfighter attack and there is a total loss of life in the crew of eight.

Seven men's lives are ended following a nightfighter attack on a 15 Squadron Stirling.

A Lancaster pilot's barrel corkscrew, and his gunner's hostility, works to see off a Ju88.

0231 onwards

A Stirling rear gunner replies to tracer appearing from the port quarter. The enemy aircraft moves across to the starboard quarter and is identified as a Ju88. The rear gunner again responds. The enemy aircraft moves to astern below and is then lost as the Stirling corkscrews.

Eight 57 Squadron airmen are killed following a nightfighter attack on their Lancaster.

Seven 102 Squadron airmen are killed when their Halifax is shot from the dark sky by a nightfighter.

A rear gunner replies with a short burst to enemy aircraft fire, which then drops two flares and breaks away.

A Ju88 follows a Lancaster for three minutes before the rear gunner fires. There is no response and a corkscrew ensures a loss of contact.

The crew of a 101 Squadron Lancaster bale out following an encounter between their Lancaster and a nightfighter near the Dutch coast. Six of the crew come down in the sea and lose their lives. One man is blown inland and is subsequently captured.

A Me110 on the port quarter turns to starboard, as does the Lancaster it is stalking. The bomber's gunners open fire. The Me110 banks to starboard from above. The Lancaster gunners keep firing, and bullets tear into the centre of their adversary, the engines and the cockpit. The nightfighter rolls onto its back and is seen to dive in flames.

A Luftwaffe pilot fires his cannon at a bomber, but contact is lost following a violent barrel corkscrew executed by the RAF pilot.

Five from the crew of seven survive the demise of a 103 Squadron Lancaster, and are subsequently captured.

A Lancaster corkscrews to avoid an enemy aircraft. Thirty seconds later the enemy aircraft closes from 200 yards directly behind and fires. The rear gunner responds. Shortly after, a nightfighter attacks head on into the fire from the front turret. Contact is lost.

A 106 Squadron Lancaster smashes into Dutch soil. The pilot, the only survivor from the crew of seven, is captured.

A badly damaged Lancaster is abandoned over Lincolnshire, only five of the seven crew survive.

In the above account the loss of only 20 bombers are detailed – for which crash times are known.[13] The total losses from aircraft detailed for the raid were 33 (which includes one crashing on take-off, and another was written off following an inspection of the damage caused by flak). Harry, Sam, Ken, who was credited with the Ju88, Jackie, Harry Hooper, 'Red', and Tommy, had survived another night battle over Germany; 180 Bomber Command airmen had not (seven from 102 Squadron).

Harry's last operation in the month was an attack on Cologne on the night of 28/29 June. And early in July, the night of the 3rd/4th, Harry Hughes navigated his crew once more to Cologne, the squadron's number depleted once more through five deaths and two men taken to prison camp. The Hartley crew did not take part in the raid to Gelsenkirchen on 9/10 July, 102 Squadron losing four dead, three captured, then on 13 July they were back on ops, Harry's 19th, the crew flying to Aachen. 102 Squadron sent 23 aircraft to the city, one returned early when the compass went u/s and two other aircraft failed to return. Sergeant Amos lost his life with five other members of his crew, one man surviving and captured. Harry Hughes recalled the other loss that night, proof if needed, that experience was no guarantee of survival. 'It was a very big blow when we lost Wing Commander Henry Coventry [DFC]. He was a good CO and instilled a lot of confidence into us.' The squadron diary also recorded the impact of the loss.

> The loss of the Squadron Commander together with his navigator (Flight Lieutenant King) and Gunnery Leader (Flight Lieutenant Hogg) was the heaviest blow the squadron has suffered for some time. All three were deservedly popular and thoroughly conversant with their job. Wing Commander Coventry had only been the CO since the 12 April 1943, having posted supernumerary on the 18 March. In his short time as Squadron Commander he had impressed everyone by his complete devotion to his work, his general personality and invariable courtesy to all. While it is devoutly to be hoped that he has not died for the squadron it is certain that he lived for it.

There were no survivors, the being crew buried in the cemetery at Maubeuge, France.

On the night of 15/16 July 102 Squadron was back on operations, the Sam Hartley crew and 20 others detailed for an attack on Montbéliard. The squadron diary recorded, 'One aircraft scrubbed early u/s. All other aircraft reached the target. PFF [Pathfinder] were thought to be very accurate and the bombing was concentrated. Attack might well prove an outstanding success although a crashed aircraft burning on the ground was bombed by some aircraft in error.' Harry's next three operational navigation tasks were to direct his pilot to Hamburg on the nights of 24/25 and 27/28 July and 2/3 August. Harry had nothing out of the ordinary to recall against the first two operations. Against the third he would.

> We encountered a vicious thunderstorm over Germany, which actually turned us over, with a full bomb load. We were told by Sam to abandon aircraft and the escape hatch was jettisoned. I was sitting with my feet dangling out of the aircraft, with my parachute clipped on, facing aft. I was about to bale out but I had forgotten to take my helmet off. Then Sam suddenly said, 'It's OK. I've got her.' The bomb load had been jettisoned so we turned for home, but the air

was rushing in through the escape hatch and I lost all my
charts. We flew west until we hit one of the Gee co-
ordinates, which we headed down until reaching
Pocklington.

The devastation wreaked by Bomber Command on Hamburg,
which carried out four major raids on the German port, reached
unprecedented levels. 102 Squadron did not come away
unscathed, five aircraft lost on the raids; 36 pilots, navigators,
bomb aimers, gunners, wireless operators and flight engineers
missing. Indeed only four survived, ending up behind barbed
wire. In addition the squadron had also carried out an attack on
Essen in this period which had claimed seven more airmen's lives.

Following the Hamburg raids Bomber Command's Commander-
in-Chief Sir Arthur Harris gave his opinion of the Battle of the
Ruhr: 'Nothing like the whole succession of catastrophes which
overcame the cities of the Ruhr and North West Germany in the
first half of 1943 had ever occurred before, either in Germany or
elsewhere. It was an impressive victory, but I knew that it could
be only the beginning of a serious bomber offensive.' As such he
now prepared his force for the attack on Berlin during the long
nights of 1943/44. Harry Hughes would be involved, but prior to
his first visit to the heart of Germany he enjoyed a welcome
period of three weeks away from operations; time for some rest
and relaxation. But Harry managed to get in some partying prior
to going on leave.

We were doing a samba and I was leading. I took everyone
off onto the balcony and I jumped off. That was alright and
several followed me. I took them up again for another jump
and as I sat on the balcony people were encouraging me to
jump. However a policeman had arrived by that time and
he told me that if I jumped he would run me in. Then
someone gave me a shove from behind. I fell awkwardly on
my toe, breaking a bone in my left foot. We weren't on ops
because there was a moon stand down and then we went
on leave, and by that time Sam was a flight commander so
we didn't have to do every trip. When my foot was nearly
mended I then fell off my bicycle, tore the ligaments and
had to be replastered. The doc who was going on leave the
following day said that he intended to keep me in hospital

until the foot was better. Sam came in and told me there was a maximum that night, that he had to go, and would have to take a spare navigator. 'Come on Sam,' I said, 'No way are you going without me. Let's go and see the doc.' The doc was in a good mood because of his leave. I explained the danger of not going, emphasising that I would end up as a spare and that was a sure way of getting the chop. I'd sooner go with my foot in plaster. Sam was also quite persuasive so the doc said OK providing that I came back into hospital on my return.

I attended the navigation briefing and set off on my crutches to the main briefing. There was Gus Walker. 'Where are you going flight sergeant?' I said, 'I'm going on ops sir.' 'Why?' 'Because my crew's going and I'm not about to let them fly off without me.' So we went to Berlin that night.

The squadron diary, with brevity, recorded Harry and his crew's contribution to the battle over Germany that same night. 'Attacked primary target 17,500 feet heading 350 degrees M, 165 IAS. Clear – good visibility. Markers at target seen. Bomber centre of green TI. Big glow seen when leaving.'

When we got back to base Gus Walker did his debriefing and he said to me, 'I've been hearing all about you young Hughes. I'm going to take you back to the hospital.' In the car he tore me off a strip. Then as I got out of the car he said, 'Bloody good show anyway Hughes.'

I got to bed about 5.30 am, and was just going off to sleep, when a WAAF came and put a thermometer in my mouth. Then the doc came round at about 10 am. He said, 'Flight sergeant I've got you down as an up patient. So will you kindly get yourself out of the bed and get dressed?' He added, 'Where were you when I was on my rounds last night anyway.' I said, 'Possibly I was over Berlin.' He responded, 'Get up and get out of my hospital.'

The raid to Berlin on 23 August was Harry's 24th, his crew's only operation in a month in which the squadron lost 62 airmen, 43 of them killed. One other, particularly harrowing incident occurred that month, which remains fixed in Harry's memory. On the night of 27/28 August the squadron sent 17 Halifaxes to Nuremberg, part of a force of 674 aircraft. Thirty-three of these would not be returning, one manned by a 102 Squadron crew. In addition there was a casualty on board one Halifax that did make it back to England.[14]

> The navigator on this particular Halifax, Jackie, was a personal friend of mine. We were on A Flight dispersal and they were just across from us. All the crew were all good friends, particularly the pilot, and we often went out drinking together. I would always go over and compare my charts with Jackie, see what winds we got. On this occasion the rest of the crew climbed out but he didn't. I asked them where he was and they all just looked very glum. I went rushing up to the aircraft, climbed in and found Jackie lying in a pool of blood. It was the first time I had seen somebody killed; it affected me for a short while but we got on with it.

An attack on Munich on 6 September and to Hanover on 22 September brought Harry to the conclusion of his first tour with Bomber Command. 102 Squadron's losses in the month came to two aircraft missing from which ten men died and four became POWs. In addition another aircraft crashed on return to the UK, the crew suffering injury, one man later losing his life.

Thus ended Harry Hughes's time at 102 Squadron. He had flown with a squadron that fought Harris's Battle of the Ruhr and suffered accordingly. Loss rates had been high but Sam Hartley's crew had worked together, focused on their job, fought the battle and survived. Harry was now to take up instructing duties, posted to a Stirling conversion unit, and was separated from his crew.

> It's funny how they wanted to disperse the crews as much as they could. We were all posted to different stations. I suppose it was a question of discipline and they felt that if there were two or more of us together we might be a disruptive influence. We were still quite young.

On 28 September Harry arrived at 1666 Heavy Conversion Unit and then early in April he was transferred to 1653 HCU. But training was not for Harry, he was getting impatient and wanted to get back to an operational squadron.

> I got friendly with an Australian pilot and we decided that rather than wait to go back on operations we would apply

to go back to ops on Mosquitoes.

We both wrote a letter to the group captain, were called in front of him the next day and told that they were still short of instructors, so we wouldn't be going back. We waited another couple of weeks, wrote another letter and got turned down again. That night we had a few beers and piled the furniture up in the centre of the mess. I got hold of a tin of black paint and wrote a letter to the group captain on the ceiling, as one does, and signed it with mine and my Australian friend's names. The following day we were up in front of the group captain and he said, 'Right you are both going back on operations, but no way are you going to go back on the same crew or even the same squadron.'

Harry would, however, have a chance to converse with his Australian friend at a later date.

He went back on Canadian-built Mossies, which operated at about 25,000 feet, whereas we operated at 27,000 feet. One night, I knew he was on his first trip, and as we were crossing the Dutch coast, suddenly over the VHF comes, 'Who dat up dere saying who dat, when I saying who dat down here?' So I said, 'Who dat down dere saying who dat?' 'Who dat up dere saying who dat when I saying dat down here?' Everybody was shouting, 'Who dat down dere saying who dat?' It must have been heard back in the UK but nobody said anything.

Harry began gaining experience on 1655 Mosquito Conversion Unit on 26 July 1944, and a month later he was transferred to 692 Squadron, part of 8 Group's Light Night Striking Force.

As we have encountered earlier, Don Bennett had been developing the idea of using Mosquitoes in a somewhat independent role for some time. In June 1943 Bennett acquired 139 Squadron, to go with 105 and 109 Squadron and throughout the remainder of the war the 8 Group Mosquito force would continue to grow, ultimately comprising nine squadrons. In his post-war memoir Bennett recalled the expansion and role of this force, following the addition of 139 Squadron.

This I used as a 'supporting squadron' to go in with the early markers, and also to carry out diversion raids to attract fighters from the main stream at appropriate moments during the attack. This tactic proved very successful, and often diverted the fighters away from the main target to a likely one within visual distance of it just before the main raid started. Thus the fighters might be fifty or eighty miles away before they suddenly realised their mistake. I also used this squadron for nuisance raiding – an idea entirely of my own, which I quietly insinuated into the operations of the Group, without its being particularly noticed for some time. When the C-in-C did notice it, he thoroughly approved of it and the idea grew.

Mosquito bombers were being produced in goodly numbers. They were coming out of the factories faster than had been anticipated, largely due to the nature of their wooden construction. Moreover the losses were relatively small – in fact almost negligible. I therefore adopted a policy of an expansion of Mosquitoes which had far reaching results.

Part of the expansion was the formation of 692 (Fellowship of the Bellows[15]) Squadron on the first day of 1944, which took up duties within the Light Night Striking Force flying from Graveley. The squadron went on to carry out the first operation on which a 4,000lb bomb was dropped by a Mosquito; over Düsseldorf on 23/24 February 1944.

Harry Hughes arrived at 692 Squadron on 23 August 1944, with his new pilot, Roy Montrowe[16], who had completed a tour on Wellingtons in the Middle East. 'He was a typical dour New Zealander but a lovely guy and we got on fine.' Harry was also enjoying his time flying in the 'Wooden Wonder', 'The Mosquito was great, now I was sitting up with the pilot.' But if Harry needed any reminding of the dangers of operational life it came on the day of his arrival at Graveley. Tragedy struck when Warrant Officer Collinson's Mosquito crashed shortly after taking off for operations. Collinson and his navigator, Sergeant Youens, were killed. Two days later the squadron lost Squadron Leader Bird and his navigator, their Mosquito crashing on return from operations. The squadron diary recorded: 'This was the second crew of this squadron to be killed within three days and the sad loss of these crews is most distressing.' In addition another Mosquito had crash-landed at Woodbridge that night, the crew uninjured but the aircraft a write off. Squadron Leader

Joe Northrop maintained a diary briefly describing the events at the squadron. On 25 August he noted meeting Collinson's relations and Sergeant Youens's brother to make funeral arrangements. He finished off the day's entry com-menting briefly on the losses on operations, 'Pretty rough night for 692'.

On the night of 26/27 August Harry and Roy flew their first operation with 692 Squadron, a 3 hour 50 minute flight to Kiel and back. Their task was to drop Window across the target prior to the opening of the main attack, and then orbit and drop their 4,000lb cookie. The next night they carried out a 3 hour 40 minute flight to Mannheim, a 'straight bombing trip'. The operation had not started well, Northrop's diary recorded, 'Last aircraft off, "Y", swung bodily and crashed and caught fire on aerodrome. Cookie went up but crew got away OK. What a horrible mess!!! Diverted other aircraft on return to Wyton. One missing, "P", F/O Warner. Several of the boys saw him go down over target [Warner lost his life with his navigator surviving to become a POW].' Roy and Harry closed out the month with a 3 hour 45 minute operation to Frankfurt.

Harry and Roy were operational on eight nights through September 1944. 'Mainly we operated by ourselves although on occasions we did Window opening for the heavies, going in about 30 seconds before the first Pathfinders, to give them some cover. Having done that we would go on to another target and drop our four thousand pounder.' Northrop's diary provides a post-raid summary of these specific operations.

1 September – Bremen. Straightforward.
5 September – Hanover. Operation a flop due to 10/10 cloud.
7 September – Karlsruhe. Freezing level fairly low tonight. Loads of trouble. 'N' F/O McKinnon did not get off – no brakes. Wadsworth crashed after take-off on one engine – wizard show, with cookie on. 'C' Huggett and 'O' Plum landed Manston on way home on one engine. Get to bed about half past five in the end.
8 September – Nuremberg. All cope very successfully. 'R' and 'K' landed at Manston on way back short of fuel.
23 September – Bochum. Successful.
26 September – Frankfurt. Perfect raid in half moon.
28 September – Brunswick. AOC and several guests came

to briefing and take-off. All goes well and see chaps back
by 2300 hours. Successful raid.
30 September – Hamburg. All get off OK but 'J' F/L
Huggett leaves VHF on all way round. 'H' F/O McKenzie
crashes at Warboys at 2028 and turns over. Crew not badly
injured.

During October Harry was operational on seven occasions. The
raid to Berlin on 5 October remains firmly lodged in his memory.
Northrop recorded that the 692 Squadron crew did, 'an excellent
job according to reports. 692's prestige should go up after this.'
Roy and Harry were one of the six crews that were, as the
squadron diary described, 'put on to the mail run'. Harry
recalled:

> Butch Harris came to the station on one occasion, and he
> came for our briefing. He was standing beside the squadron
> CO, Joe Northrop, as Joe was reading out the battle order.
> The spare aircraft was S-Sugar and it was a bloody awful
> aircraft. On occasions we took it, and on the way back it
> would barely get into Woodbridge [near the Suffolk coast
> and available for emergency landings]. Fuel consumption
> was terrible. As it was we were briefed for Berlin this night
> and when reading the battle order, Joe said, 'Flight
> Lieutenant Montrowe S-Sugar.' 'S-Sugar!' exclaimed Roy.
> 'What's wrong with R-Robert?' 'Sorry Roy, R-Robert's got
> a mag drop [problem with the magneto], so you'll have to
> take the spare.' Roy's response, 'S-********-Sugar sir, that
> bloody kite flies like a brick shit house.' Harris was
> standing there and his moustache was twitching, trying his
> best not to laugh. We took S-Sugar and we landed at
> Woodbridge.

One other raid of note in October was the 28 October attack on
Cologne; 733 aircraft, from which only seven were lost,
attacking the city in two separate waves. Northrop recorded in
his diary, 'Twelve aircraft on tonight after a "heavies" raid on
Cologne'. The 692 Squadron diary recorded:

> A very successful raid. Weather was clear and the target
> was already burning from the afternoon raid by heavies.
> Markers were successfully dropped on time and the
> squadron released all their bombs in four minutes. Several

crews obtained a visual of the city as the river showed up well. They bombed with the usual 4,000 pounders between 2031 and 2035 from 25,000 feet. Flak was seen slight, but accurate. On the way out several crews saw jet aircraft.

In addition, that night Northrop penned in his diary, 'Best trip for the squadron in a long time as fires still burning.' The sighting of the jet aircraft is of note, something Harry would see three days later on a return visit to Cologne, along with another type of aerial weapon. The squadron only sent two aircraft on the raid, the diary recorded:

A Windowing raid for the heavies. Window was successfully released and both crews bombed the markers at 1919½ [Roy and Harry] and 1921 hours respectively. Cloud was 10/10ths over the area and no bombing results were seen. A jet aircraft [Me262] was seen by both crews, and also a rocket bomb [V2] which appeared to come from the Rotterdam area.

This was not the first time Harry had seen the V2 rocket or the Me262.

We used to have a codeword if we saw any jet fighters – Snappers – to warn everybody else to look out for them. In September 1944 we saw the first V2s being launched. We were somewhere over the Scheldt estuary, near an island called Overflakee, which amused me. We suddenly saw what we first thought were jet fighters but they went soaring above us. Everybody was calling, 'Snappers', thinking they were jets. When we got back we were told not to talk about it.

Harry began November with a raid to Osnabrück on 2/3 November, his 45th operation. By the end of the month that tally had risen to 53. On 27 November Northrop described the operation to Berlin as the worst night they'd had for ages. From the twelve aircraft sent on the raid only eight bombed. Four aircraft suffered various problems including Roy and Harry's 'R', which bombed Osnabrück instead owing to problems with oxygen and fuel. On 29 November Harry went to Hanover, Northrop describing it as, 'All goes well and all return but Chandler has engine pack up on approach and prangs safely on aerodrome. Another daylight on in the morning – wonder when it will all end?' Both men escaped unscathed.

There was no let-up in December with nine operations, two of which were flown in daylight hours; such was the perceived diminishing threat of the Luftwaffe. On 11 December Roy and Harry flew two operations. Taking off at 0900 hours they went to Duisburg with the squadron diary recording, 'Another daylight attack in two waves, 45 minutes apart. The two flights flew in formation each led by a marker bombing visually with 4,000 pounders as his was released. No results were seen weather being 10/10ths.' On return, landing at one minute past midday, they then prepared for an evening attack on Hanover, taking off at 1658 hours, the diary noting that is was, 'not a very successful effort only one marker was seen'.

Harry finished the year with a raid to Berlin, his tally now standing at 62 operations. Opposition to the Mosquito incursions was certainly nothing compared to the opposition that Harry's previous squadron had endured in the dark nights of 1943; although the dangers of operational flying were still present. On 17 December Flight Lieutenant Brunt and his navigator Flight Sergeant Sutherland lost their lives when their Mosquito overshot the runway on return from an operation, smashing into trees and bursting into flames. Harry also recalls another of the possible dangers facing operational crews, following one flight to Berlin. 'On our return a lot of the main force heavies had been diverted to Graveley, where we had FIDO'; a fog dispersal system, whereby pipes running along either side of a runway would spray jets of burning petrol to dispel the mists.

> There was a Lancaster landing in front of us and the pilot completely misjudged the height, coming in on the top of the flames rather that the ground. It was a terrific heavy landing. Unfortunately he had a 2,000 lb hang-up, and when they hit the ground it came straight through the bomb doors. When we landed there was this bomb spinning in the runway. So Roy said to control, 'There's a ******* bomb right in the middle of the runway.' There was a deafly hush from the WAAF operators. Then presently Popeye, the control officer, came on and said, 'R-Robert message understood. Ladies present.' Roy said, 'I do apologise. It's quite an ordinary bomb, but it's ******* dangerous.'

Roy and Harry carried out seven more raids in January 1945; unfortunately missing out on a squadron attack on rail tunnels, in support of the Ardennes ground battle. It appeared that the European war was nearing a conclusion but nobody could be sure when. So operations continued and losses rose. One crew and two lives were lost on the attack on rail tunnels on 1 January and two aircraft and four lives were lost on the night of 14/15 January following a raid to Berlin. Flying Officer Morgan had been unable to land on return and informed the station that he was going to bale out. His Mosquito came to ground four miles north of Newbury. The next day the squadron diary recorded the news that Morgan had been killed. He had struck the aircraft's fin and failed to open his parachute[17]. His navigator's parachute harness was found, but not the navigator. Then on 17 January the squadron diary recorded, 'News was received late in the day that the body of Sergeant Sturrock [Morgan's navigator] had been found some 3-4 miles away from his harness. The death of both members of the crew in such tragic circumstances is deeply regretted.'

There followed a further seven raids in February, for Harry Hughes, which brought his operational tally to 76 operations; his last operation on the night of 14/15 February 1945, a 3 hour 30 minute flight to Frankfurt and back. Harry's time fighting the war was over. He had already received the DFM, and his accomplishments were to be further recognised with the award of a DFC. However, Harry carried out one further flight of note prior to the end of hostilities in Europe, on 19 March 1945.

> I was sitting in a beautiful leather chair, given to us by the Argentinians, in the flight office, minding my own business when in came the station CO and asked me if I was doing anything. I said no and he then told me I would be flying with him, and to bring some Gee charts. I went out and found them loading up a four thousand pounder on the aircraft we were to fly. I asked the groundcrew how much fuel we had got, 'Full tanks and full drop tanks'. On that particular day there was a gale blowing down the 1,400-yard runway. Grant said, 'We are going to see if we can get off the short runway in this wind.'
>
> We taxied to the start of the runway and revved her up to pretty much maximum, waited until the wind was right and let her go. We got airborne and went and dropped the

cookie on the live bomb target in the Wash. We landed safely and he reported that it wasn't possible to take off using the short runway. I said, 'Thanks very much!' He responded that a lot of pilots would not have waited until the wind was strong enough.

Harry remained with the squadron waiting for a posting, 'they didn't know what to do with us' until 9 May, the day following the end of the war in Europe. The squadron diary noted on 8 May, 'Squadron was stood down. <u>VE Day</u>. Most of the air crew personnel took advantage of the special 48-hour pass and departed to celebrate victory in their diverse ways'. Harry, of course, joined in. 'We went into Cambridge and drank too much. I remember there was a bowl of tulips. I ate them all. I was hungry.'

After the war Harry was given a four-year extended service commission and initially received a posting to ferry Mosquitoes across the Atlantic, 'but when we got there they didn't want us'. He was sent on indefinite leave following which he began ferrying aircraft out to the Far East; Mosquitoes, Beaufighters and Dakotas (which he had the chance to pilot) to Burma. He was then transferred to Transport Command, took a categorisation exam, and did well enough to take on responsibilities with VIP flights. Following two and a half years in the Far East Harry returned to the UK, left the RAF and took a job in the City, selling ships; including the sale of the Royal Mail ship *Highland Princess*, on which he had sailed to Canada in 1941.

Sixty-two years since the end of the European war, Harry reflects on his time in service.

It is a very mixed feeling. I was proud to have been a part of Bomber Command, there was a sense of achievement. But there was always a feeling of guilt in the background, that you tried your best to suppress, that you killed a lot of people. The German propaganda and the anti-bombing people in the UK kept us aware of that.

I think people nowadays want to know more about the bomber offensive. I am asked many more questions than immediately after the war, when people seemed envious, bordering on jealousy, over the fact that you had a couple of gongs; although others did respect you. However there were a lot of people in Bomber Command who got no decoration whatsoever. I would certainly like to see recognition of the groundcrews. They would always be there waiting for you to come home, no matter what time of night it was. The first thing they would do is take a torch and ask, 'God what have you done to our aircraft?'

We had heard Churchill in his 1941 speeches saying that the only way of attacking Germany was to bomb them. He was quite definite about it and then after the war he completely deserted us. We didn't get a mention on VE day. Here we were, at times the only ones taking the war to Germany. We suffered all those very heavy losses and we didn't even get a campaign medal.

There was no alternative to the bomber offensive. We felt at the time that we were saving our own people's lives, and the lives of those in concentration camps, by shortening the war. I think a lot of us possibly needed counselling after the war; today we would be, for the very fact that we had killed so many people. I was on the Hamburg raids, which were horrendous. I do still ask myself today what, if I get to the Gates of Heaven, Saint Peter is going to say to me.

Squadron Leader Tony Iveson DFC

Chapter 9

Fighter Boy to Bomber Boy

Irene Leigh served as a driver with the Women's Auxiliary Air Force during the war, with both Fighter Command and Bomber Command.

Bomber Command was better. It was more interesting. Spitfires were not interesting, but Lancasters were. Even now if I see one I have tears rolling down my cheeks. But it was sadder, sitting up in flight control waiting for your boys to come back. It wasn't until a day later that you might hear he'd landed somewhere else, or not come back. I never had a boyfriend, it wasn't worth it, you'd never know if they'd come back.

With all his training complete, Tony Iveson prepared to join a front line squadron. He had already fought the enemy from the seat of a fighter aircraft, in the defence of his country, now he was to captain the crew of a Royal Air Force heavy bomber, taking the fight directly to the opposition. It had been recognised that he had great potential as a bomber pilot; so much so that Tony had been asked to take up operational duties with the most famous unit in Bomber Command – 617 Squadron. As he recalled when asked if he would like to volunteer, 'I was speechless... it was the greatest.'

Tony Iveson was born in 1919, the son of a First World War veteran who served with the 2nd Battalion Royal Fusiliers and bore a 'terrible battle scar on his chest'.

> My father was wounded on the first day of the Somme [1 July 1916], at Beaumont Hamel. He climbed out of a trench and within about ten yards he was hit. He lay there all day; fortunately he was strong enough to survive, someone found him and he was recovered. He was wounded again later in the war, at Ypres.

Tony's father became a policeman after the war and raised his family in York, a city which Tony had great admiration for and where he felt very lucky to grow up. Tony was one of four boys, and he, along with two of his brothers, would serve in the forces in the coming war; the younger brother being below age for service. 'One of my brothers was in the Yorkshire Hussars and another joined the merchant navy as a radio officer. I think he had the worst war of all of us, involved in the Atlantic convoys, Malta convoys and the invasion of North Africa.'

Tony had finished his schooling at Archbishop Holgate's grammar school in 1936 and was articled to train as an architect. Other interests also took his fancy.

> I always wanted to fly from being about ten years old. I had my first experience as many others did, with one of Alan Cobham's flying circus visits. Then I tried to persuade my

father to let me take a short service commission in the RAF but he was against it. His generation was more concerned with security and he felt that I would fly for four years and then what; all I could do was handle an aeroplane. In those days there weren't any commercial prospects. He was adamant that it was no job at all.

There were one or two horrific films about in the thirties concerning the war and I had heard the stories. Not that my father talked a lot but my uncle was also in the army and sometimes when a few of the friends got together I would listen in. One knew a lot about trench warfare.

When it became obvious that another war was pretty near and conscriptions were going to be introduced I persuaded my father to let me apply for the RAF Volunteer Reserve. I joined in 1938, flew for about a year before the war at No 4 E&RFTS at Brough near Hull in Yorkshire.

Here were a whole bunch of people like myself who wanted to fly. We flew an aeroplane called the B2; a Blackburn-built biplane rather like a Tiger Moth but you sat side by side in the B2. After about 50/60 hours on that I graduated to a beautiful aeroplane called the Hawker Hind. Again a biplane with a 330 horse power engine and one really felt one was flying. Then the war broke out at which point I had about 70 hours in my logbook.

Tony heard Neville Chamberlain's famous broadcast confirming the nation was at war in the Station Hotel, Hull.

It was no surprise. Afterwards we all went to some pub and had a very splendid lunchtime session, because they really didn't know what to do with us. We spent a couple of days lying around in barracks and then they sent us home, saying give us a ring every day. Then it became give us a ring every week. Then it became don't call us we will call you. I actually went back to work having gone through a tearful farewell with my family when I first left. It was six weeks before we were called up and I went down to Bexhill to an initial training wing.

The thing we did most was to play rugby, about five times a week. We were also marched around on the seafront, had lectures and had our jabs. That went on until early December.

At this stage I really knew nothing much about the German air force at all except what we had seen on the newsreels concerning the attacks on Poland. We did know that they had been operating in Spain, and we were under the impression that the Luftwaffe was a pretty formidable force.

From Bexhill Tony was posted to No 5 Flying Training School, Sealand, near Chester, training on the Miles Master 'a lovely low winged monoplane, a step towards responsibility as a fighter pilot.'

Sealand was just a grass field at the time and the winter was pretty grim. Our flying was spasmodic and around Easter time we were shipped across to Speke near Liverpool; Sealand was practically unusable, these were the days before runways. But then I got appendicitis and went south to Halton for the operation, where they whipped it out. This slowed my training down, but the rest of my course went on. They sent me to Montrose to another FTS (No 8), where I started my advanced course again. So I went into an operational squadron about two months after my mates and I think that is the reason why I am here today because of the 14 of us on the course on Masters at Sealand only about four of us survived the Battle of Britain. Had I gone through with them it's more than likely that I would not have survived, I wasn't a brilliant fighter pilot by any means.

From Montrose Tony went to an operational training unit (No 7) at Hawarden, near Chester, where he began to get to grips with the aircraft he would be going to war in. 'They had a Spitfire on a trestle in a hangar and we were told to get in it and memorise all the instruments and controls. Then along came an instructor and I was blind folded and asked where the flap lever was, mixture control, pressure gauge and so on.' Tony would come to appreciate the Spitfire as a beautiful aeroplane, and lovely to fly. But the first tentative attempt to get the fighter airborne proved a challenge for this and many other new pilots.

The first flight was always tricky and everyone on the airfield knew when someone was flying a first solo. They all came out to watch. There was a great deal of torque and

OTU Spitfire

if you didn't watch it the aeroplane very much wanted to wander off to the right. So you had to apply full rudder. There were no dual Spitfires of course, so your first flight in a Spitfire was the first one and alone.

Came the day when I was told, 'There it is, fly it.' I trundled the aircraft to the downwind end of the grass field at Hawarden, then a couple of swallows – the moment had come. I carried out the take-off checks and then turned into the wind, opened the throttle and it felt like I had suddenly been hit in the small of the back. The tail came up and it started to swing. I thought I had corrected it, then bounce, bounce, bounce and I was in the air.

The first one I flew didn't have a constant speed propeller; there were two speeds, coarse and fine. I took off in full fine pitch and when off the ground pushed it into coarse pitch; it almost felt as if it had stopped as it changed pitch. I then changed hands; taking my left hand off the throttle having screwed it up, then left hand on the stick, and with the right hand, selected undercarriage up and then pumped it up. You can image with the right hand pumping the left hand wanted to pump as well so the aeroplane, as often happened, was doing a series of curves!

Once settled down at about 1,500 feet I looked back and the airfield wasn't where I thought it should be, having not taken into account the swing. I had been told to fly for about twenty minutes and then the moment came when I thought, 'God I've got to get this thing back on the ground.' So it was down wind, then turn across wind and then motor it in, bounce a couple of times and then a great sigh of relief that I had done it. I then taxied back and the flight sergeant thanked god that the aircraft was still in one piece.

Whilst at the OTU Tony met a friend of his from his days at Brough, and began to see what the rigours of warfare could do to a man. Lionel Pilkington had served with 73 Squadron during the Battle of France. He had been in the thick of the air battle making a number of claims, but also having force-landed twice, been hit a number of times, and received burns to his face. On the return to the UK he had been posted to Hawarden as an instructor. Tony recalled that when he first met him, 'he was a changed man, he really was. One sensed that he had had a pretty bad time and was still getting over it.' Pilkington would go back on operations in 1941, losing his life on 20 September.[18]

On completion of his training, with a mere ten hours of flying Spitfires in his logbook, Sergeant Tony Iveson received news of a posting from No 7 OTU to 616 'South Yorkshire' Squadron, Auxiliary Air Force, at Leconfield. After Tony arrived there the squadron moved to Kenley in 11 Group, where the Battle of Britain was at its most intense; 616 Squadron was thrown into battle immediately and losses began. 'I finally got my way down to Kenley at the beginning of September 1940, but they had moved from there to Coltishall. They were only in the front line for a short while; they had such terrible casualties and were pulled out very quickly. They were a chastened lot.' Tony caught up with the squadron at Coltishall and a few days later, 9 September, the whole squadron once more moved to Kirton-in-Lindsey. Tony recalls his experience flying in the Battle of Britain.

> The squadron did not have any time to train us. I had not fired my guns at any kind of targets, carried out no formation flying; the squadron CO had little time for sergeants. The need was there of course for pilots but we were chucked in really with very little experience.
>
> One lived in a very strange state of mind because people went off and never came back. One sat in dispersal all dressed up, with the aeroplanes just a few yards away, with your parachute actually in the seat. You would be listening for a certain telephone, which always seemed to have a different ring and resulted in the corporal yelling 'scramble' and you belted to your aircraft. Looking back it was a strange experience living with that at such an early age, and day to day.
>
> I had a fair amount of respect towards the enemy pilots. I didn't have any strong attitude, most of us felt that if you

got a bead on an enemy aircraft it was a machine not a man. You didn't really think about the people in it. One saw a few parachutes of course. I don't think I had any particular hatred for them.

I don't think I ever doubted that we would win the war. I think when it got into October/November, when the Luftwaffe turned their attention more to night bombing, I think we realised we had staved it off. When they attacked Russia in June 1941 we heaved a sigh of relief because had they not done that and really concentrated on trying to invade Britain in 1941 then it might have been a different story.

Over the course of the first six days that Tony spent with 616 Squadron, nothing of note occurred; a much needed time to recover following the attrition of August 1940. On the morning of 16 September squadron pilots would once more be in action. Blue Section, which included Tony Iveson, scrambled at 0922 hours that morning.

Three of us took off for a convoy patrol off the coast. We were cruising round and suddenly there was a lot of flak around us. We discovered that there was a Junkers 88 fairly high above us, which the navy had decided to shoot at despite the fact we were there. Anyway we went off after it; this was my first brush with the enemy and I was still fairly new on the Spitfire. By then I only had about 15 hours. As it was I got left behind by my more experienced flight commander and number 2. When I finally caught up with the Ju88 he was trailing smoke. Now I had been told to get in fairly close, and as I did so the gunner opened fire and hit my machine. We then broke off and I lost him. I don't know where he went I just couldn't find him, and there I was alone way out over the North Sea. I thought the best thing to do was to head back for the UK and after a while I became conscious of the fact that the engine wasn't running properly, the temperature seemed to be creeping up and the pressure was going down. The upshot was that basically I had run out of time and sky.

I was lucky that I could prepare for hitting the sea. I opened the hood, put the door down, took off my parachute harness, and took off my flying helmet and leads.

I was only linked to the aeroplane with my Sutton harness. I had been told that if you had to you should try to land along rather than into the waves, and not to put the wheels down obviously because you would just turn over. I put down a little flap, about fifteen per cent. I was lucky – I got down and the sea wasn't very rough. It bounced once; I had forgotten there were two bounces. I didn't know, I don't think anybody knew then. I bashed my face on the windscreen surround and was covered in blood. Then I stepped out onto the wing and the aeroplane disappeared beneath me.

I think I was one of the rare few to have got away with ditching a Spitfire. Fortunately I finished up near a convoy. After about 40 minutes in the water a minesweeper sent out a boat to pick me up.

Tony had to rely on his Mae West to keep him afloat.

It was a bit cold, I had lost a flying boot and I was beginning to feel I was getting soggy. I could see the minesweeper when I was on top of a wave and similarly they could see me. I really was lucky that they got to me. When I got aboard I felt even better because they stuffed me full of rum!

The following day a boat was sent out from Lowestoft to pick Tony up, and on his no doubt welcome return to dry land he was driven to Coltishall.

I was still in my uniform which they had dried and it was very stiff. I had no flying gear at all because that had gone down with the aeroplane. At Coltishall they said, 'We've got a Spitfire here to be delivered back to your squadron at Kirton-in-Lindsey. You had better take it.' I got into the aircraft, with no parachute, they had put a sort of cushion underneath me, no helmet and with a bandage on my face. I flew to Kirton-in-Lindsey and I don't think anybody thought there was anything strange about it. In fact they sent me on leave for nine days.

On 11 October Tony was posted south to 92 Squadron, at Biggin Hill, part of 11 Group, to replace losses they had suffered. Yet as the month progressed Tony recalled, 'things were beginning to slow down and apart from fairly routine patrols and interceptions, I didn't see anything very exciting.' Early in 1941 Tony was posted away from the squadron. He's still unclear exactly why.

> I suppose the movements of the Air Ministry as far as postings were concerned were very mysterious. You just suddenly found you were posted. I was sent to a central flying school along with two or three others. Perhaps they thought I wasn't a very good fighter pilot. I am pretty sure I wasn't. They just did not give you enough training, although I have always contended that fighter pilots are not made. I really learnt to fly while I was a flying instructor. I was much more at home later on, with the bigger aircraft.
>
> To be a fighter pilot the qualities you need are quick reactions, split-ass flying. You don't fly by the book with fighters. A good fighter pilot doesn't care what position he is in, and he has no regard for the aeroplane. I say this with admiration because that's how it had to be. You had to be a natural and be comfortable in any flying position; haul your aircraft around with violent manoeuvres. You also, of course, needed to be a good shot and I think the real top fighter pilots had a very aggressive spirit; people like Johnnie Johnson and Douglas Bader. Fighter pilots are born. There was an incredible Canadian called Screwball Beurling, who flew in Malta. He was totally disinterested in discipline and authority, but as a fighter pilot he was an absolute natural. He could still knock the enemy off, even if he was upside down or on top of a loop; he was a splendid shot. Top class fighter pilots are a breed apart really.

Tony graduated as a flying instructor in the spring of 1941, his assessor stating that he 'should make a useful flying instructor with experience'. This he would prove eventually passing on his knowledge to a total of 251 students, flying for 1,501½ hours. Following a short period at an EFTS at Meir instructing on Magisters, he was posted to Rhodesia, to take up duties training aircrew as part of the Empire Air Training Scheme, 'where we could carry out the training in good conditions without interference from the enemy.' The journey by sea took six weeks, in convoy with HMS *Repulse*, 'it was a comfort to see that zooming around', via Canada, then Freetown and on to Durban, 'where a lady in white was standing at the end of the quay singing and welcoming us.' Tony was to spend almost two years training airmen from August 1941 to June 1943: firstly on Tiger Moths, at Induna just north of Bulawayo; then Harvards, at Thornhill, near Gwelo; and finally on Oxfords (near Salisbury). Tony described the conditions for training as 'absolutely perfect'.

> At elementary training we used to start at five or five-thirty in the morning, winter or summer. We would be flying with the new pupils in smooth conditions for about the next four hours. Then the second lot would come along because by that time convection made it a bit bumpy. But you could rely on almost 30 flying days out of 31. The situation for anybody was just wonderful; we had everything on the station, swimming pools, tennis courts, squash courts; we played rugby and cricket. The local people were incredibly hospitable. We were altogether apart from the war outside. It was a great life. What impressed me, and I was a 21-year-old flying instructor with the responsibility of sending people solo, was that the RAF system had developed to the point where you could take an 18 year old who had probably never seen an aeroplane close-up, and within five weeks you could not only have him flying solo by day but solo by night.
>
> I had some splendid farmer friends nearby with whom I spent time and through them I met a lot of other people including the then Prime Minister Godfrey Huggins who came one day for tea, being an old friend of the family. One could say from my experience that ninety-five per cent plus were fully supportive of our being there and did everything they could to help the many thousands of aircrew who passed through Rhodesia.

In Rhodesia, the instructors and their trainees were far from the fighting, but not from danger. Whilst there Tony would witness death although fortunately not on the scale of some other training establishments.

> We sadly lost one instructor during my stay in Rhodesia. On a cross country whilst doing some low flying he hit a cable, which stretched across a valley. Otherwise I think we had a very successful and accident free period.

And of course, as expected when a group of young men were together, there were lighter moments.

> There was one amusing incident one night when the mess caught fire. We lived in huts around the mess and I was woken by lots of noise and a glow. I rushed out and there was everyone hurrying about. The mess was engulfed in flames but the piano had been rescued and someone was playing it, pretending to be Nero, on the lawn outside. Some other brave soul went in and brought out our bar books, then somebody else with more sense said, 'don't be bloody silly chuck them back in the fire!'

Despite enjoying his time in Rhodesia, Tony was still hopeful of a return to action. 'All the time I think one was trying, hoping, one could come back to operations some time, but it was a very good life for a young man, it was very healthy with lots of sport.' In the middle of 1943 Tony's hopes would be realised, although he did not follow the usual procedure for a return to operations.

> I had a taxiing accident on the very morning when I had signed a form, following on from a letter from Command, along with all the other instructors, saying that taxiing accidents were to cease; they were unnecessary, a result of carelessness and there were far too many of them. We signed to say that we had read and understood the order. Anyway I went out and whilst running my Tiger Moth from a landing onto the apron I touched the wing of another Tiger Moth; we had no brakes. I was immediately put under close arrest by my CO who was furious that within an hour or so of him getting the order stating that such accidents should cease, and my signing it, his station had promptly committed the first taxiing accident. I was quickly released through open arrest, which did mean that I could still do my job. My colleagues were very sympathetic towards me; they might have swayed the CO a bit. Nevertheless the outcome was that I was summoned to Salisbury in front of the air vice-marshal commanding the group and asked if I would accept his punishment which I did. Rather than a court martial he fined me £5, knocked six months off my seniority and a red endorsement was to be entered in my logbook.
>
> About six weeks later I was again summoned by my CO,

he was furious. He read out to me a statement from London, which said that, 'this officer should not have been dealt with summarily; he should have been court martialed. Therefore his fiver is returned, his seniority is restored and his logbook has to be cleaned up.' The CO never forgave me for that and he had me posted back home as quickly as possible. Otherwise I might have stayed in Rhodesia until the end of the war – some did.

Tony travelled to Cape Town where he spent six weeks, having to cable his father to allow him an overdraft. 'I did some flying with the South African Air Force, but I got bored doing nothing.' He then sailed across the South Atlantic on a Liberty Ship arriving in New York where he had 'five riotous days. Without telling my father I got on the telephone and persuaded my bank manager to let me have some more money. It was a bit expensive there and we wanted to see the town. Although we did meet a lot of hospitable people and an RAF uniform and wings did help.' Tony then crossed the Atlantic to Greenock, Scotland on the *Queen Elizabeth*, 'with about 16,000 American troops; 8,000 below for half a day and 8,000 on deck and then they would change over. I saw the biggest poker games I have ever seen in my life. I travelled in a state room, but with fifteen other people.'

We arrived at Greenock and came ashore in a little boat from the side of the liner. When we got to the quayside there was a band assembled, along with all sorts of dignitaries. We said, 'Well thank you very much.' 'It's not for you', they said. 'This is to welcome the Americans.' Half-way across the Atlantic many of them had put up a medal, because they were then serving in the European theatre of operations.

It was August 1943 and Tony was posted up to an advanced flying unit (No 14) at Banff in Scotland to fly twin-engine Airspeed Oxfords, 'for which I was already qualified. I was very cross about this posting because I wanted to go back to Fighter Command.'

There was a group captain there who was a pilot from the first war with a Military Cross; he went for me because I had been a bit stroppy. But he didn't want me to stand to attention and be ticked off. He said, 'Take off your hat and

sit down and tell me what's wrong with you young man.'
We talked and he said, 'Look there is only one command
which is hitting the enemy now and that's Bomber
Command. Fighter Command are doing a great job but
their days are slightly passé. We want the best people for
Bomber Command and you are one of them.' I got smaller
and smaller and smaller. He said, 'Now come on, promise
you will be a good lad, the next time we meet in the bar I'll
buy you a drink.' I had been overspending a bit for my
rank. He said, 'We'll get you through the course as quickly
as possible. Perhaps you can do an awful lot of night flying
if you haven't done it in this country; but you have got to
go through with it.' I promised him I would and I did.

Tony's next posting was to No 14 OTU at Market Harborough,
with a satellite at Husbands Bosworth, flying Wellington ICs and
Xs, accumulating just over 50 hours flying time, which included
a leaflet drop in northern France. Tony, at the OTU and
subsequent heavy conversion unit, also began to assemble, and
establish a relationship with, the men he would be entering the
air battle with; an all-British crew.

My navigator, Jack Harrison, from Sheffield, was the first
to approach me. He had a bomb aimer with him, Frank
Chance from London. Jack had peeked at my logbook and
knew I had a lot of flying time. We then found our gunners,
Ted Wass (rear gunner) from Peterborough, and Lesley
Smith (mid-upper gunner) from Edmonton, who used to
eat razor blades as a party trick. Alan Tittle, from Stafford,
a very quiet young man, joined us as the wireless operator
and Desmond Philips from South Wales came in as our
flight engineer.

The crewing up process seemed to work, at least no one
could complain afterwards that they had been forced into
a crew, which may have been the case had the flight
commander just picked a series of names. One of my
friends told me that he had been sorted out by a rear
gunner who was much older than the rest of them. The
story came out that they knew my friend had had a crash
at an operational training unit in a Wellington, so they
said, 'We've chosen you because you've had your crash
and you might be more careful next time.' My crew

actually came together very well.

From OTU Tony went on to fly Stirlings at the heavy conversion unit at Winthorpe (No 1661), 'because there weren't enough Lancasters for training.'

> Finally we went to what was called 'Lancaster Finishing School' at Syerston, Nottinghamshire, where we did ten hours on a Lancaster – a beautiful aeroplane to fly. A real pilot's aeroplane and I was very fond of it.

Tony's crew was, in the main, new to operations.

> Lesley Smith had served for quite a long time and had survived a crash in a Wellington at an OTU in Scotland but the others were all going on their first tour. In retrospect the way we crewed up was very strange but it seemed to work. We were just put together in a group and told to sort ourselves out. What I found was that some of the other aircrew had done a bit of homework and so they knew a bit about the pilots. I was a flight lieutenant, and some of them had actually discovered the kind of flying we had done before, so I had three or four chaps who wanted to join me. I suppose they thought that with an experienced pilot they had more chance. As it turned out there were 14 crews on that course which meant 98 aircrew and within about six months there were only ten of those 98 left in this country operating. The others were either dead, missing or prisoners of war and that was in 1944. So the chop rate was pretty high even in those days.
>
> I decided I would like to go to 49 Squadron with a friend of mine. Commanding the squadron was someone I had met at Banff and he had come across to a dance and sort of signed us up. On my clearance day at Syerston, whilst I was going around all the departments obtaining signatures to say that I hadn't walked away with a pair of silk flying gloves or flying boots or something which I shouldn't have, I was making my way round when I heard a call for me over the station tannoy. The wing commander flying wanted to see me right away. Of course I immediately wondered what I had done wrong. When I got to his office he asked if I would like to volunteer for 617 Squadron. I was speechless. We all knew of 617 Squadron; it was the

greatest and one couldn't have hoped to have got anywhere near it – they were all supposed to be aces. He said, 'Well your flying record is pretty good', by that time I had about 2,000 hours anyway, 'and I have spoken to Wing Commander Cheshire and he said he would be delighted to meet you. So if you agree we will take you over there tomorrow.' I was asked if my crew would be OK and I responded that I was pretty certain they would come with me. I left and called my crew together and told them what was proposed. They were all very enthusiastic.

The next day I was flown across to Woodhall Spa where I met Leonard Cheshire who, with his incredible charm, gave me a feeling I was the chap he had been waiting for. At that time there were many of the survivors from the 1943 Dams raid who were just about to leave and it wasn't long after I joined them that Leonard Cheshire also left and was replaced by Wing Commander James Tait, known as Willie Tait, who would finish the war with a DSO and three Bars and a DFC and Bar. Tait was a quiet, very reserved man, but he had a great reputation and settled in well.

Tony joined 617 Squadron at a time when the Normandy land battle had been raging for six weeks, the Allies were still meeting heavy opposition on the ground, with the army commanders under pressure to break the stalemate. Bomber Command had been fully committed to supporting the invasion and 617 Squadron had played its part in the assault on the Normandy beaches and the subsequent breakout; carrying out numerous special operations. It had deceived the enemy in the hours prior to the landing, using Window to simulate on German radar a convoy approaching the Pas de Calais, far to the north of the actual landings. It had attacked and blocked the Saumur rail tunnel to prevent German reinforcement reaching the battle area. It had sought to counter the German secret weapon threat, bombing, with some success, the V2 installations at Watten and Wizernes, the long-range gun at Mimoyecques, and the V1 launch bunker at Siracourt.

On the ground the opposing forces ground away at each other, the Allies eventually breaking the thinning German line, and by the end of July were poised to break out of Normandy into Brittany and towards Paris and the Seine. Key to the Allied success was winning the battle of the build-up. Men, weapons and supplies had to be transferred by sea from England to Normandy, at a faster rate than the Germans could redeploy forces along rail and road routes. Vital supplies streamed across the English Channel and they had to be protected. Not only could the RAF protect against airborne attack, but bombers could also counter one specific threat from the U-boats, attacking their 'nests' along the Atlantic coast of France. Throughout the invasion the air campaign was overseen by a daily meeting in England of the air commanders. By August the presence of U-boats was regularly reported at the meetings. Something had to be done, Bomber Command was called in, notably the special bombing skills of 617 Squadron.

Flight Lieutenant Tony Iveson joined 617 Squadron on 22 July 1944, the first pilot to go to the squadron without any operational experience. Tony soon began settling into his new life on an operational bomber squadron – different in so many respects to his previous fighter experience, 'There were of course three years plus in between and I had matured a bit.' Tony found a terrific esprit de corps expressed in a typical casual air force way.

> We had 130 odd aircrew, not all officers, and we lived in a wonderful hotel in Woodhall Spa called the Petwood Hotel. I found it a terrific atmosphere; we had Australians, New Zealanders, Canadians and a couple of Americans, as well as a variety from all over the British Isles. When I joined most of them were very experienced. There was some scepticism about me being a 'sprog' on bomber operations; 'What the hell are they sending us now', and, 'They'll have him for breakfast'. One had to live up to a very high standard. But they certainly made me very welcome.

On 31 July Tony flew with Flight Lieutenant John Williams to attack the rail tunnels at Rilly La Montagne. 'I sat alongside John and watched him go through the motions.' The squadron were carrying 12,000lb 'Tallboy' bombs; specially designed by Barnes Wallis, the man behind the development of the 'bouncing bomb', to fall at speed and penetrate deep into a target before exploding.

On this raid John Williams brought his Tallboy back, the

target being identified too late for a good run. Others did manage to hit the target with the 617 Squadron diary claiming, 'The operation was successful, several bombs seen to burst close to the aiming point.' The success came at the cost of one notable member of the squadron and his crew; Bill Reid, holder of the Victoria Cross. Moments after releasing their Tallboy his Lancaster was struck by bombs from above, smashing out one of the port engines and seriously damaging the fuselage. Reid and one other member of his crew survived and were captured. The rest of the crew lost their lives.

617 Squadron were operational on 1 August; but the raid to the large V1 site at Siracourt was abandoned, and on 4 August they attacked a railway bridge at Etaples. Tony did not take part in either operation but on 5 August 1944 his abilities were to be called upon and he prepared for his first operational flight with 617 Squadron at the controls of a Lancaster, detailed to attack the U-boat pens at Brest, using 12,000lb Tallboys. He lifted his Lancaster I ME554 at 0952 hours, one of 15 Lancasters and two Mosquitoes detailed by 617 Squadron. 'We flew as a gaggle and I remember flying over the south coast, seeing Jersey and the sunlight glinting on the green houses. It was a beautiful day.' At the target, and from 16,550 feet, Tony's Tallboy fell, precisely on midday, his post-raid report recording, 'Aimed at corner and allowed false height setting. Bomb fell on A/P [aiming point].' The squadron summed up the operation as 'very successful', despite one aircraft returning early owing to engine failure and the loss of Flying Officer Don Cheney's Lancaster. Cheney and two of his crew evaded capture, one man was caught and three men lost their lives.

Tony now had his first special bombing operation noted in his logbook, and he would be adding more in the weeks and months to come. Each of the raids he was on required precision bombing, and to aid accuracy the squadron was using the Mk IIA stabilised automatic bombsight (SABS). Tony describes what it was like using the equipment and how it felt to be on a bomb run.

We were the only squadron to have it, a kind of computer into which information such as altitude, air pressure, wind velocity, airspeed and temperatures were all fed. We had several wind finders in the squadron so eventually a mean wind was decided upon by the CO's navigators. We all used the same wind, so if it wasn't quite accurate we were all, as a group, drifting in the same direction. On the bombsight was a glass reticle on which was projected a 'sword', with a blade and a hilt. The bomb aimer would get the point of this light sword on the target and then see whether it drifted on or off. If it drifted off then he had a control which activated a little instrument in front of me with a pointer, and if that pointer moved off the centre line then I would bring it back very carefully with a gentle back turn. We had to maintain strict altitude and we had to maintain a strict airspeed. The bomb doors opened some way ahead of the target so we would settle down at this airspeed, and fly straight and level for quite some time to the target area. I would put my seat down and concentrate entirely on the instruments and try and forget what was going on outside; keeping the aircraft absolutely dead level and dead straight so the target was travelling straight down the line. Then about ten seconds before the bomb left us I got a red light; it meant hold it rigidly and then when you lost five tonnes you knew something had gone. You held for a little while longer to get the photograph because the camera was lined up to activate at the time the bomb struck the ground, taking a series of photographs. Then you had to clean the aeroplane up and get the hell out of it.

On 6 August the submarine pens at Keroman, Lorient, were targeted; two Mosquitoes and 14 Lancasters detailed (only 12 actually taking off) to take part in the late evening attack. The squadron diary recorded, 'The operation was successful, though heavy flak opposition was encountered. All aircraft returned safely, several being damaged.' Wing Commander Tait, flying in a Mosquito VI, carrying two red TI recorded, 'Target was easily identified from the Ile de Croix where the bombing run commenced. Bombs fell in a quick salvo and were concentrated on the projecting span on which the pens are built. I did not see any wild bombs. Smoke prevented accurate observations.' Tony recorded his contribution to the raid, 'Bombing appeared well concentrated and up to the standard of the attack on Brest.'

The following day the squadron detailed a Mosquito and nine Lancasters, including Tony Iveson's, to attack Lorient the following evening. 'The aircraft were recalled whilst over the target area as it was believed that USA ground forces were at the outskirts of the port.' Earlier in the day the squadron suffered further loss; Flying Officer Warren Duffy and Flying Officer Philip Ingleby killed in a crash at Wainfleet Bombing Range. Such loss would of course, be felt most by the next of kin. Squadron friends could not dwell on the fate of their colleagues; they would have to re-enter the air battle within days.

> By that time we were acclimatised to losses. We had been at war for getting on to five years. All of us either in training or on operations had lost people we knew. Although you were saddened it didn't make you think any more seriously about your self. Mr and Mrs Ingleby came down to Woodhall Spa and stayed at the Spa Hotel, our drinking hole. After a few days we became embarrassed. They were naturally desperately sad. We had all said how sorry we were, but we could not go on doing it everyday. They were seeing us all cheery and having a pint and I found it an embarrassing situation.

The U-boat threat was again countered on 9 August; one Mosquito and 12 Lancasters to the pens at La Pallice. The attack was recorded as very successful, with several direct hits being observed. Tony's Tallboy fell at 1301½ hours from 17,550 feet, 'First two bombs seen, one on port of dock gates to left hand corner and one direct hit in centre giving big orange flash.'

Tony would not be operational again for two weeks. In the meantime of course the war was always with him. The squadron ensured a presence at the funeral of Ingleby at Coningsby on 10 August; Duffy's body was taken by train to Harrogate and buried next day at the regional cemetery. That day 617 Squadron again attacked La Pallice, on 12 August the U-boat pens at Brest, and similarly to Brest the next day, but this time to sink the ships at the port and prevent them being used by the Germans to block the port should it fall into Allied hands. It was submarine pens at Brest again on 14 August. Flying Officer Pesme (a bomb aimer) was killed instantly when some flak shrapnel tore into the nose of Flight Lieutenant Pryor's Lancaster. Pesme would be interred in Harrogate cemetery. On 18 August the squadron carried out a 'successful' attack on La Pallice; a job they had tried two days earlier, frustrated by cloud cover at the target.

On 24 August Tony Iveson took Lancaster I PD238(H) to the E-boat pens at Ijmuiden, on the Dutch coast, dropping his Tallboy at 1427½ hours from 15,900 feet, 'Bombing concentrated. There appeared to be three direct hits on direct centre'. Then on 27 August Tony again piloted PD238 (H), one of 12 Lancasters and a Mosquito, to bomb the shipping at Brest. The 617 Squadron crews took off loaded without their usual Tallboys, the supply having temporarily dried up. As such Tony went with twelve 1,000lb bombs. 'We felt it was rather useless going with these piddling little bombs, we couldn't be sure of aiming them properly.' Over the target Tony released his load from 17,850 feet, 'One hit seen out of six sticks and target became obscured by smoke. The vessel was seen to be on fire.'

Tony now had half a dozen bomber operations under his belt. What is noticeable is the complete lack of any mention of aerial opposition to his or any other of his colleagues when flying into enemy airspace in daylight. Of course these operations had so far taken place over enemy occupied territory; Tony was yet to fly over Germany. But such an undertaking four years earlier, in the days of Benny Goodman and Tiny Cooling's first tours, or indeed during Joe Petrie-Andrews's and Harry Hughes's early days, would have been nigh on suicidal. So where was the Luftwaffe? In the first instance the RAF and USAAF fighter pilots were holding the aerial ring around Normandy; the Allies certainly held local air superiority. Secondly, much of the Luftwaffe's weaponry was held in Germany defending the skies over the homeland from the American daylight bomber formations and their long-range fighter escorts. Tony and his contemporaries were reaping the benefits won by the men who preceded them; men who had switched the air battle from over Britain, to the night and daylight defence of Germany.

Chapter 10

Special Operations

Tony Iveson's next operational duty was to try, with his colleagues, to eliminate from the war the threat that Winston Churchill had nicknamed 'the beast'; the German battleship *Tirpitz*. In the preface of John Sweetman's book *Tirpitz – Hunting the Beast* he commented on the perceived threat the *Tirpitz* posed to the Allies. 'The spectre of her emerging into the Atlantic to wreak havoc along trade routes and among troop transports or to join powerful enemy warships in French ports presented a truly terrifying image.'[19] The battleship, with her formidable armament, threatened the Arctic convoys and forced the hand somewhat of the Royal Navy who had to withhold a sizeable presence in northern British waters, ready to counter any forays by 'the beast'. The destruction of, or at least the incapacitation of, the *Tirpitz* was deemed paramount, Churchill would be constantly demanding attacks, and various attempts were made. Early in the war Bomber Command made some ineffectual efforts to strike the battleship, suitably summed up by John Sweetman as 'pinpricks'. And there was further frustration as the war progressed. In January 1942 the *Tirpitz* moved to Norwegian waters. The German Navy's Commander-in-Chief Grand Admiral Erich Räder sought to 'protect our position in the Norwegian and Arctic areas by threatening the flank of enemy operations against the northern Norwegian areas and by attacking White Sea convoys... to tie down enemy forces in the Atlantic, so that they cannot operate in the Mediterranean, the Indian Ocean or the Pacific.'[20] Not that the *Tirpitz* would be a mere inactive threat; operational forays would be necessary.

212

Allied aerial reconnaissance along with reports from agents in Norway continued tracking the *Tirpitz*'s movements. When the opportunity arose Bomber Command, Coastal Command and the Fleet Air Arm made further attempts to neutralise the threat. They failed along with an attempt by the Royal Navy using 'chariot' torpedoes and midget submarines, to fully eliminate the *Tirpitz* from the Royal Navy's strategic thinking.

At the end of August and beginning of September 1944, Allied intelligence had received information that the *Tirpitz* was carrying out sea trials. Bomber Command's 5 Group was called in to intervene; as Wing Commander Tait put it: 'It was at this stage that Bomber Command took over the job of haunting the battleship.' Those attacking had at their disposal the use of Tallboys, that could penetrate deck armour and rip open the battleship from the inside, along with 'Johnny Walker' (JW) mines; these, with the use of hydrostatic valves, would fall and rise in the water. When Tony Iveson was first told that 'the mines would jump around and strike the underside of the ship', he considered it 'a crazy idea'.

Early in September Wing Commander Tait, described in one report as, 'a youthful veteran RAF pilot with a unique and long record of operational success' had been entrusted with leading the planned attack on the *Tirpitz*. Tait set about preparing his crews for the task ahead. Tony Iveson recalled:

> We were playing football one day and the CO was called to the ops room. He came back and said something's on but finish the game chaps. We didn't know what.
>
> We started practising formation flying at night with lights on – not a very happy occupation. Anyway that was abandoned and we then started doing low flying up and down the canals and over the sea. Then we began long-range flights at different altitudes and different airspeeds. We had flow meters fitted so we could see exactly how much petrol each engine was using. We were told we were going on a long trip and the idea was to fly as economically as possible, hence the various experiments.

Tirpitz lay within Kaa Fjord and the attacking crews had to achieve surprise to prevent effective use of a smoke screen. The Lancasters were to carry Tallboys and JW mines. In addition to the deployment of 617 Squadron, the Tallboy-carrying abilities of 9 Squadron were also called upon. Range was of course a major problem, particularly for the aircraft carrying the Tallboys and planners began to explore the use of Russian airfields. Various landing grounds were examined but eventually Yagodnik was settled for, 15 miles to the south east of Archangel, with the *Tirpitz* lying 680 miles away. The attacking Lancasters were to be split into two forces. Force A consisted of twelve Lancasters from each of 9 Squadron and 617 Squadron carrying Tallboys. They would bomb the *Tirpitz* and then fly on to Yagodnik; refuel and then fly home. Force B consisted of six Lancasters from each of 9 and 617 Squadron (one of which was Tony Iveson's) which were to carry JW mines, and after bombing they were detailed to return directly to their Scottish bases. However plans were changed at the last moment owing to concerns about the variable weather and it was decided that the whole force would fly to Yagodnik and operate from there.

So on the evening of 11 September, twenty 617 Squadron Lancasters took off from Woodhall Spa and set course for Yagodnik. Aiming for the same destination were eighteen 9 Squadron aircraft (one of which had to return early), along with a 463 Squadron Lancaster detailed to film the raid. In addition two 511 Squadron Liberators filled with spares and supplies made their way to Yagodnik. A 540 Squadron Mosquito, which would take on reconnaissance duties, took off for the same destination the following morning. All the crews left without the benefit of knowing what the weather was going to be like the further north they went. As Tait recorded in his report of the *Tirpitz* attacks:

> For the raid, as with all operational flying, success depended primarily upon accurate meteorological forecasting and the difficulties on this account alone presented a formidable problem in view of the extreme range of the operation, and ultimately it was not possible to send aircraft off free of considerable doubt concerning the weather conditions likely to be encountered in remote Northern Scandinavia and Russia.

As it was the weather did cause problems. Indeed the flight to Russia was notable for Tony Iveson in more ways than one.

> On my birthday we were despatched to Russia. We flew out from Lincolnshire to the north over the North Sea past

Scotland and the Shetlands, turned into Norway and went down low up the coast and over the mountains into Sweden turning north in the gulf of Bothnia. I suddenly saw a town ahead of me, right at the top end of the sea between Sweden and Finland. It was all lit up and I hadn't seen an illuminated town since Rhodesia. As we got closer I saw a lot of flak come up below but in front of me. I read that as saying, 'If you fly over our town we will be a bit more serious'. It was a bright moonlit night so we turned and they put up a few bursts just to make sure we got the message. We went round the town then pressed on.

We eventually finished up on a disused Russian airfield at a place called Onega on the White Sea. We got mixed up with our communications. We were given a code for the wireless operator to use but sadly someone had forgotten the difference between the Russian and English alphabet. So after sculling around for a long time I saw this big field and decided to land in it. It turned out to be Onega and they couldn't believe we had come from England. We had been in the air 12 hours and 15 minutes.

Owing to concerns about landing with the JW mines Tony had jettisoned them in a lake. Soon after he landed a colleague joined him.

Just after I touched down another aircraft from the squadron arrived, flown by 'Nick' Knilans, one of our Americans. We were taken into Onega, where we met a major in the Red Army and fortunately there was a hospital ship in the harbour where we got an interpreter who spoke English. He asked us where we had come from and we pointed at a map of Europe on the wall. He couldn't quite believe it. We had a phone number so he rapidly established our credibility.

Later in the day Tait came to Onega in an old biplane and he was able to guide Tony and Knilans to Yagodnik. The poor weather, low cloud and rain, and problems with communications had not just hampered Knilans and Tony's attempts to find Yagodnik. Others had encountered similar obstacles. Late on the morning of 12 September thirteen of the expected Lancasters had still failed to show at Yagodnik. News slowly filtered through of the whereabouts of the absentees, all of whom had reached Russian soil, but not all the aircraft would be available for operations. Aircraft were written off and abandoned, some giving up 'spare parts' and thirty-one Lancasters were eventually gathered at Yagodnik, although not all these were serviceable for operations.

The crews now began to settle in at their new base and await the right conditions to carry out the attack on the battleship.

> They put us up in an old ferry steamer and during the night we awoke and found the place was crawling with little bugs; we were all bitten and I finished up sleeping in my flying socks over my pyjamas, my flying sweater and silk flying gloves. We had a service aircraft Liberator that came out with our doctor as well as our technical chaps and all he brought with him was calamine lotion!

On 13 September Tony took off for Kegostrov, with six Russian groundcrew on board to try and salvage what they could from one of the Lancasters that had been written off – Squadron Leader Wyness's. Tony picked up Drew Wyness, who would be his 'second pilot' on the forthcoming operation. Wyness had been one of Tony's pupils during his short stay at Meir in 1941 and they had become great friends. On return to Yagodnik Tony's aircraft was loaded up with the JW mines, taken from Flying Officer Carey's Lancaster.

As it was, following the cannibalisation of the wrecked aircraft, in total, on 14 September, twenty Lancasters were available to carry Tallboys and six to carry JW mines. But the weather intervened once more.

> We had to spend a few days at Yagodnik. Each day the Mosquito went out to check conditions, because we didn't have any reliable weather forecast. If on return he fired a red light we stood down; played cards and football. But on 15 September it was a green light and off we went.

Wing Commander Tait recorded the scene that morning.

> Final briefing, at which the local Russian (naval) commander, captains and personnel were present, was held in the open under bleak conditions amid bleaker surroundings. In the near distance the menacing outlines of the waiting Lancasters relieved the monotony of the background of weather-beaten hutments, dim-coloured flat earth and grey winding river. The briefing, more correctly a

few last words, had barely reached its quiet conclusion when the roaring motors of the low flying Mosquito broke the stillness and galvanised the small knot on the ground into swift action. In no time the airscrew blades of the huge bombers commenced to whirr in aggressive chorus as they warmed for take-off and at approximately 0800 hours on this eventful 15 September 1944, the first of those intrepid few Lancasters rolled down the runway at the head of the noisy procession. The battle was on!

The plan of attack had of course changed. The attacking force would fly at 1,000 feet to the Finnish border then climb. Leading the way would be three 9 Squadron Lancasters determining the wind, who would then join Force A; the Tallboy-carrying Lancasters, which were to attack first in four waves. Force B would be carrying the JW mines.

It took just 23 minutes for 17 Lancasters from 617 Squadron (Nick Nilans' aircraft having been repaired), ten 9 Squadron Lancasters and the film unit Lancaster to get airborne. Tait's report recorded the sight as the Lancasters, 'streaked across the flat steppe over forests of tall pine trees and scattered small lakes and with the approach of the Finnish border the steppes gave way to hills.' The Lancasters climbed, reaching a small lake a hundred miles from the target, and the final approach was made. Tait recorded, 'the Lancasters, steadily gaining height... headed their persistent way north until in the far distance ahead appeared the cigar-like small object of their circuitous journey – the *Tirpitz*!' Tony Iveson's first view of the battleship was over the top of the front turret of his Lancaster.

> At the same time I saw smoke generators starting up all around the mountains around the fjord. By the time we got to bombing position she was covered in a cloud of smoke. It was a very efficient defensive system and although we pitched our bombs into where we thought she was, all we could do was damage her, but not too seriously.

The attacking force approached the target in favourable conditions, Tait recalling, 'one by one the aircraft opened their bomb doors and the attack began.' It was estimated that the smoke screen did not start until about eight to ten minutes prior to the first bomb release. The flak batteries did their best to oppose the Lancasters, Tait recalling, 'the surrounding air soon became extremely unhealthy for the airmen. Much to their relief, however, the firing was inaccurate.' Those attacking the *Tirpitz* with Tallboys would later report problems with smoke. 'By the time the first Lancaster reached the bomb-release point, the smoke screen entirely covered the battleship except for the tip of one mast and it was on that object that the leading aircraft lined their sights.' As the bombing progressed a few were either unable to bomb or had hang-ups although it was reported that there had been one probable hit. Those dropping the JW mines had similar problems, Tony later recording that the target was completely obscured by the smoke screen.

With 'the party over' as Tait put it, 'the planes swept majestically on their way out to sea.' The film unit Lancaster flew back to the UK, the attacking Lancasters back to Yagodnik, where they refuelled. Over the course of the next few days the airmen brought their Lancasters back to the UK. Flying Officer Frank Levy's Lancaster failed to return, and a later investigation discovered that he had hit high ground, off course, south of Trondheim. Nine men lost their lives; Levy also had some members of Drew Wyness's crew as passengers.

Post-raid reports, reconnaissance and intelligence from Norway quickly proved that the *Tirpitz* was undefeated. 'We were relieved that that particular trip was over but disappointed that we hadn't been able to deal with her knowing full well we would have to try again.' Tony certainly would be returning for another attempt on the *Tirpitz*, but other duties came his way in the meantime. In the next few weeks, he would also have the opportunity to throw himself around the sky like a fighter pilot once more.

> We were lucky on 617 Squadron because we had two Mosquitoes and two Mustangs. I was able to fly them both and I certainly loved flying the Mustang [mark III]. I saw it and lusted after it; read the handbook and flew it. Beautiful aeroplane.
>
> The Mustang in the early part of the war wasn't a great success but somehow they put the Merlin into it which transformed it and it was just a beautiful aeroplane to fly and it became very very effective. As an ex-single engine pilot, because I had flown Hurricanes as well as Spitfires, I just loved it. We used to do what we called fighter affiliation; the Lancaster would go up on a test and I would

ask the pilot if he'd like me to do a few fighter attacks on him. He could then practice the corkscrew. I would come in from high up in a Mustang and zoom down on this Lancaster whose pilot would go through the motions. We used to have a lot of fun.

On 23 September Bomber Command carried out a successful attack on the Dortmund-Ems Canal. 617 Squadron was involved but Tony Iveson's contribution was frustrated, his post-raid report recording, 'Lancaster I ME554, time up 1915, time down 2350, 1 x Tallboy, 2145 hours, 16,000 feet. Saw red TI clearly at 2142 hours. Made run on this but about 15 seconds before intended bombing TI disappeared under cloud. Made two more runs but could not pick up TI again. Called off. Bomb brought back.'

On 3 October 617 Squadron was involved in an attempt on the Westkapelle sea wall on Walcheren Island, as Tony recalled, 'a rather drastic method of trying to get rid of the Germans from the island.' From Walcheren German gun batteries could attack shipping on the approaches to the vital port facilities at Antwerp. As it was the attack by the men from Woodhall Spa was abandoned, the main force of 250 bombers managing to fulfil the objective, the sea pouring in through the breach, before the 617 Squadron crews arrived. Tait flying in a Mosquito recorded, 'Reached target at 1455 hours. Bombing by the main force was still proceeding. The wall was already breached and water had flooded inland to a distance of about 1 mile into streets of Westkapelle. After consultation with the Deputy Leader I decided that the job was done and ordered the force to return.' There was not an endless supply of Tallboys and they were not to be used lightly.

Four days later 617 Squadron would be dropping their Tallboys on the Kembs Barrage, on the Rhine north of Basle. Thirteen aircraft were detailed for the operation, their objective to destroy the lockgates and hence prevent the Germans flooding the area and hampering any future Allied land advance. The plan was to have seven aircraft circling and bombing at height, and drawing the flak, with six aircraft bombing from 600 feet, using Tallboys with delayed-action fuses. Tony Iveson flew as one of the high bombers. On approach to the target Tony's bomb aimer, Frank Chance informed his skipper, 'Christ, there's a Lanc beneath us.'

I suddenly saw this Lancaster, flown by Paddy Gingles, and he had the gunnery leader on board, Scott Kiddie. I saw Scotty in the rear turret looking up at us and our Tallboy. He told me afterwards that he thought I was going to put it in his lap.

Over the target Tony released his Tallboy from 8,500 feet. 'Our bomb fell on the left bank of the river about 400 yards south east of centre of target.' Other crews also had difficulty. Squadron Leader Fawke, bombing from 8,100 feet: 'Bomb hung up for five seconds after release and fell on west bank of river. We had to do three runs before the bomb came off.' Flight Lieutenant Sayers, from 7,300 feet: 'Opened bombs doors and bomb fell out immediately, buckling door as it went.' But others had more success, notably Wing Commander Tait, bombing from 600 feet: 'Our bomb landed in the correct position ten yards short of the target.' Flight Lieutenant Kit Howard was unable to release his Tallboy on the first run and turned for another.

> Kit was a real warrior, with a big long moustache. He had a revolver and a knife in his belt; he really went to war. I heard Kit say Q – Queenie going round again and then James Tait saying, 'No, abandon, abandon'. But Kit went round, on his own, and he was blasted from the sky.

This decision cost the entire crew their lives as the aircraft fell to light flak. Drew Wyness's Lancaster was also hit by flak on the run up to the target, at 600 feet. Tony watched as his friend's Lancaster lost height, Wyness then ditching it in the Rhine, with 'a big splash'. The crew survived and managed to get into a dinghy but their ordeal was far from over. As they headed for the Swiss shore German machine-gun fire claimed the lives of three of the crew. The remaining four men were captured and after spending a short time in jail they were then taken back to the Rhine. On the bank of the river they were shot. After the war the man who shot the 617 Squadron airmen was captured and held for trial. He managed to escape and the trial was conducted *in absentia*. He was found guilty but the death sentence was never carried out.[21]

On return from the Kembs Barrage raid Tony Iveson prepared to meet a good friend for dinner that evening.

Drew Wyness and I had arranged to meet Chris Melville, a

colonel from the King's Own Scottish Borders. They had previously been training in the highlands of Scotland. We had got to know them by inviting them to a dining-in night at Petwood. They brought their pipers and Nick Knilans got their pipe major so drunk he was sent back to barracks in disgrace.

Drew and I had had lunch with Chris on the day of the Kembs Barrage raid and he had driven us to the airfield in his jeep. Chris was a big fellow, a Scottish rugby international and a hell of a nice man. I now had to tell him that Drew would not be coming with us. We sat on the stairs in the Spa Hotel and when I told him tears just rolled down his face. He said, 'It's really my first brush with war.' Somebody he had lunched with was, within a few hours, as far as we knew, dead in Germany. It really shook him.

Tony Iveson to this day still recalls with sadness and some anger the loss of his good friend.

Many a Remembrance Day I place a memorial cross with Drew's name on it. He was a tall handsome man, bursting with life. I often wonder if he had a premonition, and that he should get in as much of life as he could. He was a lad for the ladies, in the nicest possible way. It was a great shock to me and I was outraged when I learned about his fate. If he had been killed in a crash then that was the luck of the game. But he wasn't, he was taken out and coldly murdered.

On 28 October 1944 Tony, who had recently been recommended for squadron leader rank, would be reacquainting himself with 'the beast'. In the middle of October intelligence came through of the *Tirpitz* making a move west, and aerial reconnaissance would locate the battleship four miles from Tromso, near the island of Haakoy. The move also brought the *Tirpitz* within range of a direct attack from Scotland; 617 Squadron's qualities, along with 9 Squadron's, were again called upon. As Tony Iveson would recall, because of the long flight, the squadron would need to make adjustments to its weaponry. 'They took out all the armour plating from our Lancaster, took out the mid-upper turret and the front guns, the flare chute, in fact anything to lighten the aircraft; and put an extra fuel tank in the fuselage.' On 28 October the squadron airmen made the move to their northern advanced base and in the early hours of 29 October nineteen 617 Squadron and twenty 9 Squadron Lancasters became airborne, all carrying Tallboys; Tony Iveson taking off at 0122 hours. The 5 Group operational order required Tony, along with his colleagues, simply 'to sink the *Tirpitz*'. A report written by Tait at a later date again sets the scene, initially praising the work of the 'erks' who had laboured to get the adapted Lancasters airborne.

> Here once again was conclusive proof of the high merit of the groundcrews, due to whose splendid efforts every one of the heavily loaded machines got off the ground comfortably, completely dispelling any real anxieties over the dangerous experiment.
>
> Strictly according to schedule the Lancasters, burning as before navigation lights at their wing tips and one bright orange light on top of the fuselage to assist in maintaining rough formation, joined together and in picturesque parade against the night sky headed out over the sea, keeping down below 1,500 feet once again to avoid detection by enemy radar. A little later the last home landmark – the northern tip of the Orkneys – was left behind and the sound of their motors died away in the eastern distance.
>
> Approaching the Norwegian coast, feint streaks of light heralded the approach of dawn, which finally broke strong and clear.

Following the long flight in good weather, the crews arrived at their destination, which the 9 Squadron diary recorded as covered with 'considerable medium cloud...' with tops at about 6,000 feet'. Tait recalled that the cloud was, 'almost completely shielding the German battleship from the bomber's view; despite this handicap however, a normal approach was carried out during which anti-radar strips of metal-covered paper were shed in large quantities by the formation and the attack was pressed home as accurately as the occasional small gaps in the cloud permitted.' Tony Iveson would release his Tallboy from 15,000 feet at 0750 hours: 'Results unobserved'. Others would record similarly, some would be bringing their Tallboys back, but not Flight Lieutenant Bobby Knights: 'Bomb seen to enter water and explode about 20 yards off starboard bow and ship rocked considerably. Made several circuits after bombing and saw thick brown smoke billowing from vicinity of midships. Shortly after bomb exploded, observed explosion from starboard bow, followed by thick black smoke.' Flight Lieutenant Hamilton would record, 'own bomb believed direct hit on bows followed by big flash. Saw two bombs, followed by another, drop close to *Tirpitz*, believed to be near midships.' Flying Officer Castagnola reported: 'Saw bomb fall towards *Tirpitz* followed shortly afterwards by flak and column of smoke.' In fact a few crews, from both squadrons, had reported seeing strikes on the ship and explosions. But as Tait reported when the crews returned they were, 'tired out after their long 12½ hour record flight and despondent at the frustration of their skilled and strenuous effort.' As Tony recalled, 'it was then two rounds to the *Tirpitz*.' One 617 Squadron Lancaster failed to return; damaged by flak Flying Officer Carey put his Lancaster down in Sweden, the entire crew repatriated at a later date.

Subsequent intelligence, aerial reconnaissance and Ultra intercepts proved that no hits had been scored and the *Tirpitz*, though shaken, was still afloat. On 29 October 5 Group's AOC Air Vice-Marshal Ralph Cochrane sent a message to try and alleviate the frustration of his crews: 'Congratulations on your splendid flight and perseverance at the target. The luck will not always favour the *Tirpitz* and one day you will get her.' Within days Cochrane would be planning to send his crews on the long flight north once more.

Tony would return to Tromso at a future date and it was either on this next raid or the final Tromso raid that he had cause to thank his flight engineer for probably saving the crew's lives.

It was when we were on take-off, with the Tallboy and full tanks. We had Merlin T24 engines and were able to get about 28lbs boost on each. It meant going right through the gate, assisted by my flight engineer, Desmond Philips, holding that until airborne. I would lever the left hand throttle to counteract the torque, the engineer following me up. I would then move both hands onto the controls. On this occasion the port outer didn't work properly; it didn't go through to 28lbs boost. So we went off the runway and on to the grass. Desmond was watching very carefully and he throttled back the starboard outer to give me directional control. We bounced and got it off the grass. One of our other pilots was on the peritrack and he said he ducked as we went over the top. If there had been a hangar in the way we would have gone straight through it. If Desmond had panicked we would all have died. He was very calm, it just happened, he didn't say anything. We got to about 500 feet and then I started to shake.

Cloud had been the major problem to overcome on the previous attempts on the *Tirpitz*. With the year now in its eleventh month, the planning for further attacks had to consider the diminishing hours of daylight; a raid had to be carried out in November. The meteorological conditions in the Tromso area were kept under close scrutiny. Early in the month an opportunity appeared to arise; the squadron diary recording, '4 November – Nineteen aircraft detailed for operations. Aircraft were despatched to an advanced base in Lossiemouth. Gale warning announced in the evening. 5 November – Operations cancelled through adverse weather conditions and aircraft returned to own base.' Frustration again.

We had been after *Tirpitz* for nearly a couple of months and we knew that daylight was coming to an end in Tromso. On the way back to Woodhall Spa with the Tallboy, I flew back over Filey Bay, south of Scarborough, where I used to go as a kid on holiday and play on the sands. I flew right down on the deck and looked at the deserted beach, on a grey November afternoon, pondering whether there would ever be happy laughing children down there again.

A few days later there did appear to be an improvement in the weather, and 617 and 9 Squadron crews again moved to their northern Scottish bases. In the early hours of 12 November the Lancaster engines burst into life and despite some problems with

617 Squadron Lancaster (adapted for *Tirpitz* attack)

frost and ice, conditions were good. The Lancasters became airborne and set out, passing the Shetlands, once more on a long and somewhat familiar flight.

> We flew through the night across the North Sea over Norway onto a lake in Sweden, which was our rendezvous. As we were approaching Norway there was a thin slither of dawn on the horizon and as it increased I saw a Lancaster in front of me. I pulled up alongside it, to find that it was the CO, and Micky Vaughan the rear gunner was giving me two fingers. I flew in formation with Tait and out of the lightening sky came Lancaster after Lancaster, quite dramatic. From there we flew to Tromso. It was a clear morning, absolutely beautiful, the sun was shining and you could see for a hundred miles. I think we knew that we had a great chance of disposing of her there and then.

Tait again gives the background.

> The sea crossing [was] as uneventful as its predecessor, although slightly colder. Once again dawn was breaking as they neared the coast of Norway and crossed in on the same track. The scene now before them was picturesque and clear, broken only by patches of low cloud over the lakes and thus screening them from the anxious eyes of the navigators. The red sun hung low over the distant horizon, turning the snow-flecked hills to a deep pink, in striking contrast to the crystal-clear blue depths of the shining lakes revealed through occasional breaks in the cloud umbrella. Once more the bombers banked and climbed into bombing formation as they altered course northwards. Soon the now familiar outline of the *Tirpitz* came into view ahead, and at a given signal the great machines swung their bombs doors wide open and converged to the attack.

Inaccurate flak greeted the bomber aircrews, but there were, fortunately, no fighters. The crews were expecting opposition as Tony Iveson recalled.

> We had been told beforehand that a German fighter unit had been moved to Bardufoss, which was about 40 miles away. We were very lucky. Had they got amongst us I think there would have been very few of us left. It was a clear sky, we were a long way from home and we only had four .303

guns in the rear turret against their cannon, no mid-uppers. No I don't think we would have had a very happy time.

Where were the fighters? An officer from the *Tirpitz* would later provide an answer.

> We knew well in advance we were to be attacked and we requested the presence of fighters. The request was granted and the take-off was reported to us. When [the] Lancasters came into sight from the south we enquired as to the whereabouts of our fighters only to discover that they had flown to our old berth at Kaa Fjord and they now did not have enough petrol to return to us and engage the Lancasters.[22]

In good conditions with little opposition, the Lancasters seized their chance. Those first into the attack had a clear sighting of the *Tirpitz* before smoke covered the battleship. Wing Commander Tait was first to bomb at 0841 hours from 13,000 feet. 'We did not see our bomb burst, but the initial bombing was concentrated on the vessel. When we arrived steam was coming from the funnel.' Eight aircraft then claimed to bomb at 0842 hours; their post-raid reports sum up what they saw.

> *Flying Officer Castagnola;* 12,650 feet. Our bomb fell on the centre of the superstructure. There was a direct hit, at the same time a cloud of smoke followed and the ship became completely obscured by it.
> *Flying Officer Gingles;* 13,200 feet. Centre of ship. We think we obtained a direct hit. We did not see further results as we were hit by flak and had to turn away.
> *Flying Officer Sanders;* 14,000 feet. Two bombs, one of which was ours, went down together and both appeared to hit the edge of the ship near its centre. Bombing appeared generally concentrated. Only one wide bomb.
> *Flying Officer Lee;* 14,400 feet. The ship was obscured by smoke just after we bombed. Our bomb went straight down into the centre of the smoke. All bombing we saw appeared very well concentrated and firing from the ship ceased after the first bombs went down.
> *Flight Lieutenant Knights;* 13,400 feet. Our bomb fell about ten yards off port quarter. We saw the first four bombs go down as follows: On or near starboard quarter;

starboard bow; port bow and near funnel. We remained near target area until end of attack and saw large explosions at 0851 hours and a smaller one at 0853 hours. Before we left we saw the *Tirpitz* listing heavily to port. Bombing by 617 was concentrated and accurate. Four of 9 Squadron's bombs (using Mk 14 Bombsight) fell approx. 200 yards, 500 yards, 3/4 mile, 1 mile.

Squadron Leader Iveson; 13,000 feet. Our bomb fell in the centre of the smoke pall which covered the ship when we attacked.

Flying Officer Watts; 13,800 feet. We did not see our own bomb burst but saw one possible direct hit, one overshoot and two wide.

Flying Officer Joplin; 15,200 feet. Our bomb fell in the smoke which covered the ship. One direct hit and two near misses were seen.

Tony adds to the reports above with his personal recollection.

I couldn't see very much because you can't see over the front of the Lancaster's nose and the turret, but we looked down afterwards and saw lots of smoke and saw bombs going down. We knew that we had pretty well got her. Once we had dropped our own bomb there was only one thing to do – leave.

Smoke was now hampering the attack, but the remaining 617 Squadron crews would also return with optimistic reports: 'Heavy explosion seen... We saw at least one direct hit which was followed by a big column of reddish brown smoke... a fire was seen on board... Immediately after the first bombs fell a red glow appeared followed by a big column of black smoke... There was a big explosion on the ship at 0851 hours.' And so on.

Following in the wake of 617 Squadron were the men of 9 Squadron, releasing 11 Tallboys. One aircraft lost an engine to flak and made for Sweden, from where they would later be repatriated.

The Lancaster crews now had to endure the long flight home, the pilots further tested when the weather showed it was not quite beaten, forcing the crews to land at numerous northern destinations. On 13 November the 617 Squadron crews made the flight back to Woodhall Spa. News of the raid had obviously travelled faster, the squadron diarist being able to record, 'confirmed *Tirpitz* sunk. Crews welcomed by ground staffs and the band of the Border Regiment.'

Initial post-raid reports therefore suggested success, which would be backed up by agent reports and further reconnaissance. The *Tirpitz* had indeed been hit – fatally; Tait's Tallboy was later credited with the first strike, follow-up strikes and near misses could not, with certainty, be accredited to crews. But what was certain was that by the end of the raid the *Tirpitz* had turned 'turtle' – the beast was no more, the threat extinguished.

On return to Woodhall Spa the celebrations began, Tait recalling, 'in the traditional youthful fashion of the RAF', and congratulatory messages flooded in. The King conveyed his 'hearty congratulations to all those who took part in the daring and successful attack on the *Tirpitz*'. The Secretary of State for Air, Sir Archibald Sinclair commented: 'The War Cabinet have invited me to convey to you and all concerned their congratulations on the brilliant achievement of Bomber Command in sinking the *Tirpitz*. The series of attacks on Germany's most powerful battleship were pressed home with great skill and determination against formidable opposition. The destruction of the *Tirpitz* must rank with the finest feats of Bomber Command and marks a further stage in the crumbling of German power.'

Despite this the war was not going to be over before that Christmas as some wished. Hitler fought on and the Allies needed to cross the Rhine to enter and overrun Germany. On 8 (19 aircraft) and 11 December (17 aircraft) Tony Iveson took part in two Tallboy attacks on the Urft Dam, at the head of the Roer valley. American troops were preparing to cross the river and did not want the Germans to flood the valley during the operation. On the first of the bombing attacks Tait called off the raid owing to thick cloud. 'The force orbited for some time making runs on various directions but it was impossible to bomb.'

I took a royal marine with me on this raid. An operation had been scheduled where we were going to drop airborne boats in Bergen fjord, with an explosive charge in and a marine; a crazy idea. They were with us about four weeks before it was scrubbed. Anyway I took a marine with me as he wanted experience of an operation. On the raid my flight engineer said to me, 'Christ skip, the soldier's turning blue.' We quickly sorted him out; he wasn't getting the proper oxygen supply. I received a strong balling out from James Tait afterwards as we had sneaked the marine on board without permission.

On 11 December the crews were able to bomb the dam, Tony Iveson recalled seeing the effect of a Tallboy exploding, 'it was the first time I saw ripples in the ground'. Tony's post-raid report recorded.

Lancaster I ME554
Up – 1245 hours
Down – 1740 hours

1526 hours. 8,400 feet, 1 x Tallboy. Bomb believed to have exploded just to the left of the overflow about one third of the way down. First bomb that exploded hit the dam itself quarter of the way down. One other bomb seemed to fall to the left of the overflow about twice as far away as ours and about the same height. Other bombs fell into the water and did not explode. Another overshot in the water and did explode. Just as aircraft left the target area an explosion was seen right on aiming point.

The attacking force had met with some success, with thirteen feet taken off the top of the dam, although the Germans managed to prevent the breach deepening, by lowering the water level.[23]

On 15 December Tony's Lancaster was one of seventeen 617 Squadron aircraft that carried out a fairly successful attack on the submarine pens at Ijmuiden; Tony dropping his Tallboy at 1503½ from 9,400 feet. 'We did not see our bomb burst owing to smoke but saw two slightly overshoot and one direct hit, also two undershoots.' On 21 December he was part of an attack on the synthetic oil plant at Politz, recording, 'Over target from 2151-2205. Saw many yellow TIs. Did not see the flashing V. Bomb sight toppled on first run. Target not identified, and decided not to bomb after three orbits.'

That was a shambles. A long penetration and marking a single target at night. They expected too much of us. On return we orbited Woodhall Spa but couldn't get in because of the fog. So we went to Coningsby which had a contact strip; sections of green, amber and red, very concentrated strong lighting. With my bomb aimer in the nose peering through the fog, we eased down.

617 Squadron had deployed 16 aircraft on the raid, most of the pilots landing their aircraft in fog at Coningsby on return. The wing of Flying Officer Joplin's aircraft struck the ground whilst attempting to land at Ludford Magna, cartwheeling the Lancaster; two men were killed, the pilot and two others badly injured.

The following week weather curtailed flying. Christmas was celebrated, as was the departure of Wing Commander Tait (who was awarded a third bar to the DSO) and Group Captain Philpott. Group Captain John Fauquier took over the squadron, 'a very tough Canadian indeed – a warrior'. 617 Squadron closed the month out with an attack on E-boat pens at Rotterdam on 29 December and bombing cruisers in Oslo fjord on 31 December, neither of which Tony took part in.

In the opening ten days of January poor weather prevented operations a number of times. On 11 January snow was cleared from the runways in the hope of use for operations, but with no improvement in conditions the 617 Squadron aircrews were prevented from going to war, until the next day that is when 16 Lancasters and a Mosquito flew to the U-boat pens and shipping in Bergen, accompanied by 9 Squadron crews. Following the liberation of France, and the loss of the French ports, the Germans had moved their U-boats to Norwegian bases. In October 1944 Bomber Command had carried out attacks, with some limited success, but there had also been civilian deaths. Hopefully the combined experience of 617 and 9 Squadrons could improve matters with their precision bombing and accuracy.

Fourteen of the 617 Squadron Lancasters took off between 0830 and 0846 hours, Group Captain Fauquier lifting his Mosquito at 0841 hours. Flight Lieutenant Dobson was delayed, lifting off at 0915 hours. Squadron Leader Tony Iveson was also delayed. The brakes had failed on his usual aircraft F-Fox.

I found we had no brake pressure as we were leaving dispersals so I took over the reserve aircraft [Lancaster I NG181]. It was another daylight operation, and they hadn't put back the armour plating or the mid-upper turret.

To change from the usual aircraft was another of the

superstitious concerns of Bomber Command airmen. Familiarity of course fosters a feeling of safety; as did some other 'routines' that aircrews went in for.

> I always had a St Christopher and I am sure many others had little mascots. I'm not sure if I was over superstitious but it was rather interesting that the only time I did not fly Fox on an operation, I took Mike and I got clobbered. Whether it would have been any different had I been in Fox I don't know. I made Fox my aeroplane and as a flight commander I had a bit of pull in that direction.
>
> The aircraft did vary to some extent. One got very used to one's own aeroplane, handling the engines for instance, and perhaps the odd flying idiosyncrasy. I think you got attached to it, I think everybody got attached to their own aircraft.

As it was, early on 12 January 1945 the main element of 617 Squadron set course for Bergen, without Tony Iveson and his crew.

> They went via Peterhead where they picked up an escort of a squadron of Polish pilots on Mustangs; then across the North Sea to Bergen. By the time we got airborne we decided that we would cut the corner. If we just followed on the track we would have been a long way behind. In doing so we caught them up just off the Norwegian coast and I took my position. There was no wind and when we did the first run the CO wasn't satisfied; we said we would make another run. Then somebody at the end at the rear let go a Tallboy, which when it exploded, threw up so much dust that the target was almost covered. We went round about two or three times and I told my gunners to keep a look out for the Mustang escort. My gunner then alerted me to approaching fighters. The next thing I knew there was tracer flying all over the place and an engine exploded and caught fire. Various other things happened to the aircraft, and she wanted to stand on her tail.

Tony's post-raid report recorded: 'Port inner engine caught fire, port tail plane, port rudder and rear turret u/s. Rear turret guns jammed. No elevator or rudder trim, only slight elevator control. Captain warned crew to prepare to abandon aircraft.'

We were being attacked by Focke-Wulf 190s, and I do remember that one of them did an upward roll right in front of me. I thought, 'You cheeky sod!' It was literally right in front. We were coping with the situation because as a crew we had carried out our drills frequently. We stopped the respective engine, feathered the prop and took the necessary measures to deal with the fire, which fortunately went out; otherwise we wouldn't be here today. But there was more damage. The trimming wires to the elevators had been shot through which is why she wanted to stand on her tail. I had my knee between my seat and the stick, and my bomb aimer came up and gave me a hand. We flew into the flak, hoping the fighters wouldn't follow us and then we decided to quit. We got rid of the bomb, we just had to jettison it into the sea, and the intercom was out – the power coming from the now useless port engine. I started wondering what had happened to the others, hearing nothing from them. My flight engineer, Desmond, went back and found the rear door open, with three helmets on the step. He then managed to gather up the wires from the trimming tabs on the rear of the elevator, was able to tie them up, which had tremendous effect, and gave me some sort of control. We staggered back at pretty low altitude across the North Sea to the Shetlands and Sumburgh. The hydraulics had gone so we had to blow the wheels down with the emergency air system. We were on the approach when a Spitfire with a stopped propeller came round in front of me, so we had to go round again.

Tony's aircraft was a write-off. Alan Tittle, Ted Wass and Lesley Smith saw out the war as POWs. For his achievements on this raid, and taking into account his previous operational duties, Tony was recommended for a DFC. News of the award was made public in the *London Gazette* on 16 March 1945.

On the Bergen raid the 617 Squadron force had split its attack between the U-boat pens and shipping. Those attacking the pens were hampered by smoke, a number of crews having to make five runs and some Tallboys were brought back. John Fauquier's post-raid report recorded:

Height 7,000 feet. The floating dock was only visible from above although runs were made from various directions, and as smoke from the pens was drifting north, I ordered the dock forces to attack shipping. One motor vessel was seen to receive a direct hit and sank within two minutes. Two other ships were attacked but not hit and there was no visible damage.

The raid was certainly a success, despite the difficulties over the target. Twenty-three Tallboys were reported as having scythed their way into the U-boat pens causing severe damage, a minesweeper was sent to the bottom, and a cargo ship had to be beached. A price was paid however. 617 Squadron lost two crews. Flying Officer Ian Ross ditched in the sea, the crew managing to climb into a dinghy. An air-sea-rescue Warwick found the crew and dropped a lifeboat, but the arrival of an enemy aircraft forced the Warwick away. The lifeboat and the men in the water were then strafed. None of Ian Ross's crew survived; only the body of Flying Officer Ellwood was ever given up by the sea. Flight Lieutenant John Pryor did not return; his aircraft came down in Norway, all of his crew bar one being made POWs. Flying Officer Kendrick, on leaving the aircraft, struck his head and his parachute failed to open. He died from his wounds a few days later. In addition 9 Squadron also lost one aircraft.

The operation to Bergen proved to be Tony's last with the squadron, and he departed in February 1945.

> The adjutant asked me what I would like to do and I expressed an interest in an operational training unit. I went to Abingdon and the HQ of 92 Group. They offered me a flight commander's job at a Wellington OTU. I thought this was settled and then within a couple of days of returning to the squadron I was seconded to BOAC. I have no idea why; one of the mysteries of the RAF. I was what they called a junior captain of BOAC and wore the dark blue uniform; I was still a squadron leader of the RAF. BOAC along with Qantas, being quite far sighted, decided they wanted to reopen the route to Australia. This was actually to happen before the end of the war in Europe and they were anxious to establish themselves. The only aircraft which would fly the distance was the converted Lancaster, the Lancastrian. They wanted experienced Lancaster pilots. The turrets and

other surplus equipment were taken out and they put two 500-gallon tanks in the bomb bay, which gave us 3,140 gallons. It had an endurance of about 17 hours. The route to Australia was via Marseille, southern Sardinia, Malta, with the first landing at Lydda airfield, near Tel Aviv; about ten and a half hours non stop. The next leg took you via Kuwait, down the Persian Gulf to Karachi, to Ceylon. We would hand over to the Qantas crews at Karachi or Ceylon. The next leg before Singapore was recaptured was to Darwin; that was 15 hours. Then Darwin to Sydney. As a passenger you could fly the whole route from UK to Sydney, Australia in 72 hours elapsed time. What sort of a wreck you were after that much time in a noisy Lancaster, as you staggered out at the other end, I do not know.

Not only did Tony make the flights on the Australian route, he also flew a number of times into Iraq and Iran, and a delivery flight in a Lincoln to the Argentine Air Force in Buenos Aires. Tony returned to the RAF in 1949, taking up duties with Transport Command, eventually leaving in the early 1950s. 'I listened to my dad, seriously, for the first time.' Tony joined Waterlows, the printers, and then went into television with Granada. Following this he had a career in corporate public relations. He retired in April 1990 and went to live in France for nine years. Under the persuasion of his three daughters (seven grandchildren) he then returned to England where he now resides.

Tony looks back with justified pride at the opportunity he had to fly with Bomber Command's most famous unit.

Morale was sky high in 617 Squadron. It was a great squadron. We had experienced crews and we did a lot of practising and training and there was an extraordinary spirit. We were determined to be good; all of us felt that way. The squadron would have taken on anything. I am not boasting but there was just a feeling of competence and capability. I was comfortable with the Lancaster and in the situations we flew. I felt I had grown up; if things went wrong it was in my own hands, my own experience, my own skill, my own capability. And that stayed with me into later life.

We could hit things even in those days from 16-18,000ft.

We could hit them with one bomb – a Tallboy. Photographs we took and evidence gathered after the war proved it. The *Tirpitz* from 18,000ft looked about the size of a match stick, but we hit it. Didn't dive-bomb it; we hit it from straight and level, high level bombing. We were a very confident squadron and I was very proud of being in 617 Squadron because of its traditions. One felt one had to do one's best to maintain them. Then suddenly about four months later we were as out of date as the bows and arrows of Agincourt. After Hiroshima precision bombing disappeared.

Tony did his part in keeping the memory of 617 Squadron alive post-war; acting as the squadron association's secretary for 24 years. He also spent some time on the Bomber Command Association committee in the 1980s. When he came back from France in the late 1990s he attended a Bomber Command Association Christmas lunch and was persuaded by the secretary Doug Radcliffe and Sir Michael Beetham to rejoin the committee. 'You don't say no to a marshal of the Royal Air Force.' Within a year Tony was asked to take on the chairmanship of the association, a position he holds to the present day.

Tony reflects upon the post-war treatment of Bomber Command.

At the end of the war Bomber Command was very badly served by the Prime Minister. Churchill wrote a scurrilous memo about introducing the theme of 'terror bombing' – his phrase. And he didn't mention Bomber Command in his speech at the end of the war. Churchill was behind all the policies to do with bombing Germany then all of a sudden the rug was pulled from underneath. Harris tried hard to get a medal for Bomber Command and we all supported that; not so much for ourselves but for the groundcrews. A skilled fitter or armourer who had served on a bomber station out in the wilds, in all kinds of weather, had no more to show for it than someone who had been in a store in the middle of England and filled in a few forms.

Lots of historians pounced on the 600,000 civilian deaths in Germany and we've had this reputation of really not doing much beyond destroying cities and killing innocent people, which we always resented. I think there is becoming a more sensible view, taking into account the difficulties of the early days of the war, no navigational aids, no marking aids, inadequate aircraft, very low bomb loads. Consider what Germany did to Europe, including Russia, the way they behaved in the countries they occupied, killing millions of civilians quite deliberately. Why they think the Germans should sit in their homeland fat and happy with foreign slaves doing the work for them, living on the loot, and nothing should happen to them – it's beyond me. We just had to take the war to Germany otherwise the war would have been fought over here. The Bomber Command offensive took the war from the rooftops of London into Germany. The air war was fought over Germany and in 1945 they were still using the same bombers as they used in 1940. They never developed a four-engine bomber like ours with the capacity and the range. They would have done it if they hadn't been forced to build thousands of fighters for defence. And if you consider the man who fired the torpedo from a U-boat as a target, and in the rules of war you can kill him, then what about the man who makes the periscopes and the torpedoes, he's just as skilled and necessary to the war effort.

The war historians who were critical of Bomber Command are a dying breed. I think the perception's changed and we've seen how brutal, nasty and difficult it was. Any time you take a decision, you act on what you know then and how you assess it. Our commanders took rational decisions. Harris had the burden of deciding that the whole command would go on a raid and he knew he was going to lose 40 or 50 aircraft and the aircrews. More than any other commander he was regularly committing in the order of 5,000 chaps to battle maybe twice a week, maybe three times. How he carried the burden I don't know, yet it had to be done. We simply could not sit back and do nothing.

In 1958 Air Vice-Marshal Don Bennett CB, CBE, DSO, wrote:

Great Britain and the Empire have, in the goodly time of ten years since the end of the war, strangely failed to erect any 'Nelson's column' in memory of Bomber Command, the most powerful striking force in all British history. There is not even a Bomber Command campaign medal... We are not bitter, for we know in our own hearts just what we did – and that is our reward – the truest reward of all.

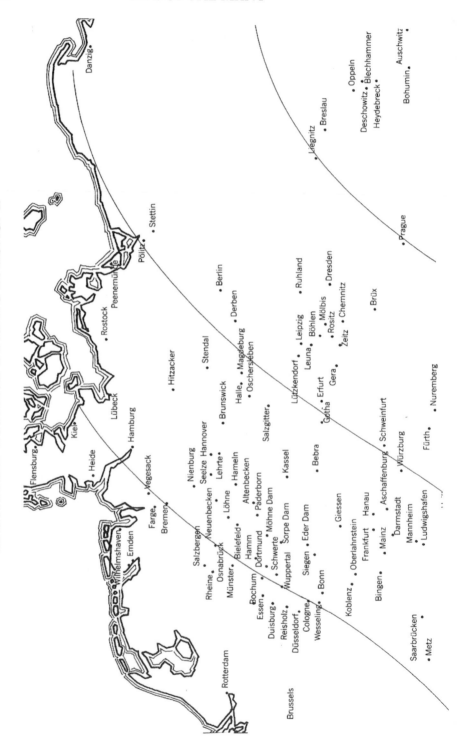

MAIN ALLIED BOMBING TARGETS IN EUROPE

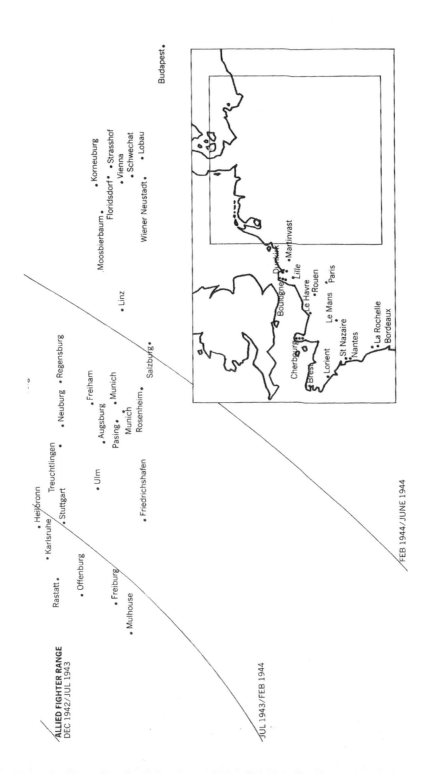

Appendix

Details of the principal Bomber Command aircraft types flown by the airmen featured in the book.

Avro Lancaster

Type: four-engined seven/eight-man mid-wing monoplane heavy night bomber.

Powerplant: Mk I and III, four 1,460hp Rolls-Royce Merlin XX, 22, 38 or 224, 12-cylinder liquid-cooled, supercharged in-line engines; Mk II, four 1,650hp Bristol Hercules VI 14-cylinder air-cooled two-row radial engines.

Dimensions: span 102ft, length 69ft 6in, height 20ft 4in, wing area 1,297 sq ft.

Weights: empty 36,457lb, loaded 68,000lb. With 22,000lb bomb, 72,000lb.

Performance: 287mph at 11,500ft, cruising speed 210 mph at 12,000ft, service ceiling 24,500ft (with bomb load), range with 14,000lb bomb load 1,660 miles.

Armament: Defensive – 2 x .303in Browning mgs each in Frazer-Nash nose and dorsal turrets, four in Frazer-Nash tail turret; some aircraft had 2 x Browning mgs in downward-firing ventral turret. Offensive – max bomb load 14,000lb. Special aircraft, either 1 x 22,000lb or 12,000 deep penetration bombs, 1 x 9,500lb Upkeep bouncing mine.

Production: 7,373.

De Havilland Mosquito

Type: twin-engined two-man mid-wing monoplane bomber.

Powerplant: Mk I and IV, two 1,460hp Rolls-Royce Merlin 21,22 or 25 12-cylinder liquid-cooled supercharged in-line engines; Mk IX and XVI, two 1,680hp Merlin 72 and 73 or

1,710hp Merlin 76 and 77 engines.

Dimensions: span 54ft 2in, length 40ft 6in, height 12ft 6in, wing area 454sq ft.

Weights: Mk IV, empty 13,400lb, loaded 21,462lb; Mk IX, empty 14,570lb, loaded 22,780lb.

Performance: Mk IV, max speed 380mph at 17,000ft, service ceiling 29,100ft, range 2,100 miles. Mk XVI, max speed 415mph at 28,000ft, service ceiling 37,000ft, range with max bomb load 1,485 miles.

Armament: Defensive – none. Offensive – Mk IV, max bomb load 2,000lb; Mk IX and XVI, max bomb load 4,000lb, plus 2 x 500lb bombs under wings.

Production: 7,781 of which 1,690 were completed as unarmed bombers.

Handley Page Halifax

Type: four-engined seven/eight-man mid-wing monoplane heavy night bomber.

Powerplant: Mk I, four 1,145hp Rolls-Royce Merlin X 12-cylinder liquid-cooled supercharged in-line engines. Mk II and V, 1,280hp Merlin XX. Mk III and VII, 1,650hp Bristol Hercules XVI 14-cylinder air-cooled sleeve-valve supercharged radial engines. Mk VI, 1,800hp Hercules 100.

Dimensions: early production aircraft, span 98ft 10in, length 70ft 1in, height 20ft 9in, wing area 1,250 sq ft. Late production aircraft, span 104ft 2in, length 71ft 7in, height 20ft 9in, wing area 1,275 sq ft.

Weights: Mk I, empty 36,000lb, loaded 60,000lb; Mk III, empty 38,240lb, loaded 65,000lb; Mk VI, empty 38,900lb, loaded 68,000lb.

Performance: Mk I, max speed 280mph at 16,500ft, service ceiling 19,100ft, range with 8,000lb bomb load 1,060 miles. Mk III, max speed 282mph at 13,500ft, service ceiling 18,600ft, range with max bomb load 1,030 miles.

Armament: Defensive – Mk III, 1 x Vickers K GO mg in nose, 4 x .303in Browning mgs each in Boulton Paul dorsal and tail turrets. Offensive – max bomb load 13,000lb.

Production: 6,135.

Vickers Armstrong Wellington

Type: twin-engined five-man mid-wing monoplane medium night bomber.

Powerplant: Mk I, two 1,000hp Bristol Pegasus X and XVIII air-cooled radial engines. Mk II, 1,145hp Rolls-Royce Merlin X in-line liquid-cooled engines. Mk III, 1,500hp Bristol Hercules XI sleeve-valve radials. Mk X, 1,675hp Bristol Hercules VI/XVI radials.

Dimensions: span 86ft 2in, length 64ft 7in, height 17ft 5in, wing area 840 sq ft.

Weights: Mk Ic, empty 18,556lb, loaded 28,500lb. Mk X, empty 22,474lb, loaded 36,500lb.

Performance: Mk Ic, max speed 235mph at 15,500ft, service ceiling 18,000ft. Mk III, max speed 255mph at 12,500ft, service ceiling 18,000ft. Range with 4,500lb bomb load 1,540 miles.

Armament: Defensive – Mk Ic, 2 x .303in Browning mgs in Frazer-Nash nose and tail turrets, 2 x manually operated Browning .303in mgs in beam positions. Mk III, 2 x Browning .303in mgs in Frazer-Nash nose turret, four in Frazer-Nash rear turret, 2 x manually operated Browning .303in mgs in beam positions. Offensive – Mk Ic, max bomb load 4,500lb. Mk III, max bomb load 4,500lb.

Production: 11,460.

Sources and Bibliography

The context of each of the airmen's stories is based upon a considerable amount of primary source material; notably squadron, group and command records at the national archives. Tiny, Benny, Joe, Harry and Tony's personal stories are drawn from interviews (conducted by myself and the Imperial War Museum), their own writings and their logbooks and I have constantly sought to tie up the information that is provided by the veterans with official records. Much of the background information concerning the campaigns the 'Five' flew in has been accumulating in my mind over many years now, but I must make mention of a few publications, which are invaluable tools to any researcher of the Bomber Command story. Martin Middlebrook and Chris Everitt's *Bomber Command War Diaries* provide an excellent summary of the ongoing campaign. Jonathan Falconer's *Bomber Command Handbook* helps the researcher with an excellent overview of Bomber Command's organisation and the detail of operations. And Bill Chorley's extraordinary feat producing the *RAF Bomber Command Losses* series, receives particular appreciation from this author.

Below is a bibliographical list of all the publications that have been of help in putting this book together. The publication dates are the editions consulted, rather than the first year of publication.

Bennett, D C T *Pathfinder* (Frederick Muller Ltd, 1983)
Clutton-Brock, O *Footprints on the Sands of Time* (Grub Street, 2003)
Chorley, W R *RAF Bomber Command Losses of the Second World War – 1939-1940* (Midland Publishing, 2005)
Chorley, W R *RAF Bomber Command Losses of the Second World War – 1941* (Midland Publishing, 2006)

Chorley, W R *RAF Bomber Command Losses of the Second World War – 1943* (Midland Publishing, 1996)

Chorley, W R *RAF Bomber Command Losses of the Second World War – 1944* (Midland Publishing, 1997)

Chorley, W R *RAF Bomber Command Losses of the Second World War – 1945* (Midland Publishing, 2004)

Churchill, W *The Speeches of Winston Churchill* (Penguin, 1990)

Cooper, A *Beyond the Dams to the Tirpitz* (Goodall Publications, 1991)

Darlow, S *Victory Fighters* (Grub Street, 2005)

Darlow, S *D-Day Bombers – The Veterans' Story* (Grub Street, 2004)

Darlow, S *Sledgehammers for Tintacks* (Grub Street, 2002)

Falconer, J *Bomber Command Handbook* (Sutton Publishing, 2003)

Goss, C *It's Suicide but it's Fun – The Story of 102 (Ceylon) Squadron 1917-1956* (Crécy, 1995)

Harris, Sir Arthur, Marshal of the RAF. *Bomber Offensive* (Greenhill, 1998)

Holmes, R *Acts of War, The Behaviour of Men in Battle* (Cassell, 2004)

Liddell Hart, B H *History of the Second World War* (Papermac, 1992)

Middlebrook, M and Everitt, C *The Bomber Command War Diaries* (Midland Publishing, 1995)

Tedder, Lord *Without Prejudice* (Cassell, 1966)

Terraine, J *The Right of the Line* (Hodder and Stoughton, 1985)

Webb, A B (compiler and editor) *At First Sight – A Factual and Anecdotal account of No. 627 Squadron Royal Air Force* (published by Alan B Webb, 1991)

Wilmot, C *The Struggle for Europe* (Collins, 1952)

Endnotes

1 *The Bomber Command War Diaries*, Middlebrook, M, and Everitt, C (Midland Publishing, 1996)

2 Tiny's logbook was lost during the war and the 9 Squadron operations record book is very brief on detail. I have been unable to confirm that Tiny was operational on 20/21 May and there is therefore a possibility that Tiny was actually operational the night before.

3 Further details of training losses are given in Harry Hughes's story.

4 *The Rise and Fall of the Third Reich* Shirer, W (Secker and Warburg Limited, 1991)

5 *The Bomber Command War Diaries*, Middlebrook, M, and Everitt, C (Midland Publishing, 1996)

6 *Bomber Offensive*, Harris, Marshal of the RAF Sir Arthur (Greenhill, 1998)

7 *Ibid*

8 Statistics from www.arnold-scheme.org – Dr Gilbert S Guinn

9 *The Bomber Command War Diaries*, Middlebrook, M, and Everitt, C (Midland Publishing, 1996)

10 *Sledgehammers for Tintacks*, Darlow, S (Grub Street Publishing, 2002)

11 *Bomber Command 1939-1945 Reaping the Whirlwind* Overy, R (HarperCollins Publishers, 1997)

12 *The Bomber Command War Diaries*, Middlebrook, M, and Everitt, C (Midland Publishing, 1996)

13 *RAF Bomber Command Losses of the Second World War – 1943* Chorley, W R (Midland Publishing, 1996)

14 There is a little confusion with regard this incident. It has also been recorded that the Halifax actually landed at Tangmere. However Harry remains convinced that the aircraft came back to Pocklington – and it would be hard to disagree considering his vivid recollection of the incident.

15 The 'Fellowship of the Bellows' was a group of Anglo-Argentinians who raised money for RAF aircraft; with the 'Bellows' there to 'raise the wind'.

16 Roy Montrowe's name was recorded in official records at the time as Roy Momo.

17 *RAF Bomber Command Losses of the Second World War – 1945 Chorley*, W R (Midland Publishing, 2004)

18 *Those Other Eagles*, Shores, C (Grub Street, 2004)

19 *Tirpitz – Hunting the Beast*, Sweetman, J (Sutton Publishing Limited, 2004)

20 *Ibid*

21 *Footprints on the Sands of Time: RAF Bomber Command prisoners-of-war 1939-1945*, Clutton-Brock, O (Grub Street, 2003)

22 *Beyond the Dams to the Tirpitz*, Cooper, A (Goodall Publications, 1991)

23 *Ibid*

24 Bomber Command aircraft specifications based upon Jonathan Falconer's *Bomber Command Handbook* (Sutton Publishing, 2003)

Index